Canon and Canonization
British Movement Poetry

Canon and Canonization
British Movement Poetry

Charu Sheel Singh

AKHAND

AKHAND PUBLISHING HOUSE
NEW DELHI (INDIA)

Published by

AKHAND PUBLISHING HOUSE
L-9 A, IST FLOOR, STREET NO. 42
SADATPUR EXTENSION
DELHI-110094 (INDIA)
CELL- 0-9013387535, 0-9968628081

Canon and Canonization British Movement Poetry

Edition 2010
ISBN 978-81-910525-0-3

The responsibility for facts stated, opinion expressed or conclusions reached and plagiarism, if any, in this book is entirely that of the author/editor. The publisher bears no responsibility for them whatsoever.

Printed in India
at Tarun Offset Printer, Delhi

For my mother
Who gave me bread
And my father
Who gave me water

Foreword

No exclusive critical examination of the poetic manifestoes of Davie, Amis, Wain, Conquest, Hughes, Larkin, Tomlinson and Gunn, together, exists in books on British poetry after 1950 as presented here. Blake Morrison's book is more a study of poetic relationships of Movement poets, their general beliefs and tradition; Michael Schmidt and Peter Jones's book on British poetry after 1950 is a critical anthology; Calvin Bedient's book offers brief, though penetrating, comments on post-War British poets whom he finds "difficult, 'American' in the way it approaches its subjects cold, indeed in a cold sweat, without help, alone in an undefined silence." This book, for the first time, examines statements on poetic theory, made by poets above from time to time.

The first two chapters form a dialectic in themselves arguing and counter-arguing upon the nature of poetry and its relation to people. The first chapter is concerned with Movement poetics whose aim was to bring simpler parts of melody and rhythm back to proper orchestration. It considers in detail Robert Conquest's anthology on British poetry of the fifties, *New Lines*, I & II, and D.J. Enright's *Poetry of the 1950s.* Chapter II is a study of the reaction that followed Movement aims and ideology, made manifest first in Alvarez's anthology, *The New Poetry* (Penguin, 1962). It also examines Davie and Alvarez's claim for a new seriousness and new aestheticism as criteria for new poetry.

The remaining three chapters on Hughes, Gunn, and

Tomlinson both apply and illustrate the poetic theory and practice of poets under discussion. The poets' choice is my own as is the choice of their poetic collections analysed (heavily limited for want of space). In spite of at least five books on Hughes's poetry by Hirschberg, Gifford and Roberts, Keith Sagar, and Ekbert Faas, Crow myth as well as the source of certain other images and symbols remains unlocated. My chapter on Hughes locates them considering in detail Hughes's religious position which has also not been specifically dealt with by available scholarship.

An analysis of Thom Gunn's *Moly* is done in Chapter IV. *Moly* has received some unfavourable reviews, and has not been extensively analysed. Charles Tomlinson's *Seeing is Believing* and *Renga* form two masterpieces in themselves, and their close analysis has long been due. Instead of going through the whole range of poetic collections of poets studied and offering comments in a generalised or journalistic manner, I have concentrated on a close textual analysis of collections I consider important of the entire written work a poet has done. Moreover, what is seldom realized, and even not realized at all, is the fact that apart from Ted Hughes, Gunn and Tomlinson have also been making subtle uses of myth either in individual poems or in their poetic frameworks. *Moly* and *Renga* will illustrate the point. This tradition extends to Geoffrey Hill's *Mercian Hymns*.

Since the work of art is at the centre of my critical discussion, I have, time and again, made poets' statements as meaningful referents for the illumination of intentions and concepts, images and symbols, which, otherwise, would have remained in the dark. I have taken poet to be an empirical particular whose relationships with objects refer, represent, signify and symbolize levels of adjustments, degrees of involvement and communication. This empirical particular I also take to be a text, who though always being dragged, sometimes to the hazards (as in Hughes) and sometimes to the deep and meaningful silence (as in Tomlinson), is always building bridges of conscious adjustment and patterns of control over its medium (as in Gunn). The poet and the poem

I view as married partners whose spirits demand liberation without walls of flesh, but whose walls of flesh again invite them to copulate and multiply relationships. The struggle is my theme throughout.

A belief in noumenon, the "other," has been consistently occupying the poetry of poets studied, and the Muse, who had been imprisoned in the fifties within the confines of an empirical and earthly city, is finally released in the open spaces of mystery that bodies over our existences. The Conclusion gathers important findings and places Blake Morrison and Andrew Motion's anthology on British poetry (1982) in perspective.

To Edward T. Larrissy of the Department of English, Warwick University, I am grateful for reading my chapters, correcting and commenting upon them; to Professor C.J. Rawson of Department of English, Warwick University, I have incurred debts words cannot tell; his love and encouragement it is difficult for me to parallel. To Peter Larkin and Audrey Cooper I owe thanks for readily helping me with the books I needed; to the staff at the inter-library loan I express my deep gratitude their promptness in getting for me necessary books has been exemplary. The study would still not have been possible had British Council not awarded me scholarship from India to study at Warwick University for one year. I sincerely thank British Council for the financial help. This book appeared under a different title when it was published first. The change in the title gets us in to the groove.

Varanasi **Charu Sheel Singh**

Contents

1

Urban Muse in Empirical Locale

The chapter will consider Robert Conquest, Kingsley Amis, Donald Davie and Jahn Wain's statements on poetic theory and try to discover principles of poetic composition which became conspicuous and characteristic of a group of writers generally known as having given birth to the Movement. The first part will establish the context by examining the nature and implication of relationship among poets under consideration; the secand part will put up the case by prominently focussing attention an the poetic manifestoes of each of these poets, while the third part, i.e., the Conclusion, will gather important findings and attempt a comparative evaluation. It will also make such necessary generalisations as are warranted. The main burden of the chapter, however, will be to see above poets, acting and reacting, within the framework, conscious and unconscious both, of a certain specific climate of literary norm, with regard to style, diction, syntax, tone, subject matter, and, in fact, the attitude to poetic composition as a whole. The chapter will try to arrive at a Movement consensus, ethic, or code, if one would wish to call it.

I

Answering a questian from Clive James concerning his first

contact with Robert Conquest, Amis said: "I had a poem in *New Poems* 1951. I had only a toehold in the London literary world and would come from Swansea to London just for a party for the publication of that book. I came down and met Bob. He told me fifty limericks and the whole of his sequel to *Eskimo Nell,* which is better than his original. I had to be put on train afterwards. After that, I was in *New Lines,* the idea for which was all Bob's."[1] Amis had applied for a scholarship to St. Catherine's College, Cambridge, which he failed to obtain. He won, however, a place at St. John's, "one of the less pretentious Oxford Colleges," At St. John's, Amis met Philip Larkin, who was already there, for the first time. Larkin recognised in Amis "the presence of a talent greater than my own."[2] As a consequence of this friendship Amis dedicated *Lucky Jim* to Larkin. Recalling his expericnces about the first idea of *Lucky Jim,* Amis told Melvyn Bragg: "When Lucky Jim was conceived . . . I went up to what was then the university college of Leicester, to see my old friend Philip Larkin, who was working in the university library there. He said: 'one for a cup or coffee in the Common Room,' and after about ten minutes, I said to myself: 'You know, my God, somebody should do something about this, because this is totally unchartered territory'.[3]

Larkin later said: "*Lucky Jim* was published in 1954—but of course we'd been exchanging letters and showing each other our work for a long time, and I think we laughed, at the same things and agreed largely about what you could and couldn't write about, and so on."[4] Furthermore, at St. John's, Larkin and Amis were under the same tutor, Gavin Bone. An important moment came when John Wain joined the company of Larkin and Amis in 1943. Wain recalls that Larkin was finishing his undergraduate course that spring and in the summer went to take up a job in Wellington, Shropshire. Wain humbly recalls that acquaintance with Larkin has been of "greatest importance"[5] to him. "Had it not been for the accident that I occasionally saw him reading the newspapers in the common room, I should not have known of his existence. And he knew of mine, if at all, only slightly.

We became friends later."[6] Larkin was fairly respected among his friends and often drew the motley crew which shouted "Philip's coming up." In this crew was Amis whom Wain met some time in 1944. Amis had a copy of Larkin's *Jill* which he sold to Wain. Amis himself was writing a novel at this time and Wain recalls that he would never have written *Hurry On Down* if he had not read Amis's novel which was never published. Wain even founded the literary magazine *Mandrake* in 1945 in which Larkin, Amis, Jennings and Wain published their poems which later came to characterise some of the qualities of the Movement poets. Outside the Oxford trio of Larkin-Amis-Wain, the other important literary friendship which developed was between D.J. Enright and Robert Conquest. Both had been contributing their poems to the *Listener* and the *New Statesman*, and Enright particularly liked Conquest's "Reflections on Landscapes" describing it as "cold, intelligent and self-contained."[7]

Donald Davie, the last, and perhaps now the most important, of these poets, was at Cambridge when most of the Movement activities were taking place at Oxford. In 1974, in the famous article "The Varsity Match," Davie wrote: "Ten or twelve or perhaps fifteen years before, those same Oxford pubs where Fuller and Hamilton drank Worthington, had seen John Wain and Kingsley Amis, with presumably one or two others (Wallace Robson? Arthur Boyars? sometimes Philip Larkin?), preparing for the assault that, by way of Wain's radio programme *New Soundings*, established itself as "the Movement," recorded in Robert Conquest's anthology *New Lines* and George Hartley's magazine *Listen*. Ten or so years before that the plotters in the pubs were Wystan Auden and Stephen Spender; and ten or so years after John Fuller and Ian Hamilton they were, I suppose, Michael Schmidt and Grevel Lindop and Gareth Reeves."[8] Although Davie seems to have been aware of the activities of other poets under consideration, there is little possibility of his having met them in the fifties. Davie, nevertheless, had been anticipated by his unknown Oxonian colleagues, for recalling his attitude to poetry then, Davie wrote: ". . . the first of my all too many manifestoes about poetry, printed in those years mostly in Cambridge magazine, characteristically genuflected towards the author of *The Waste Land* and *Four Quartets;* and staked out whatever position they timidly sought to maintain, by veering a very few points away from something that Eliot had said in print."[9]

Of his first acquaintance with Amis, Davie recalls in his autobiography: "It was I suppose one day in 1960 or 1961 that, about one o'clock, the phone rang in the turreted polygonal room in Caius which I had taken over from Charles Brink. I was just finishing a supervision, and got rid of my pupils in a hurry when the voice on the phone identified itself as Kingsley Amis, in Cambridge for the day and asking me to lunch with him. Kingsley Amis was one of several people I had hurried to get acquainted with, some years before, when our names had been linked together by commentators in a literary manifestation of the 1950s which got itself called The Movement—itself I believe, an important phenomenon for historians of English society and culture, since it represented the first concerted though unplanned invasion of the literary Establishment by the scholarship boys of the petty bourgeoisie."[10]

Amis, in that year, had moved from Swansea to Cambridge and soon was under attack from F.R. Leavis, who resented Amis's appointment and described him "a pornographer." Davie and Holloway, however, came to Amis's rescue in a Faculty Meeting. Later also, for once ". . . he (Amis) came to a Caius dinner as Joseph Needham's guest, when my guest was his and my friend Robert Conquest."[11] We might well sum up one aspect of these relationships by having recourse to Davie's statement: "I'm like Wain and Larkin and the others in not being product of the provinces known to the tourist, but of Industrial Midlands, in my case the South Yorkshire eyefield; and like nearly everyone in the group I'm a product of the lower middle class, that is, of a stratum of British society in which the life of the mind is not taken for granted as taking part of everyone's time, but rather where if it is honour'd at all, has to be struggled for, and therefore embraced with more tenacity, fervour. . . . Accordingly, my history is the history of my education and duplicates that of all the rest—a winning of-way to one of the ancient universities by competitive examination, rather than going there as a matter of course in the case of products of more privileged classes, such as Spender, Auden, Lehmann, Connolly, and almost every other writer of previous generations that you can think of."[12]

One of the most curious things about the Movement has been the denial of its existence by those who gave it birth. In an essay Davie wrote in summer 1959, he recalls how the Movement poets ridiculed and deprecated its very idea, as, on the other hand, they kept it going. Davie even acknowledges that Movement poets went much further than halfway to meet the reader and whenever "we were challenged or flattered or simply interviewed", we pretended that "the Movement didn't exist, that it was an invention of journalists, that we had never noticed how Larkin and Gunn and Amis had something in common, or that, if we had noticed, it didn't interest or excite us."[13]

It can be easily perceived that after the Movement Davie has done more to rehabilitate and give it a shape and a texture. Clearly, something which doesn't exist cannot be created. How it is that the journalists created the Movement? Amis's view is more balanced and gives us the right perspective: "We weren't consciously a group. One doesn't start work that way perish the thought. A style emerges a lot more gradually and a lot less wilfully than that. . . . The idea that you plan, let alone plot with others, is absurd."[14] Even here Amis is not putting the thing as it really came out later. When Enright and Conquest brought out their anthologies, Conquest made a modest statement that "these poets do not have as much in common as they would if they were a group of doctrine-saddled writers forming a definite school complete with programmes and rules. What they do have in common is perhaps, at its lowest, little more than a negative determination to avoid bad principles."[15] However, the trouble with all these statements is that those who create history do not know what they have done, and if they knew it, perhaps the history would lose the intensity and force of the character of its events and the task of the literary historian would be over. Anthony Thwaite quite rightly thinks that "the nine poets in these anthologies... were as firmly saddled with a common label as any doctrine could have possibly achieved."[16] Wain also holds that these poets "were united more by their dislikes than their likes", but goes on to add, "But a broad similarity emerged, and began to be seen in their work. For a brief moment, there was a 'Movement' and it *d'd* cohere."[17]

"Poetry is the sound of human speech at those times when it comes closest to the speech of the angels and the speech of the animals,"[18] wrote Wain. Glancing backward a little we discover that Auden-Spender-Day Lewis in the thirties propounded a poetics of the writer's concern with social reality and emphasized objective and impersonal approach. However, the objective became subjective at some crucial point either in the life of the poet or the social environment. Moreover, poets of the younger generation (Dylan Thomas and George Barker among others), were not happy at the "mental gymnastics" which the poets of the Eliot generation propagated both in poetry and in criticism.[19] It amounted to the suppression, or at least the inhibited use, of language and subject matter.[20] Ian Hamilton goes to the extent of saying that the".. . notorious forties, has been thoroughly written off in most contemporary pigeon-holings. It has popularly become the decade dominated by the punch-drunk Apocalypse, the foaming horsemen. . ." and goes on to quote John Wain on his diagnosis of the forties: "If we find much of it impossibly overblown, exaggerated, strained, rhetorical, all we have to do is to remember it was produced under impossible conditions."[21]

Dylan Thomas's statement in 1934 that "the more subjective a poem, the clearer the narrative line," sounded the first note of demarcation between the poetry of the thirties from that of the forties.[22] It became impossible for the poet of the forties to maintain the tradition of the objective approach or shapeliness and intelligenee in the general chaos and confusion or contradictory theories and principles. Poetry does not exclusively grow out of social reality much less out of any theories about it. It grows from within one's own self, and once the self or the social reality is disturbed, communication with the reader becomes a lie and poets sit on the high pedestal of flamboyant rhetoric and inflated vision to balance the dry salvages of the leavenings of history. G.S. Fraser remarked: "The obscurity of our poetry, its air of something desperately snatched from dream or woven round a chime of words, are the results of disintegration, not in ourselves, but in society."[23]

The work done by Tambimuttu during this period is remarkable. In the second issue of *Poetry London* (April 1939) he wrote: "This paper exists as a platform for poets who require more freedom than that afforded them in the papers of little hencoops and cliques, in order to work well. It is a protest against the modern suppression of free speech in verse . . . we will give the public what they want. . . ." In this climate of change (Eliot, Auden, Spender witnessed all)[24] the poetics of concrete and hard imagery, rhetorical discipline, intellectual order and impersonalist ethic became a silent witness to the poetry of self-expression which labelled it as outdated, over-stretched, and even irrelevant to the purpose. These poets, who called themselves Apocalypse poets, said that they stood for "greater freedom, economic no less than aesthetic, from machines and mechanistic thinking." Other important poets of this period, Henry Treece, G.S. Fraser and J.F. Hendry claimed: "No existent political system, Left or Right, no artistic ideology, surrealism or the political school of Auden, was able to provide this freedom." Concepts like "A good poem is a response to a human situation and not an exercise in linguistic technique;[25] "What our man, or woman, required is what fits verse for rendering in those ways: absolute clarity, heavy rhythms and noticeable rhymes with some break in the lines preferred at the end of the line. Subject matter must suit the occasion by being public, popular, what unites the individual with some large group of his neighbours;"[26] "It was, I believe, in response to this situation that 'modern' poetry, and the 'modern' arts generally, grew up . . ."[27] became recurring features of poets who disliked the tradition of classical objectivity, continued so relentlessly by Richards, Leavis and Empson, after Pound and Eliot. Their views on poetry were replaced by a poetics of subjectivism which found the contours of limited social framework sufficient guide to, and material for, the work of art. Such an art was soon to become the coterie of poets and not of the reader, for the latter was consistently baffled by the poet's occasional use of personal myth, metaphor, symbol and idiom.[28]

When we come to the fifties, the poets under consideration found themselves, on the one hand, as having provided an alternative to the mythic, symbolic and allusive poetry of T.S. Eliot, Pound and others; on the other hand, in their revolt against the poetry of the forties, these poets propagated "conservatism," "building up" and "consolidation" as safest virtues. The ground on which they stood, gave nothing to them, except excessive discipline, excess of style, which murdered the vital links of the being of Apollo, and the inflated diction, distorted metaphor, and personal use of myth, which took poetry away from the common man; Christ became not the herdsman among his flocks but the Official Priest, sitting in the foundationless Imagery-Museum. The poets of the fifties, legitimately, and with a lot or justification, undertook to cleanse the temple and ask the Muse to sit, as in ancient times, and sing in conversational tone, simple, straightforward diction, and rhythms which could be normally breathed by the man on the street and rhymes which could be easily sung by mothers in the kitchen-rooms. John Wain explained the poet's position and the task ahead:

"The world had been dragged by two decades of meaningless peace and then suddenly battered nearly to death by global war. Worse, that war had ended with the fearful savagery or Hiroshima and Nagasaki; at last man's fingers had closed round the lever that, once pulled, would bring universal destruction. At such a time, when exhaustion and boredom in the foreground are balanced by fear and guilt in the background, it is natural that a poet should feel the impuls to *build.* Writing in regular and disciplined verse-forms is building in a simple and obvious sense, like brick-laying. Too simple, too obvious? Perhaps. But we were all very young and were doing the best we could to make something amid the ruins."[29]

The notion that excess of feeling had impurified diction, and the unexpected breaks in syntax had shown, far too much, a break in sensibility, gained ground. Kingley Amis, John Wain, who were the regular reviewers to the *Spectator,* and Donald Davie on the other side, discovered irony, wit, syntax, morality, as safe guides to the health of the poetry of the period. We shall soon see how most of the Movement poets took refuge in the eighteenth-century verse-forms and sensibility, and drew their models from it. Of the objectives and aspirations of the Movement poets, I refer to part of the article Anthony Hartley wrote in 1954 in the *Spectator:* "It is bored by the despair of the forties, not much interested in suffering, and extremely impatient of poetic sensibility, especially poetic sensibility about 'the writer and society.' So it's goodbye to all those rather sad little discussions about 'how the writer ought to live,' and it's goodbye to the Little Magazine and 'experimental writing.' The Movement, as well as being anti-phoney, is anti-wit; sceptical, robust, ironic, prepared to be as comfortable as possible in a wicked, commercial, threatened world which doesn't look, anyway, as if it's going to be changed much by a couple of handfuls of young English writers."[30]

II

The pioneers of the Movement in English poetry were D.J. Enright and Robert Conquest whose anthologies[31] delineated the outlines and were in the nature of first manifestoes as an argument in the art of the current necessities for poetic composition. Robert Conquest began his Introduction to the anthology by analysing the state of current poetry and public taste, often flashing back upon the old traditions of poetry writing in English. Conquest's tone, throughout, is modest, and his modesty, sometimes, takes an ironic tinge, and sometimes, assumes piercing satirical airs at the state of affairs.

Eliot had said that every generation must interpret the past for itself and Conquest rightly says that in the history of English poetry during the 1920s, 1930s and 1940s, groups of writers with "different attitudes" and taking "different positions" emerged and contributed their share to the writing of poetry. Analysing the 1930s John Wain wrote: "It was the last age, consciously and feverishly the last, in which people had the feeling that if only they took the trouble to *join* something, get a party card, wear a special shirt, organise meetings and bellow slogans, they could influence the course of events. Since 1946 nobody above the Jehovah's witness level has taken this attitude; are we right or will the sixties think us as silly as we think of the thirties?"[32] Conquest found in 1950 that the attitude of people to poetry has become corrupt; a certain undiscriminating atmosphere has helped to develop the "vicious taste" of the people, and the view that poems should be diffuse, sentimental verbiage, hollow technical pirouettes, and above all metaphorical, gained uncalled for momentum, with all its debilitating, corroding, and nerve-shattering repercussion. Residual nuisances like social-realists, the Lallans-mongers, the Church-furnishers, and the neo Georgians, were able to maintain themselves. It was against such practices that the Movement poets refused to surrender, to subjective moods and social pressures, which render all the emotional and technical gifts worthless. The Movement poets aspired to a genuine and healthy poetry, though they were fully aware that the task of correcting the vicious public taste was not an artistic problem purely; perhaps, not a Kipling or Hardy, but a small community of Lesser talents could contribute its share for the betterment or public taste and thereby of poetry.

Kingsley Amis, dwelling upon the problem of style, makes a brief survey of English poetry agreeing that before the seventeenth century, there was a single style in which a poet could move from grave to gay and *vice versa.* But".... Metaphysical style strained the language, forced it into behaviour much more unnatural than anything Shakespeare imposed upon it, . . . the second attack had come from Milton, the only English poet no one could call light in even the remotest sense. . . A sufficient variety of forms lay ready to hand, from the loosest ballad or song metre to the strictest simulacrum of high verse in heroic couplet or decasyllabic quatrain. With this there went an equally wide range of manner or method, from satire, which for the most part is aggressively sensible, to what is called nonsense."[33] Amis is writing an Introduction to light verse and it is his burden to dismiss the notion that light verse is funny and its language decorous and artificial. It is also believed that light verse prepares for parody and is unsuitable for decent seriousness; that it deals with "low" rather than "high" diction and subject-matter, and that its chief weapon, whether it be "rustic, technical, colloquial, facetiously anachronistic, or vulgar, ill-bred, obscene" is impropriety, Amis cites Swift as an example who was writing *vers de societe* and still did not opt for satire (as his non-use of heroic couplet would indicate). And then Amis drives home the point: "We are dealing with a kind of realistic verse that is close to some of the interests of the novel: men and women among their fellows, seen as members of a group or class in a way that emphasizes manners, social forms, amusements, fashion (from millinery to philosophy), topicality, even gossip, all these treated in a bright, perspicuous style."[34]

Donald Davie, whose early poetics derives largely from the eighteenth century theory and practice of poetry, considers that one of the greatest virtues of eighteenth century poet was that he considered every subject fit for poetry (which is not to hint at the poetry of commitment): " . . . eighteenth century poetry *does* talk like folks of this world; and indeed a main intention of this anthology is to show how much of it does so. Of poets not represented here, Swift almost throughout, and Pope much of the time, use a language that is conversational, not to say colloquial. . . . As the century wore on, however, the language of poetry became more divorced from the language that was spoken; though there are striking exceptions like Cowper, and one has to distinguish between Johnson and Goldsmith, who admitted spoken usage as a relevant consideration. . . ."[35]

John Wain thinks that English poetry has seen more changes since 1910 than before it and that most of these changes have been abrupt. Once there was a change from the "exhausted remnants" of Victorian poetry to the "glittering sparsity" of the Imagists. The thirties succumbed to "easy, flowing poetic journalism." As compared to these changes the forties and fifties brought about changes which were "staggeringly complete and far reaching."[36] One has but to agree with Mr. Wain that "It is impossible to love the soul of poetry without loving her body, and every reader who ever felt deeply the strength and beauty of this supreme form of literary art. . . has been willing. . . to pay attention to matters of form."[37]

Perhaps this is where the forties made way to the fifties to come and take charge. While the fifties poets continued to value Wordsworthian virtues of "spontaneity" and "sincerity", they equally emphasized on a poetry of the *Polis* as Wain said, or a poetry of "urbanity" as Davie said. In other words fifties poets were trying to make use of the best in romantic and classic traditions. Robert Conquest wrote on the ideology of Movement poets: "On the more technical side, though of course related to all this we see refusal to abandon a rational structure and comprehensible language, even when the verse is most highly charged with sensuous or emotional intent."[38] John Wain later wrote: "Ever since the late eighteenth century, sincerity and spontaneity (seen as opposed to conventionality and artifice) have been highly valued, as when Wordsworth called poetry 'the spontaneous overflow of powerful feelings'. What we are seeing in our century is partly a natural development of this tradition; anything that sounds like rhetoric and lofty style is avoided, very much as modern television actors try to sound and look like ordinary people in ordinary situations, where the old tragedians never tried to sound ordinary. All this is legitimate, and interesting work can come out of it, . . ."[39] What Robert Conquest was trying to do was to set in order the "simpler part of melody and rhythm" of the orchestra which was "completely out of its depth with harmony and orchestration", "the restoration of a sound and fruitful attitude to poetry, of the principle that poetry is written by and for the whole man, intellect emotions, senses and all."[40]

Post-War poetry concerned itself too much with language and poetic process, and forgot that poems are made not only of the intellectual backbone, which is the first lesson to be learnt, as Conquest would agree with John Wain; but, that poems are also made of "the flesh of humanity, irony, passion or sanity," which is the second lesson, and which is not always learnt. As for Wain's advocacy, as also of Davie's and Amis's, of Empsonian discipline and rigour, Conquest would agree, but he would be quick to emphasize the other side: "Intellectual frameworks can be filled out with bad materials as well as good and Empsonianism has been almost as much a vehicle for unpleasant exhibitionism and sentimentality as the trends it was designed to correct."[41]

One of the most important changes that the Movement poets were trying to bring about, was to bring poetry down to earth. This is obviously not so simple as it sounds. Davie, remarking upon Wordsworth's originality, wrote: ". . . it is important to realize, where his originality lies. .. Wordsworth is original in his attitude to the subject, in making the light fall upon it from an unforeseen direction; in this instance, by treating the plight of the beggar, not from the beggar's stand-point, but from the point of view of community which maintains him and so derives spiritual benefit from the beggar in its midst."[42] Kingsley Amis, because he did not find this very thing in the attitude of Keats towards his subjects, criticised him for dwelling too much in the world of imagination and making the simple obscure and learned: "Even in his best poems Keats devotes himself too uncritically to 'the world of imagination.' Even the 'Ode to a Nightingale' . . . is full of frigidities, of appeals to the remote and merely fanciful. What else are the references to hemlock, Lethe, the Dryad (tautologically) described as 'of the trees'), Flora, the blushful Hippocrene (seen as a kind of Greek red sparkling Burgundy, and apparently sedimented at that), Bacchus and his pards (brought into effect a translation into poeiese of the unpoetical notion of getting drunk)? Such entities are, as Jeffrey observed of the subject of 'Hyperion,' *too far removed from all the sources of human interest.* And to string together counters of this kind, to use 'Olympus' faded hierarchy' as correlatives for what are evidently the most passionate feelings, was a favourite procedure with Keats. . . ."[43]

Fifties poets could not think in terms of a poetry divorced from human language and human feeling, which leads us to a metaphor devoid of the *zeitgeist,* the intensity, the mood of the common man, the primitive man, who is the real source of all artistic forms, and whose language is the language incorporated into human passion with an its feelings of love, hate, life, death, even questions concerning immortality and the ultimate destiny of human soul. Such a poetry is meaningful because it is meant for the people who gave it birth and made its existence possible. It was keeping these things in mind that John Wain said: "Poetry, however we define it. . . and I think the simplest bedrock definition is 'anything that makes language dance and sing as well as just speak'. . . is extremely a necessity of the human spirit."[44]

Kingsley Amis's attack on Keats, earlier, is not that Keats did not concern himself with simpler human emotions, but that his treatment of those emotions was too learned; in other words, Keats failed to find a suitable objective correlative for his feelings for the common man. This may, sometimes, be equally true of Wordsworth in practice. The treatment of any subject has to make room for personal tilts, even idiosyncracies. When Wordsworth speaks of "the gaudiness and inane phraseology" of the writers prior to him, he in fact is applying their own criteria to their own poetry and practice. "Sobriety", for instance, is an eighteenth century virtue not only in the use of literary language but also in life and manners, and when Wordsworth emphasized sobriety of style and diction, he was obviously having in mind the "gross and violent stimulants" which are already present in the subject and attitude of Langhorne as is shown by Davie. Davie rightly says that sobriety is something that ought to be "carried into, and reflected by the very minutiae of poetic style." He further says: "In the subjects they choose and in their attitudes to those subjects, in their unwillingness to raise their voice above the tone of measured conversation, in their respect for common sense and a sense for proportion, they are all remarkable for sobriety."[45]

In the fifties, the sense, the diction and the sentiment, all had been denatured;[46] perhaps Wordsworth, and perhaps tho "School of Dryden, would become the torch-bearer and lead poetry away from the quagmarish cliches of the impotent metaphor of the forties and the political metaphor of the thirties! The sanity of art must be restored at any cost. It should, therefore, not look surprising, when Davie said, paradoxical though it might seem, that "Wordsworth is rather the last poet of the eighteenth century than the first of the nineteenth."[47] The eighteenth and the early nineteenth centuries are immediately relevant to, and present us with, a poetic situation similar to the one in the fifties. As Conquest has said that younger poets, and poets of lesser talents, almost dote upon their heroes who have extended the range of art, as if extension itself is a sign of quality. No wonder then, in their search not to become their own selves, but Pounds and Eliots and Butterfields, they close their eyes to the immediate present, and concentrate on the past which has already become the slum of history hidden beneath the changing clouds of time. These poets attempt "an absurdly inflated search for novelty through an attempted blend of the flashier and the more irrelevant features of past schools."[46]

The meaning of the inheritance of tradition varies from age to age and surely it is not a self-conscious act of will. Similarly, the insistence upon experiment and novelty in experiment do not depend for their origin on "self-consciously" doing something: "The idea of creating a new, or of reviving an old, poetic culture (by an effort of will) is the baisic fallacy."[49] Poetry, likewise, cannot substitute medical surgery and improve the lot of those who are devoid of poetic sensibility. Tho poet is a dedicated being and what he is dedicated to is not something outside the outlines of his own being (and his being includes society, nation, etc., only through and by the medium of the poetic process) but something which is inherent in him; something which is giving him inspiration and energy to assimilate social, national and universal rhythms, which, when heated into the crucible of his mental furnace, flows out as easily as the uninhibited speech of the man on the street. The poet, then, is not only in harmony with the conversational idiom, but the more sobre and gentler psychic rhythms of history become part and parcel of his personality and articulation. It is of these things and considerations gone away that Amis had to say: " . . . nobody wants any more poems on the grander themes for a few years, but at the same time nobody wants any more poems about philosophers or paintings or novelists or art galleries or mythology or foreign cities or other poems."[50]

Donald Davie brought the entire problem of poetic malady on to the poetic diction, pure and impure, and poetic syntax, and his earlier two books[51] are best attempts to understand the Movement and elaborate its principles. Amis had written the above because he knew poetry writing had fallen into some fame-hungry, irrational, and unpoetic minds, who know not the noble tradition of English poetry, and therefore, could not chalk out their own course of action. The problem of diction is not with poets like Shakespeare and Hopkins, for they can use any word to the best purpose. The problem of diction is felt by poets of lesser talents, who try to create effects, which the use of their diction, or the social milieu thereof, would not permit. For all poetry, good or bad, is written to generate effect of some sort on the reader and a good or pure diction comes out of a selection of language on reasonable principles for reasonable purposes. Conquest wrote: " . . . the pleasure of poetry is not the pleasure of thinking 'how clever I am,' or 'how moral I am,' or 'how mature I am,' but the objective non-egotistical pleasure 'I like the effect. . .'! But the essential is the direct enjoyment, not indulgence of the comfortable feeling 'the author and I are one up on your peasants."[52]

The rejection of one's highly valued poetic virtues like objectivity and impersonality by the forties poets was easy, its substitute difficult. Poetry became the churning ground for different vocabularies, idioms, definitions and theories, while the Muse continued to lament the poet's essential separation from the object of his experience: "The ideal poetic state is purely instinctual, emptied of opinions, reduced to a simplicity, "as Wain seems to agree with Gottfried Benn's opinion, and therefore, "The impulse towards openness of texture, which came in during the 1950s, was necessary and liberating."[53] Elaborating the need for the kind of poetry that grew up in the fifties, Wain wrote: "The mechanised intricacy of the modern world has bred a great desire for simplicity and spontaneity. This much is obvious. What is not quite so obvious is that it has also bred a desire for the inchoate. The things we have to deal with from morning till night, from motor cars to television sets, from sky-scrappers to business corporations, are all so *finished*, so remorselessly contrived and carried out to the last detail, that we begin to long for something that is fragmentary and suggestive, something that we can complete for ourselves."[54]

Elsewhere, dwelling upon the etymology of the word "modern," Wain said that it grew out of the Latin word *modo,* which means "just now," and *modernus* is the adjective from which we derive the word "modern." Wain draws home the point that the arts which grew up between 1912 and 1945 "were characteristic of an epoch of social impatience."[55] This social impatience thought very low of tradition, and therefore could not produce a work of art which could be worth emulating for by the younger generation. The fifties poets did not take any literary model from the forties; instead they went back to the eighteenth century to draw their models from: "In the eighteenth century, most poets believed that what dignified man and distinguished him from the brute was his faculty of reasoning; so the poetry they wrote was reasonable and intellectual; and the diction they chose included many words for operations of the reason, such as generalisation and analysis. In the nineteenth century most poets glorified man's will of his passion or his sensibility, rather than his reason; and their diction changed accordingly."[56] The poetry of every period can only adjust and readjust itself to the demands of a particular sensibility at a particular time. It is possible and desirable on the part of the poet to be aware of the tradition behind him to which he can turn on points of crises, formal or semantic. Davie wrote that his time in Russia has taught him that a "writer's sole duty is to report what was, *as it was;* and that in the interest of serving that overriding obligation, he must be prepared to be numbered among the criminals, the perverts, the barbarians, even the unfeeling administrators."[57]

All Movement poets emphasize urbanity, sobriety, and sincerity, and a return, time and again, to the eighteenth century prosody and diction. As Davie thinks, diction in poetry in particular and literature in general, is the product of the prevailing ideologies of the time. Spenser's diction, says Davie, is courtly-humourist; Johnson's diction is pious and bourgeois, while Yeats's diction is rooted in Irish culture. Style, as different from diction, constitutes the great tradition of English poetry; style unconsciously assimilates diction; poets like Chaucer, Milton and Pope have created a style; poets like Gray, Goldsmith, Johnson and Wordsworth have developed a diction out of it. Dryden, Johnson and Crabbe draw upon a common stock of artifice and convention.

The poet has a responsibility to his society for correcting and purifying the spoken language. The poet should not become frigid, much less get lost in his own ivory tower. Frigidity gives sense of impropriety, while the highly metaphorical use of language lends artificiality to the tone. Language varies according to genres. For Wordsworth language becomes unchaste when devoid of its common use. "Wordsworth", says Davie, "dare leave no margin of operation for taste and judgment; because he thought he found, among readers of poetry, only vicious taste and unstable judgment.

Wordsworth had no such confidence in his readers as Goldsmith had in his. When he lost confidence in his public, the poet was thrown back upon confidence in himself. When this confidence, too, was shaken, it masked itself as hysterical arrogance. This is one way of describing the Romantic revival."[58] Kingsley Amis, reacting against romantic poets' use of language, wrote:

> Over all, a grand meaning fills the scene,
> And sets the brain raging with prophecy,
> Raging to discard real time and place

And then comes the advice:

> Better, of course, if images were plain,
> Warnings clearly said, shapes put down quite still
> ... ...
> Within the finger's reach, or else nowhere;
> But complexities crow the simplest thing,
> And flow the surface that they cannot break.[59]

Davie goes on to add that Romantic poets affected the Sublime rather than the Pathetic, and therefore, Wordsworth, though he purified the written language, let the spoken language suffer: "A chaste diction is 'central,' in Arnold's sense; it expresses the feeling of the capital, not the provinces. And it can do this because it is central in another way, central to the language, conversational not colloquial, poetic not poetical. The effect is valuable urbanity, a civilized moderation and elegance."[60]

Because of different social contexts of each age, literary forms continue to change their colour and texture in terms of language as well as subject-matter. That is why, Wain remarked that in spite of the fact that the eighteenth century set a very high value on the epic poet, failed to produce one. Augustans were not in a position to nourish an epic poet because of their "prevailing rationalistic and urbane atmosphere."[61] The course open to the poet of the fifties is to choose from a variety of cultures and traditions. But "one demand, in return, the imagery museum will henceforth make on every artist. He will have to take the reader, listener or looker into his confidence. The poet will have to say to his reader, 'This is how I propose to work—along these lines, starting from these conventions'; there will have to be an element of invitation, with the poet saying to his reader, "Will you come with me? Shall we share this experience?"[62]

Davie told Alvarez once: "I still maintain that with all the skill, with all the delicate ear, with all the pleasure you take in sheer verbal manipulation you do not in this way get good poetry. A good poem is necessarily a response to human situation."[63] Elsewhere also Davie has said: "I cannot help being personal. For like any other literary man of my generation in the English-speaking world I find myself, as I turn the pages of Tate's *Collected Poems,* repeatedly brought up short by poems and parts of poems that recall my past to me. . . ."[64] Combine, as a poet should, the intellectual with the emotional, he should in no case lose his contact with the "visual and the emotional events," as Conquest put it. In his "Post-Script 1975" Davie again comes to the same point and recalls that in the 1950s poets wrote as if they had a contract with the reader as was possible in the eighteenth century. Davie believes: " . . . those of us who have survived as writers from the 1950s into the 1970s it is still the only honourable stratagem that we can practise—to act *as if* the writer and his readers were still the civilized people that they may have ceased to be."[65] Society has changed with the times and concepts of justice, leisure and productivity have undergone a similar change, according to Wain. What we now have is a bourgeois public which can look at a work of art as an utterance on behalf of humanity, without asking whether it can serve particular causes. Wain agrees with the view that "The modern arts command a large public because they offer work in a bourgeois idiom and they address a bourgeois audience. Since most of the people who take any notice of art—who go to concerts, buy books, frequent art galleries—are middle-class, they naturally attend to the middle-class artist."[66]

The way open to the modern poet, therefore, is where he thinks the writers of the succeeding ages have gone wrong in imitating the ancients: ". . . it is just here that the modern poet can cut in: our objections are silenced as soon as the poet, when he uses a style from the past, makes it plain to the reader that he knows what; he is doing-that this is a conscious pastiche or a conscious parody."[67] Once the poet, reader, and the people have got in touch with each other, the writer may take a backward glance at history to formulate his own vocabulary of terms-symbols and images. Wain wrote: "In some epochs of literary history, poets are on the whole content with the forms which have been working well for their civilisation, expressing its thoughts and aspirations and dreams, telling its stories, portraying its scenes: thus the Augustan poets, more or less from 1660 to 1750, were largely content with the end-stopped couplet (called the 'heroic' couplet because it was associated with epic poetry. . .), or with certain well-tried lyric measures; again, the Victorians, willing though they were to experiment with a wide range of forms, tended to feel happier with patterns that had been used before and were associated with recognizable purposes: ten syllable blank verse for high narrative, the sonnet for passionate reverie, or formal address, the ode (however structured) for lofty rhetoric and high meditation. When the modern idiom came in, the reigning conventions were at once passed under searching and sceptical review: to express modern view of the world, it seemed to many, must involve breaking the old forms. But what to replace them with?"[68]

Obviously, one should go back from the deluge, confusion and chaotic formlessnes of the forties to the confident heroic couplet and urbane diction of the eighteenth century. History is a kaleidoscopic conglomeration of images in which events, the poetic forms, lie, sometimes dead; sometimes half-breathing, and sometimes just about to die; it is the duty of the poet in crises to go into that region with all sincerity and devotion at his command, and revive and bring back to life those poetic forms and sensibilities which fit in into the mould of his age. He should further inject in his chosen images a new life by the sheer stroke of his genius so that the monuments of history become the living ornaments in the now and the immediate present. This is what purification of diction implies. Taking his title of the chapter from Eliot, "The Language of the Tribe," Davie says: "For if the poet who coins new metaphors *enlarges* the language, the poet who enlivens dead metaphors can be said to purify the language."[69]

Purity of diction is a historical need and forms put of a continuous episode in the history of the poetry of every nation. The dead metaphors are offered by poets of previous generations as well as by "studied conversation" and "artless prose." It is the poet who recreates, redefines, these metaphors, the eternal lineaments on the continuous ebb and flow of the current of time. Davie found that "the best eighteenth century verse strikes us as active, weighty, governed by the forceful verb."[70] In such a verse, sound becomes the necessary concomitant to the sense, and the verse is what it says. The dancer cannot be separated from the dance, nor the dance from the dancer, and if poetry has been able to strike harmony between form and content• on the one hand, and the poet and the reader on the other, what more do you want out of it? Form must mimic the matter as Wain says, and if you "escape from" form, you escape from all the poetic effects worth having for.[71]

Amis explains that for the modern poet: "A sufficient variety of forms lay ready to hand, from the loosest ballad or song metre to the strictest simulacrum of high verse in heroic couplet or decasyllabic quatrain. With this there went an equally wide range of manner or method, from satire, which for the most part is aggressively sensible, to what is called nonsense. . . the writer plays on a set of tensions, between closeness to the model and distance from it, the plausible and the entertaining, what makes a fair parody and what makes a good poem in its own right".[72] The fifties poet could even look into such eighteenth century literary devices as Personification, Generalization, and Circumlocution for his own purposes, and assimilate them into the texture of his idiom. It all depends upon the metaphorical force a writer is able to throw upon and inject into words. Johnson throws metaphorical force from noun to verb and produces personification. Wain says: "The instinctive naturalness with which Johnson uses this kind of language—concrete and abstract at the same time—is illustrated by the fact that he doesn't seem to have heard of the rule that Personification has to have a capital letter and Non-Personification must do without one."[73] Whereas Davie could advocate the use of such devices by his sheer reliance upon the inventiveness of the poet, Wain seems more sceptical, and remarks that "Modern writers simply don't use language with that degree of generality; if they did, they would be postulating a social infrastructure that is just not there."[74]

It is often thought that the eighteenth century poets were lofty in tone and with the use of devices like personification, generalisation, and circumlocution went away from the conversational idiom of the people. Davie contradicts the whole notion: "The lofty style uses the speech of the court; the mean style, the speech of merchants and yeomanry; the base style, the speech of menial trades and the peasantry. However much the social structure may have changed since Puttenham's day, there is no excuse for supposing (as we often do) that the loftier the verse, the less conversational."[75] Throughout his thesis in *Purity of Diction,* Davie takes pains to show that it is not the words which grow old; it is the poet's sensibility which loses its vitality and becomes senile because of the vicious tastes of a particular milieu, and the poet loses all sense of inventiveness and metaphorical force in language. "This circumlocution is neither good nor bad in itself. When it is good, it ensures a consistent tone of discourse. And if, as I.A. Richards maintained, tone is an aspect of meaning, then to preserve a consistent tone is one way of defining meanings and purifying the language."[76]

Some pedagogues in our time think and want others to believe, Davie says, that Romanticism was a series mental aberrations which we must disown.[77] Davie rightfully acknowledges that it is the Romantic poets who permanently transformed the physical land into mental landscape.[78] However, when Wordsworth was advocating that there is no essential difference between the language of prose and that of poetry, he was deriving his inspiration from the language used in the eighteenth century natural philosophy: "Literary history can show us, in many languages, examples of prose influenced by verse; with English poetry, at the moment, it is the other way round. Since it is not given to any human artist to be so original that he breaks free of *all* influences and still remains an artist, a poet who throws away all the aids designed for him by his predecessors in poetry ends up leaning on one crutch alone, the crutch of prose."[79]

As long as a poet uses deeply and seriously metaphorical language; as long as he handles aptly syntax and the conversational idiom, he can make words poetical otherwise unpoetical, and thereby purify the language. Poetic language depends upon, and is often influenced by, prose: "In Shakespeare the prosaic is only a momentary shaft of light through the foliage of metaphor. In Pope it is superbly clear and taut, but always pointed, limited in tone. In Wordsworth what seems to be statement is really rumination. Where this strength occurs in poetry, that poetry must be said to have the virtues of good prose. . . This strength of statement is found most often in a chaste or pure diction, because it goes together with economy in metaphor; and such economy is a feature of such a diction."[80]

There is a poetry in prose and a prose in poetry, and the division of literature into genres is a critical necessity, and at one level is irrelevant. Wain believes that all literature exists within the single act of integrated perception of the imaginative realm. But at another level imaginative perceptions search for forms: "Great poetry results when the poet who receives this strength is able to match it with his own native vitality. Neither will do without the other."[81] It is a fallacy, as Wain holds along with Davie, that traditional rhythmic patterns are divorced from the common flow of language. People do speak in iambic pentameter only if we keep our ears open (your face is dirty. Do you ever wash?). "All the metrical patterns that have served poets faithfully are still serving ordinary speakers. The rhythms of the Anglo-Saxon alliterative metre are so pervasive that one cannot talk in English for two minutes without the whole repertory of them. And rhythms from outside English, such as the Alexandrine and the hexameter, are very apt to occur in speech."[82] Here Wain more or less summarised the argument of Davie's *Articulate Energy.* Davie agrees with Wimsatt's statement that "In fact, words have no character as rhymes, until they become points in a syntactic succession."[83] Language at its highest pitch, mood and intensity, is not a system of grammatical rules and the poetic license can make verb of nouns, or adjectives of nouns and so on: ". . . a case for syntax other than symbolist syntax in poetry can be made to rest upon just these grounds—that a movement of syntax can render, immediately present, the curve of destiny through a life or the path of an energy through the mind . . . in my view the enthusiasts for presentation, for embodiment, have been ill-advised in ignoring the part that authentic syntax can play in bringing about all that they hope for, by miming a movement of the mind or of fate."[84]

Poets in different periods, under the garb of stylistic or thematic innovations, merely shift trends of emphasis with varying degrees of novelty. "Clarity, heavy rhythms, strong rhymes and the rest are the vehicles of confidence, of a kind of innocence, of shared faiths and other long-extinct states of mind,"[85] felt Amis. Urbanity, strength, clarity, sincerity, *polis,* conservative, conversational idiom, in a way, summarise the whole attitude of Conquest-Amis-Wain-Davie party. Interestingly enough, the chapter, in which Davie summarises the whole argument, is titled, "The Reek of the Human." Here Davie refers to Wordsworth's poem "Complaint of a Forsaken Indian Woman" and emphasizes the essential human predicament of the poem. ". . . there is nothing left; for diction, metre, rhyme, imagery, all are made transparent for the truth to shine out through them. This poem is not a world, like the world of a symbolist poem, 'closed and self-sufficient, being the pure system of the ornaments and the chances of languages.' It takes meaning only as it is open to another world; unless it refers to that other 'real' world, it is meaningless. Its syntax articulates not just itself, not only its own world, but the world of common experience."[86] This is what Wain calls the absorption of a public situation by the poem: "If a poem deals with the public situation it must absorb that situation into its metaphors, its rhythms and its entire verbal fabric."[87]

Any approach in criticism, from any standpoint, will offer value judgment of some sort on the poem; the business of critical jargon, for more than five decades in poetry, has, however, been to make a poem something more or something less than it actually is. Partly, the problem is metaphysical, but partly in their attempt to be objective, critics try to hide value judgments. Conquest tells such critics that "The real way is not to conceal them in this fashion, but to recognise them."[88] A poem is a monument to the creative impulse in man, and even if the poet had to explain his own poem, he would utterly misconstrue the entire fabric of words that went into the making of his poem. The tendency of systematic criticism has been to build a theorem, a system, or order of words, and try to explain the poem in terms of values, impulse, language, structure, strategy, and so on. The attempt by recent critics to achieve "rigour" in writing and reading a poem has sometimes resulted in absurdity. This is not to say that a poem is a mysterious entity. The symbolist and anthropological critics will have us believe that a poem is its own world. Such a poem for them has pure syntax, diction, is absolute and self-contained. Such critics would let Wordsworth down because his poems smack of the natural soil, the reek of the human, as Davie says.

Davie has always stood for an approach to the poem from within a factual verbal structure. Such arguments that a poem is a mystery, and that it is beyond explanation, Movement poets thought nefarious. A poet is made of the same flesh of which words are made and have their origin in. It would be a better way of saying that the environment and situations in which certain words are used at certain temperatures of creative process, differ, sometimes largely, and sometimes slightly, from their common day-to-day use. But it would be a fallacy to believe that the roots of the tree of words are not down inside the earth but up above in the voids of the sky. "It is my case against the symbolist theorists that, in trying to remove the human smell from poetry, they are only doing harm. For poetry to be great, it must reek of the human, as Wordsworth's poetry does. This is not a novel contention; but perhaps it is one of those things that cannot be said too often."[89]

All criticism is based upon impressions and responses to the poem. However, Wain thinks, criticism sometimes fails to understand its task which is that of making the poem more communicable and an object of shared appreciation. Wain makes it clear that no poetry is an impenetrable mystery, and readers, who complain of the obscurity of modern poetry, would do well to read Shakespeare or Dante. Wain makes clear his attitude: " . . . what we need, I should have thought, is a reasonable supply of criticism that is serious without being esoteric. If it were possible to establish the basic fact that to read a poem critically (that is to say with discrimination that directs, without stifling, an alert sensibility and a full respon" siveness) is not really an impossible ideal, something to be left to the specialist, but an activity that any sensible person can hope to train himself for, with not much more equipment than his native honesty and vitality—if we could establish *that,* we might dispel a good deal of the blankness with which the ordinary educated person, in an age of prose, looks at the poetry that comes his way."[90] It will be seen by the statement quoted that Movement poets were not only trying to bring poetry down to earth; in their attempt to make poetry an object of shared and community experience, they were de-mystifying the dimensions of symbolist criticism and simplifying the jargon of American and British criticism of the thirties. On the poetry and criticism prior to the fifties, Amis wrote:

Enough of this great work has now appeared
For sightings to be taken, the ground cleared,
Though the main *purpose – what it's all about*
In the thematic sense-remains in doubt.
We can be certain, even at this stage,
That seriousness adequate to engage
Our deepest critical concern is not
To be found here. . . [91]

The concern of modern critics to indulge in "degrading thirst after outrageous stimulation" (Conquest quotes Wordsworth) has only tried to test the merit of a poem upon the criteria of "tension" and "density": "There is a spinsterish opposition to balance and proportion and in favour of 'brutal' frankness; and a demand for vigour is vulgarly satisfied by a plethora of kinaesthetic adjectives and images."[92] Such critics have forgotten the simple fact that "poetry has no 'tasks' (as, for example, to fulfil the requirement of certain critical demands) except to be poetry,"[93] and what it means, a poet-critic would know better than a critic-poet. The critics are not critical enough, or perhaps they lack creative-critical bent of mind, such critics imagine their own judgments certain and final, and "feast upon shadows in the prevailing famine of substance." As Davie told once to Millicent Dillon, on has to "unlearn" all the skills of poetic craft when the ideas are in a stage of formation and simmering up: "When I wanted to write poems I did have to consciously unlearn a great deal of those skills and disciplines which had got me where I was. And it was by studying Pasternak particularly, very intensely in the late 1950s and the 1960s, that I learned how to suppress the abstracting and conceptualizing part of my intelligence in favour of the image-making and sensuous perceptions."[94]

Movement poets' emphasis upon a close link between poetry and prose we have met before. In the *Purity of Diction,* Davie returns to this point again quoting from Pound who exhorts the poet to learn from the prose writers, while, at the same time, not to use prosaic syntax. This is what Johnson called the "prosaic discipline" in poetry. In symbolist poetics, the syntax is dislocated. Davie would even argue that this dislocation makes "unprecedented concentration of one kind of poetic pleasure;"[95] but the poetics of the fifties poets is grounded in the community feeling, and therefore, deviations from pure artistic pleasure, to the pleasure of community, have to take place. And because Mr. Davie relates the whole concept of purification to being close to the language of conversation, he goes on doubting, if it can ever be possible for a symbolist poet to "purify" language in the sense in which Dr. Johnson did it in the eighteenth century or Movement poets did it in the twentieth. For this reason too, Mr. Davie will find the well-arranged syntax, the spokesman of law and order in society, and the dislocation of it, a threat to the system.

John Wain too, always emphasizing upon the essential closeness of metaphor to the living speech, says: ,. All Eliot's theories about poetry started from the assumption, which he in turn had inherited from the generation before, that a nation's taste in poetry is dictated by a small, highly cultivated minority, whose attitudes are handed down, in an increasingly blurred form, to ever-widening circles below them".[96] Wain also goes to Pound like Davie, and remarks that one reason why *Cantos* have been attractive is "stop-and-start, jotting qualily,"[97] and the reason for the popularity of Pound's *Cantos* is Pound's habit of note-book form of writing therein. Recounting the fifties Wain says that younger ones in that decade thought of giving to the public the "right quality of feeling," "to respond to life with one's emotional priorities in the right order – that was the ideal".[98] This attitude, one will have to agree, could only *settle* for certain things, either in syntax, or in subject-matter, for its chief concern was to correct the public taste, and not to develop a highly meta-symbolist ethic about the universe of the poem. Wain said: "My purpose in life is the same as that of any artist: to perceive such truth as I am able to perceive, and to pass on to other people through the experience of the art I practise," and further, commenting upon artist's responsibility to society,

Wain says: ". . . if I didn't say that a major motive is to build bridges to other people, bridges without which I would be very lonely and frustrated,"[99] I would, Wain thought, not be telling of a major function of literature.

The impulse to assimilate people in the experience of the poem is likely to take us as close to prose as possible. That is one reason Davie praises Landor. Davie derives his meaning of urbanity from Arnold who described it as "tone or spirit of the centre, embodying the best of a civilization". It is here that Arnold spoke of urbanity as an attribute of the best prose, and the best prose for Davie becomes the sign of pure diction: "To make poetry out of moral commonplace, a poet has to make it clear that he speaks not in his own voice but as the spokesman of a social tradition."[100] What the Movement poets have been aiming at is to build a society with precise traditions of literature and manners; it is only then that the tone, which this social environment would give to the poet, should be the tone of confidence, and the diction which the poet would use will be pure. At this point one wishes that Addison and Steele were born in the twentieth century instead of eighteenth, to make the task of Movement poets easy and successful.

From the same essential concern with a public poetics,[101] Davie defends British poetry which has often, in recent years, come under attack, labelled as provincial and extremely limited in scope. Davie traces this strain in British poetry to Thomas Hardy and says: "I have in mind an apparent meanness of spirit, a painful modesty of intention, extremely limited objectives-fall into place if they are Seen as part of an inheritance from Hardy, an attempt to work out problems, especialy social and political problems which Hardy's poetry has posed for the twentieth century. And I hope to do more than merely excuse these characteristics of writing in Hardyesque tradition; I want to present them as challenging, and to ask in effect, "Are not Hardy and his successors right in severally curtailing for themselves the liberties that other poets continue to take? Does not the example of the Hardyesque poets make some of those other poets look childishly irresponsible?"[102]

The challenges which Davie has thrown here hold a great potential in themselves. The statement above asks for need of historical perspective, the perspective in the light of which we could place and judge our Miltons and Larkins. In the reprint of 1969 of *Purity of Diction in English Verse,* Davie has written, "Under a thin disguise the book was, as it still is, a manifesto."[103] In the 1952 edition itself Davie had written in conclusion to Part I of this book: ". . . it is, after all, to the would-be poet of today that I should like to address myself," and that ". . . this study might help some practising poet to a poetry of urbane and momentous statement."[104] In his second book, *Articulate Energy,* Davie again wrote: "My first book of criticism, *Purity of Diction in English Verse,* was a thinly disguised manifesto."[105] Again, much later, Davie told Dana Gioia in an interview: "Yes, there was a time when I was, and indeed it's now got itself a modest little place in literary history, and is called simply The Movement, with a capital M; and it belongs to the middle 1950s, to a period when I discovered, and half a dozen other poets subsequently my friends discovered, that though we were starting from very different points we were moving upon a common area, a point at which our different careers, and the styles we were working out for ourselves, interacted in an important way. And that moment in history is marked by what was the fighting anthology of the Movement, *New Lines,* edited by Robert Conquest . . ."[106]

In fact, when Amis met Davie for the first time, he had already read the *Purity of Diction.*[107] It was then that Davie recalled that "we had been moving, each by his own route, upon a common point of view as regards the writing of poems. That point of intersection, or an area of agreement around it, came to be called the Movement, and under that title has earned itself a footnote in the literary histories,... I like to think that if the group of us has ever cohered enough to subscribe to a common manifesto, it might have been *Purity of Diction in English Verse.*"[108] Wain also recognises that Amis's work is based on a "'steadying common sense, a real hatred of imbalance and excess, . . "[109] Someone even wrote that it was "difficult to tell John Wain's poetry apart from Kingsley Amis's," but Wain doesn't quite agree with this view and modestly recounts: "As for the so-called 'Movement,' I only wish my writing really did have the virtues of the 'Movement' as, say, Philip Larkin's does."[110] Nevertheless, Wain's principles of writing remain committed to the ideology of the Movement poets. "A writer," wrote Wain, ". . . is doing well if he understands the truth about any kind of human situation, any kind at all, and passes it on to the reader without evasion, without distortion, without smudging it into sentimentality, and above all without oversimplifying it."[111]

People have read in Davie's *Articulate Energy* another poetic manifesto. Davie, too, says that the book was an extension of the argument of *Purity of Diction.* Apart from syntax with which *Articulate Energy* is chiefly concerned, Davie is developing his theory of syntax while always having in mind the type of audience which the eighteenth century poet enjoyed. This ethic of shared experience naturally allows for a simple, straight-forward, and prosaic syntax, for every man of the poetic community cannot become an expert in deciphering subtle nuances of tone and deviations in syntax. Contract with the reader, of some kind or the other, is a traditional contract, and a poet like Ted Hughes, who rejected terms of contract of the Movement poets with the audience, had to develop a grosser contract which puts him on a par with Mick Jagger.[112]

John Wain had complained to Davie in the fifties that English verse suffers from a pervasive lack of style, and Davie is said to have approved this view privately. That was one reason for Davie falling back upon the eighteenth century which hated excess and welcomed urbanity, balance, either in style or in manners. Professors Cox and Jones, writing on the literature of the fifties, said: "Many of the new writers of the 1950s had been young men during the last war. Their writing appears to stem from a denial of the horror of such facts as Dachau, Belsen and Hiroshima, a refusal to be contaminated by the chaos in which their youth had been involved. They withdrew from politics and fighting, and tried to celebrate the inviolate quality of their personal emotions in lucid, disciplined verse. Philip Larkin's recently published *The Whitsun Weddings* includes some of the best poems written in this mode, combining lucidity and compression of meaning with orthodox meters and rhyme. . . In the novel, Kingsley Amis and John Wain tried to return to the fictional modes of H.G. Wells and Arnold Bennett, to show the problems of man in society in a conventional manner."[113] Wain agrees that this is true of his career in the fifties. In 1957, analysing the state of poetry in England, Wain wrote that learning the trade is an ideal that has been neglected for the past twenty years: "During these years, the watch-word was 'open your mouth and shout.' Now, it is 'learn your trade, sing whatever is well made.'"[114]

III

The foregoing study of the poetic manifestoes of Robert Conquest, Kingsley Amis, Donald Davie and John Wain has demonstrated that in their concern for simple but urbane language, a poetry of shared experience, for a pure and chaste diction, choice of subject-matter, treatment of traditional, often eighteenth century metres, and above all, in their basic concern to maintain in the poems a human touch or contact with the reader, the poets under discussion are seen to have an uniformity of opinion which groups these poets, inadvertently, in The Movement.

The purpose of Part I was to do the spadework for the theme in hand. It demonstrated how the personal knowledge of each of the Movement poets, of the other, helped ruminate over the state of poetry in England in the thirties and the forties, and what the poet of the fifties should and could opt for, in the best possible way, it was decided, was to correct flam-boyancy in speech, manners, subject-matter, and style.

Part II demonstrated the course of action the Movement poets took. How they tried to do away with the rigours of the concepts of objectivity and impersonality without undermining their real value; the poem as a self-contained world in itself; the poet as the supreme craftsman not caring the least for the congregations in the church or the man in society; the poem as an artifact, order of words or symbols quite esoteric; and the use of impure, unchaste diction and syntax. Literature which thinks that its purpose is to serve the intellectual elite was soon to be forgotten of. The Movement poets were trying to bring literature close to the common man which not only Wordsworth, but the writers prior to him, had done in the eighteenth century. The virtues of lucidity, precision, urbanity, clarity, chastity in diction, well-mannered rhythm of confidence in poetry and perfection in craftmanship were what these poets aspired for, as opposed to allusion, obscurity, and excess of style.

The eighteenth century discovered its models of clarity, precision of thought and contour, in the works of Horace and Virgil and other Classic Greek and Latin poets. The Movement poets looked up to eighteenth century for the purpose in hand was: "In church or chapel the unlettered eighteenth century Englishman could be nourished, at least some of the time, by a poetry like the poetry of Horace; by language that was clean, solid and intellectually sinewy as well as forcefully melodious."[115] Davie's four books on the study and style of eighteenth century language and literature speak, in themselves, of the Movement poets' interest and aims, methods and technique they were trying to adopt for their strategy in the fifties. The second section of the chapter also elaborates the principles outlined above. It inclines to the view, as the extensive quotations from each of the poet under consideration will show, that the poet is a product of society, and therefore, by the poems that he constructs, he must reflect his own sense of responsibility to it. This responsibility can best be carried out by correcting the tastes, tones, manners, even understanding, of people at a given time. The Imaginary Museum, of which Davie talks, is a museum in which a plethora of styles, cultures, sensibilities, and traditions are available to the twentieth century poet. This much ingenuity is expected of the poet that he makes a choice, and that which he choeses, he should be confident of its effects, moral or literary, upon the audience he is supposed to address. The entire gamut of this argument is of course directed to this simple fact, that the language should be conversational, and that the formal aspect should cover the virtues of the purification of diction and thereby of the language of community, nobility in style, use of traditional metres, and above all, a concern with the human.

Ian Hamilton notes that Robert Conquest's Introduction to *New Lines* "outlines the well-known virtues of clarity, honesty, intelligence and rigorous empiricism."[116] Conquest had spoken of the basically non-mystical and empirical attitude of the Movement poets. John Press also wrote: "They all display a cautious scepticism, favour an empirical attitude, speak in carefully measured accents, and examine a problem with alert wariness. Believing that the virtues of good prose are not out of place in poetry, they have room in their verse for coherent argument, subtlety, irony, and erudition, because rational men ought not to exclude from their poems those qualities of mind which have played so large a part in shaping our intellectual heritage. . . . They frown severally on loose emotional gestures, inflated rhetoric, the cult of the poet as rebel, inspired madman, or Bohemian, since these aberrations permit the fool and the charlatan to debauch their readers' sensibility and the English language."[117] John Press's statement clearly points to important characteristics of the Movement poets elaborated upon in this chapter with reference to the statements by the poets. Even John Wain, who was always conscious that he will not fit in anywhere, bad to confess that there was a "broad general agreement."

Notes and References

1. Clive James, "Kingsley Amis," *The New Review*, Vol. 1, No. 4 (July 1974), p. 27.
2. Philip Larkin, Introduction to 1975 reissue of *Jill* (London: Fortune Press, 1946), p. 17.
3. "Kingsley Amis Looks Back—An Interview with Melvyn Bragg," *The Listener*, February 20, 1975, pp. 240-41

4. Ian Hamilton, "Four Conversations—Philip Larkin," *London Magazine* (November 1964), p. 72.
5. John Wain, *Sprightly Running: Part of an Autobiography* (London: Macmillan, 1962), p. 187.
6. Ibid.
7. D.J. Enright, "Signs of the Times," *The Month* (August 1952), p. 107.
8. Donald Davie, "The Varsity Match," *Poetry Nation*, No. 2 (1974), pp. 72-3.
9. Donald Davie, *These the Companions: Recollections* (Cambridge: Cambridge University Press, 1982), p. 79.
10. *Ibid.*, pp. 134, 136.
11. *Ibid.*
12. Donald Davie quoted in W. Van O'Conner, *The New University Wits* (Carbondale, 1963), p. 121.
13. "Remembering the Movement" in Barry Alpert, ed., *The Poet in the Imaginary Museum: Essays of Two Decades* by Donald Davie (Manchester: Carcanet Press, 1977).
14. Clive James, "Kingsley Amis," *The New Review*, Vol 1, No. 4 (July 1974), p. 27.
15. R. Conquest, ed., *New Lines: An Anthology* (London: Macmillan, 1962), p. 15.
16. Anthony Thwaite, *Contemporary English Poetry* (London; Heinmann), p. 144.
17. John Wain, "English Poetry: The Immediate Situation," *Sewanee Review*, Vol 65 (1957), p. 359.
18. John Wain, *Professing Poetry* (London: Macmillan, 1977), p. 3.
19. "It seems to me that the old Arnold-Flaubert-Eliot belief in the impersonality of the work has given way to the radically different concept of art in a continual cross-fertilizing relationship with the artist's life. On these terms the existence of a work of art is contingent, provisional. It emerges from Autobiography . . ." A. Alvarez in *The Review*, Nos. 29-30 (1972), 10th anniversary issue.
20. Donald Davie maintained in an article, "Towards a New Aestheticism," that there is a prejudice for Art for Art's sake and Walter Pater.

21. Ian Hamilton, *A Poetry Chronicle: Essays and Reviews* (London: Faber, 1973), p. 55.
22. It is a different matter that such demarcation became a negative feedback for Alvarez in 1962.
23. Ian Hamilton, *op. cit.*, p. 55.
24. Spender comes nearest to pinning down the change in an interesting chapter on the poetic "I" (Short History of Pers. Pron. 1st Sing. *Nom.*") which traces different forms of self-consciousnesses from Donne to Joyce. See the review of Spender's *The Struggle of the Modern* (Hamish Hamilton) by Francis Hope, in *The Review*, No. 8 (August J963).
25. Donald Davie in *The Review*, No. 1 (April/May 1962).
26. Kingsley Amis, ed., *The Faber Popular Reciter* (London: Faber, 1978), p. 16.
27. John Wain, ed., *Anthology of Contemporary Poetry: Post-War to the Present* (London. Hutchinson, 1979), p. 10.
28. Amis rejected Dylan Thomas (and George Barker) on the grounds of "a general shift in poetic fashion." See Philip Gardner, *Kingsley Amis* (Boston: Twayne Publishers, 1981), p. 119.
29. John Wain, *Anthology of Modern Poetry* (London: Hutchinson, 1963), pp. 34-5.
30. Quoted by Ian Hamilton, "The Making of the Movement," in Michael Schmidt and Grevel Lindop, ed., *British Poetry Since 1960: A Critical Survey* (Oxford: Caranet Press, 1972), p. 70.
31. D.J. Enright, ed, *Poets of the 1950s* (Tokyo: The Kenyusha Press, 1955) and R. Conquest, ed., *New Lines: An Antnology* I & II (London: Macmillan, 1956 & 1963).
32. *The Spectator*, March 19, 1954. Mr. Litvinoff remarked that we need not wait until the sixties to know what we thought of Mr. Wain
33. Kingsley Amis, ed., *The New Oxford Book of Light Verse* (London: OUP, 1978), p. xii
34. *Ibid*, p. xviii. Amis had earlier made it clear that poetry without *Landscape near Parma*/Interests a man, so does *The Double Vortex*/so does *Rilke and Buddha*. See Philip Gardner, *Kingsley Amis*, p. 120.
35. Donald Davie, *Augustan Lyric* (London: Heinmann, 1974), p. 9.

36. John Wain, "English Poetry: The Immediate Situation", *Sewanee Review* (1957), Vol 65, p. 354.
37. John Wain, ed., *Every Man's Book of English Verse* (London: Dent, 1981), p. 23.
38. *New Lines,* p. xv.
39. John Wain, ed., *Everyman's Book of English Verse,* p. 25.
40. Conquest, *New Lines,* I, p. xiv.
41. *Ibid.,* p. xvi.
42. Donald Davie, *The Late Augustans* (London: Heinmann, 1968), pp. xxxi-xxxii.
43. Kingsley Amis, *What Became of Jane Austen? And Other Questions* (London: Jonathan Cape, 1970), p. 22.
44. John Wain, ed., *Anthology of Contemporary Poetry: Post-War to the Present* (London: Hutchinson, 1979), p. 9.
45. Donald Davie, *The Late Augustans,* p. xxxii.
46. See Conquest, *New Lines,* p. xv.
47. Donald Davie, *The Late Augustans,* p. xxxii.
48. Conquest, *New Lines,* II, p. xvii.
49. *Ibid.,* p. xvii.
50. D.J. Enright, ed., *Poets of the 1950s,* p. 17.
51. *Purity of Diction in English Verse* (London: Routledge & Kegan Paul, 1952), and *Articulate Energy* (London: Routledge, 1955).
52. *New Lines,* II, p. xviii.
53. John Wain, *A House For Truth: Critical Essays* (London: Macmillan, 1972), p. 17.
54. *Ibid.,* p. 19.
55. John Wain, ed., *Anthology of Contemporary Poetry: Post-War to the Present,* p. 10.
56. Donald Davie, "The Poetic Diction of John M. Synge" (Jan.-March 1952) in *The Poet in the Imaginary Museum,* ed., Barry Alpert, pp. 8-9.
57. Donald Davie, *These the Companions: Recollections* (Cambridge: Cambridge University Press, 1982), p. 80.
58. Davie, *Purity of Diction in English Verse,* p. 23.

59. "Against Romanticism," in Kingsley Amis, *Collected Pcems* 1944-1979 (London: Hutchinson, 1979), p. 35.
60. Davie, *Purity of Diction,* pp. 26-7.
61. John Wain, *Professing Poetry* (London: Macmillan, 1977), p. 40. Davie had earlier said, "Words like lyric, satire, epic are remnants of an old elaborate structure in which we no longer believe." *Purity of Diction,* p. 8.
62. *Ibid.*
63. "A. Alvarez and Donald Davie: A Discussion," *The Review,* No. 1 (April/May 1962), p. 12.
64. Davie, *Trying to Explain* (Manchester: Carcanet Press, 1980), p. 3.
65. Davie, *Articulate Energy,* p. xiii.
66. John Wain, *Professing Poetry,* pp. 264-65.
67. Davie, "The Poet in the Imaginary Museum," I & II, (July 1957) in *The Poet in the Imaginary Museum,* p. 54.
68. Wain, *Anthology of Contemporary Poetry,* p. 14.
69. Davie, *Purity of Diction,* p. 31.
70. *Ibid.,* p. 36.
71. " . . . the manner of a piece of writing must to some extent mimic the matter, so that one doesn't express a funeral lament in perky jog-trot rhythms or produce the verbal equivalent of trying to do a Cossack dance to a Pavane that it tends to sink out of sight." *Professing Poetry,* p. 145.
72. K. Amis, ed., *The Faber Popular Reciter* (London: Faber), pp. xii & xv.
73. John Wain, *A House for Truth,* p. 121.
74. *Ibid.*
75. Davie, *Purity of Diction,* p. 59
76. *Ibid.,* p. 61.
77. ". . .my teachers when I was young encouraged me to think that I could expunge Romanticism from my historical past by a mere act of will or stroke of the pen, and that by doing this I could climb back into the lost garden of the seventeenth century . . .", Davie, "Sincerity and Poetry" (Winter 1966) in *The Poet in the Imaginary Musem,* p. 144.

78. " . . . I would argue unfashionably that poetry may legitimately, and often does, originate in a response to landscape. . .", Davie, "Landscape as Poetic Focus" (Summer 1968) in *The Poet in the Imaginary Museum*, p. 166.
79. John Wain, *Professing Poetry*, p. 151.
80. Davie, *Purity of Diction*, p. 67-8.
81. Wain, *Professing Poetry*, p. 150.
82. *Ibid.*, p. 156.
83. See *Articalate Energy*, p. 139.
84. *Ibid.*, pp. 157-58.
85. K. Amis, ed., *The Faber Popular Reciter*, p. 18.
86. Davie, *Articulate Energy*, pp. 164-65.
87. Wain, *Professing Poetry*, p. 260.
88. *New Lines*, II, p. xix.
89. Davie, *Articulate Energy*, p. 165.
90. John Wain, ed., *Interpretations* (London: Routledge & Kegan Paul, 1962), pp. xiii-xiv.
91. "The Huge Artifice: An Interim Assessment," in K. Amis, *Collected Poems* 1944-1979 (London: Hutchinson, 1979), p. 87.
92. Conquest, ed., *New Lines*, II, p. xxii.
93. *Ibid.*, p. xxix.
94. Davie, *Trying to Explain*, pp. 43-4.
95. Davie, *Purity of Diction*, p. 97.
96. Wain, *A House for Truth*, p. 17.
97. *Ibid.*, p. 19.
98. *Ibid.*, p. 26.
99. Wain, *Professing Poetry*, p. 276.
100. Davie, *Purity of Diction*, p. 192.
101. Edouard Roditi, in an article "Public and Private Poetics" in *Poetry* (Chicago), Vol. LXIII, Oct. 1983-March 1944, held that from Homer to the eighteenth century "a vast majority of European writers was mainly concerned with imitation . . . with conforming to some standards or norms of expression, and with the avoidance of any too striking originality. . . . Such a conception of poetry led to the use . . of a relatively public

language which was rather the vocabulary of poetry than that of the individual poet."

102. Davie, *Thomas Hardy and British Poetry* (London: Routledge, 1973), pp. 11-2.
103. Davie, *Purity of Diction*, p. 197.
104. *Ibid.*, p. 107.
105. Davie, *Articulate Energy*, "Postscript 1975," p. ix.
106. Davie, *Trying to Explain*, p. 206.
107. Davie, *Purity of Diction*, p. 197.
108. *Ibid.*
109. Wain, *Sprightly Running*, p. 205.
110. *Ibid.*
111. *Ibid.*, p. 207.
112. See Davie, *Articulate Energy*, p. xiii..
113. Quoted in John Wain, *A House for Truth*, p. 213.
114. "English Poetry: The Immediate Situation," *Sewanee Review*, Vol. 65 (1957), p. 374.
115. Davie, *Augustan Lyric*, p. 10.
116. Ian Hamilton, "The Making of the Movement," in M. Schmidt and G. Lindop, eds., *British Poetry Since 1960*, p. 72.
117. John Press, *Rule and Energy*, p. 45.

2

From Prison-Hole to the Prismatic "Other"

The chapter will examine the state of poetry in England after the Movement (*i.e.,* roughly after 1956) and will try to relate points of similarity and of divergence in the poetics of Charles Tomlinson, Ted Hughes and Thom Gunn.[1] It will examine the nature of attitude that underwent a change in the climate of opinion, and could not feel satisfied by the Movement aims, methods, ideology and poetics. The first part will consider divergences between the anthologies of Robert Conquest (*New Lines,* 1956) and A. Alvarez (*New Poetry,* 1962), and will also give the reaction of the poets under consideration to the Movement poetics. Thereafter, each separate section will be devoted to examining the poetic universe in the light of the statements on poetic theory of Charles Tomlinson, Ted Hughes and Thom Gunn. The final section of the chapter will relate important findings, and try to focus on the new trends and tendencies as achievement by poets under consideration.

I

Alvarez subtitles his Introduction to *The New Poetry* as "Beyond the Gentility Principle." The context is Conquest's

New Lines where Conquest had tried to bring "simpler part of melody and rhythm" back to the proper orchestration with the aim of remedying the "rapid collapse of public taste." Conquest and the Movement poets had to oppose the view that poetry is necessarily metaphysical or symbolical, and they took it on themselves to oppose anything that amounted to "diffuse and sentimental verbiage, or hollow technical pirouettes,"[2] chiefly typified by the poetry of Dylan Thomas.[3] Social adaptiveness had burned alive the finer shades of meaning in the poetry of the poets, and the talent had come to be sacrificed to the subjective moods and social pressures. The Movement ideology, designed as it was, to correct the public taste, produced at best, a literature which is a mirror to social reality. The attempt to correct the public taste gradually amounted to conforming to it, and poets, in search for personal recognition, lost the sense of dignity of poetic grandeur while the genuine, serious poetic frameworks lay within the womb of nature weeping for want of words, with the help of which they could speak and articulate something of the mystery of life or what Eliot called, on the technical side, Donne's expertness beyond experience. Alvarez attributes it to the "relative failure of talent" and opines that the London old-boy circuit sometimes becomes "stupid, conceited, and parasitic."[5]

The Movement poets themselves found overburdened with the narrowness of their range and style and Wain was to declare: "Dylan Thomas had made his contribution to English literature and it had been a major one . . . 'Prophetic' verse was the vogue. C.M. Bowra, from the enormously influential position of professor of poetry at Oxford, pronounced Edith Sitwell the greatest living English poet. But beneath the crust of stale fatuity, a revolt was stirring. This revolt is now over, its work done, . . . The thing had been duly carried to its conclusion. . . ."[6]

In the same article Wain divides poets under three categories. The first are those who have not changed themselves in spite of social pressures (like W.S. Graham);[7] the second are those who pretend to think that there has been no T.S. Eliot, Ezra Pound, Imagists or the *Symbolist Movement in Literature.* Poets like Thomas Hardy and Philip Larkin inhabit this category. Wain is at pains to see, recognising the poetic gifts of Hardy and Larkin in particular, the conservatism of these poets, which is "Not bad, not bad at all—but how determinedly 'period'! There is an unmistakable gift at work, but why has it got to work with the materials of our grandparents' day?"[8] The third category of poets is inhabited by younger poets (like the ones under consideration) who have made significant personal discoveries, and who have found the Movement ideology insufficient. These poets have learnt their art well and taken the best from the romantic and the classic traditions to suit the need of the present. It is now public which has to conform to the taste in poetry and not *vice versa.* Conquest was indirectly hinting at Hughes and Gunn *in New Lines* when he wrote: " . . . some poets, too, were deeply affected, and men capable of moving work were encouraged to regard their task simply as one of making an arrangement of images of sex and violence tapped straight from the unconscious, or to evoke without comment the naivities and nostalgias of childhood."[9]

It was likely that Wain and Davie should develop their poetic theories with a leaning towards the academic and the intellectual, while Amis and Larkin kept on going their way of keeping close to the reader. Larkin even lamented the unfortunate merger of poet, literary critic and academic critic. Davie announced that "Poetry is not a democratic institution, and it never was,"[10] while Conquest confessed to being influenced by Gunn,[11] and thought in 1962, that "you can't programme a poet as you can a computer or something; he can't even do to him, self—the things that strike what one might call his poetic imagination adequately are not necessarily those that his political, or even his artistic, conscience (or any other conscious force) would prefer him to write about."[12] In his *New Lines* Introduction Conquest had written that if one had to distinguish the poetry of the fifties from its predecessors, the most important general point would be that "it submits to no great systems of theoretical constructs nor agglomerations of unconscious commands. It is free from both mystical and logical compulsions and—like modern philosophy—is empirical in its attitude to all that comes."[13] The trouble with this kind of poetry was that there was too little that came its way and what it thought "empirical in attitude" was the sheer localization of the world in terms of such ideas as iambic rhythms and chaste diction reflecting law and order in society; the choice in subject-matter was impoverished already. Poetry cannot live in the time-bound test-tubes of our parochial, provincial arguments, and if it is made to live, it will gyrate and revolt.

The demand to bring poetry closer to the reading public gave birth to philistinism, and the reaction against the academic, and Eliot and Pound in particular, sheltered mediocrity and such versifiers who had no theoretical or formal framework for their often unpoetic ideas. Human sciences, much less the art of poetry, are derived from, and are a reading of, the world of Nature. This Nature is both apprehensible within our rational scheme of things, and mystical in so far as our mental apparatus is endowed with certain kinds of capacities and not others. The demand from the immediate now had to give place to the demand of "the other" in poetry as we shall see, and that was one reason Davie reacted against the antagonism to academic attitude: "Academic is no bad thing to be, and in any case becomes inescapable, as the philistinism of Anglo-American society forces ap artists—not just writers—back into the campus as a last stronghold. It is a question whether the universities can rise to this emergency."[14]

As said earlier, a writing which started to correct the tastes of the reader adjusted itself to the tones, nuances, likes and dislikes of that conglomeration that is called "public", and this was, as Davie says, against the view of poetry considered as self-expression. But the result was not unexpected: "Hardly ever did we seem to write our poems out of an idea of poetry as a way of knowing the world we were in, apprehending it, learning it; instead we conceived of it as an act of private and public therapy, the poet resolving his conflicts by expressing them and proffering them to the reader so that vicariously he should do the same. The most obvious register is the absence from 'Movement' poetry of outward and non-human things apprehended crisply for their own sakes. I'm not asking for 'nature poetry', but simply for an end to attitudinizing. In 'Movement' poetry the poet is never so surrendered to his experience, never so far gone out of himself in his response, as not to be aware of the attitudes he is taking up. . . . This imperiousness towards the non human goes along with excessive humility towards the human, represented by the reader; you can be as arrogant as this towards the natural only if you assume (as I think we all assumed) that the sole function of the natural is to provoke a vocabulary of terms—'symbols,' 'images'—by which people, poet and reader, can get in touch with each other."[15]

It is evident from the statement of Davie that when poetry has been reduced to an act of public therapy, the deeper concerns of poet's relation to the world, God, and other creatures of the universe would stand isolated. Shakespeare's dramas cannot be explained in terms of a catharsis of pity and fear alone, relevant as they are to our understanding of the play. Art is more powerful than any explanations about or of it, and its success or failure is to be judged, not by seeing whether it conforms to the public taste, important as it is in itself, but by its power to stimulate and evoke in the reader a state of consiousness which, apart from having metempric, universal-metaphysical, as distinct from theological, connotations, should also be noble, sublime and innocent in the Blakean sense, or depict something of the pre-fall state when Adam and Eve lived in communion with God in the existence divine. It has been the most notable feature of the post-fifties British poetry that Hughes and Tomlinson have turned to this aspect. The other important thing in Davie's statement above is that the poet is somehow to surrender to the pre-planned attitude in his experience and in any case develop or evolve them.

C.B. Cox and A.R. Jones, writing in 1961 on the fifties,

said: "As we look back now on the 1950s, it is almost as if the 1939-45 war produced a relapse among some English writers, a psychological return to Edwardian modes of art, as a means of avoiding the terrifying implications of war. This is perhaps most clearly seen in the poetry of the Movement. Many of the new writers of the 1950s had been young men during the last war. Their writing appears to stem from a denial of the horror of such facts as Dachau, Belsen and Hiroshima, a refusal to be contaminated by the chaos in which their youth had been involved They withdrew from politics and fighting, and tried to celebrate the inviolate quality of their personal emotions in lucid, disciplined verse."[16] It will be obvious from the above account what the Movement writers were doing. However, in their search for shelter in personal emotions, the attempt to preserve the self,[17] as Cox and Jones say, wider issues of poetry remained untouched as was apprehended by Davie and Tomlinson. Cox and Jones go on to demonstrate how the works of Graham Hough *(Image and Experience),* Thomas Hardy, Robert Frost. Robert Graves, John Crowe Ransom, Edwin Muir, and John Betjeman went on to strengthen the tradition for a poetry of ideas and feelings that are part of the life of common man.

All this was good but it pinched at a vital point. This vital point asked for a "new seriousness" from Alvarez and a "new Aestheticism" from Davie. Hence the justification of Alvarez's arguments in *The New Poetry* and Tomlinson's searching and seething article "The Middlebrow Muse." It was almost baffling to note that while Pound, Williams, Stevens, Olson and Lowell continued to write experimental verse, nothing notable happened in England. Americans had no tradition of poetry writing prior to the twentieth century as Alvarez says,[18] but it is they (Pound and Eliot), again Alvarez, who "have used the genius of the English language to its full."[19] The reason for a tendency with Americans to experiment with new verse-forms and subject-matter, Alvarez says, is due to their dependence upon foreign models. On the contrary, the American Frost freely fits in the. British climate because of his poetry of manners, and not Eliot and

Pound type of cosmopolitan who in England is always a suspect virtue. ". . . I think this is why Frost has been so readily accepted in England; he is peculiarly congenial; we are easy with tradition of country poetry, simple language and simple wisdom."[20] But this was Alvarez in 1958. In 1974, Alvarez ". . . apparently so disillusioned or unillusioned now that he no longer bothers even to look at what's going on, might dismiss the whole thing—all this talk of 'two camps' and 'deadlock' and so forth—is what he once called 'gangwarfare': something which he saw ten years ago, in his introduction to the Penguin *New Poetry*. . . ."[21]

We have, by now, very well established the context which must delineate the need for a new poetry to grow and establish itself. "English empiricism had narrowed with a vengeance: if this was to be the whole extent of a poet's wisdom, then a counter-possibility had to be established. In his Introduction to *New Lines* (1956), Robert Conquest announced that poetry of the fifties, at least that part of it represented by the Movement, is 'empirical in its attitude to all that comes.' But how much was *allowed* to coine before the poet? Hadn't the deliberate narrowing—in some part of a healthy reaction against the gestures of neo-romantic poetry of the forties—been merely an excuse, one asked oneself, for the British philistine and was not the need still Arnoldian one—'to pull out a few more stops in that powerful but at present somewhat narrow-toned organ, the modern Englishman?"[22]

The statement of Charles Tomlinson is a clear indication of the *New Poetry* attitude that was to take root in England after the Movement. Alvarez begins his Introduction to the *New Poetry*, rather astonishingly, making the remark that "since Eliot removed himself into another, remote sphere of influence by proclaiming himself 'Anglo-Catholic in religion, royalist in politics, and classicist in literature,' the whole Movement in English verse has been to correct the balance experimentation had so unpredictably disturbed. Some time in the twenties Thomas Hardy remarked to Robert Graves that *vers libre* could come to nothing in England. 'All we can do is to write on the old themes in the old styles, but try to do a little better than those who went before us.' Since about 1930 the machinery of modern English poetry seems to have been controlled by a series of negative feedbacks designed to produce precisely the effect Hardy wanted."[23]

Earlier in 1958, Alvarez had said that since Americans had no tradition of poetry writing, the emphasis naturally fell upon language; and Eliot's colloquial rhythms, Cummings unfamiliar lines siding with the typewriter, and the linguistic innovations of Williams and Olson, seem to Alvarez, no more than "a series of techniques, 'gimmicks', for producing certain fashionable effects."[24] Perhaps Alvarez is not just and is exaggerating the point by placing it out of context, for why should "subsequent intense analysis of their (American poets) work"[25] be allowed to form the basis of our judgment? One will agree that mere technique will generate reptiles of feeling and nostalgias of emotion, but that the sense of "personal urgency" comes only through sticking to one's native tradition of writing, one may have his reservations against. Larkin even said in 1964 : ". . . to me the whole of the ancient world, the whole of Classical and Biblical mythology means very little, and I think that using them today not only fills poems full of dead spots but dodges the writer's duty to be original."[26] Charles Tomlinson retorted: "So Eliot, Pound, Cavafy, Seferis, Pasternak had dodged their duty? England seemed, in all senses to be becoming an island, adrift from Europe and the past."[27]

A very narrow understanding of the ancient past has been one of the major reasons for the decline of British poetry since 1940. The attempt to bring back eighteenth century into the twentieth was doomed to collide with Ted Hughes and Thom Gunn forces. A poet like Larkin who says that "(I) have no belief in 'tradition' or a common myth-kitty or casual allusions in poems or poets, which last I find unpleasantly like the talk of literary understrappers letting you see they know the right people,'[28] one is tempted to ask what is Larkin's understanding of the changing contexts for poetry, right howsoever he might be in his own case. Larkin is following Hardy's advice to Graves that constitutes one of the major negative feedbacks since 1930. Art gives one insights into the reality and dimension of being; explores being and arrives at tentative though important conclusions. Eliot did not lose his confidence in language and its possibility by trying to convey the trivial and the commonplace, or what conforms to the public taste. He explored regions that cut across the geographical barrier in his attempt to arrive at the mystery of self and life. It is advisable, taking clue from Eliot, that one necessarily doesn't start as a poet, but as a philosopher, and busies himself searching for the language and subject-matter, not only in his native tradition which in itself is a philistine concept, but in all traditions and in all languages. Only a freak would be afraid of it and call it suspect virtue; A Blake, Shakespeare, Spenser, Chaucer, Milton, Eliot, Pound, etc., will not stop at the narrow calls of parochialism;[29] their turbulent spirit will take them into regions that are yet to be explored and tones and nuances of language, unfelt emotions and feelings of history, yet to be made use of. Such a view of poetry poses challenges before the writer; asks him to explore. The poet aspires to a human tradition and to human values which enlighten, invigorate, infuse life in the dead, soul in the body, and the world's tradition, in the form of Blake's Albion, rises again from its pale languor and sees the light into the divinity of being. That, one but exclaims out of sheer innocent joy, is art; that is life; there we can go; there we can relax.

As opposed to all this, "Contemporary poetry in England, however, is no more exciting than that of America, and considerably less accomplished. Perhaps, on both sides of the Atlantic, we are going through a kind of psychological convalescence after the shocked, inarticulate poetry of the war. The work certainly has a wan, emptied-out air to it. Or perhaps the great outburst of originality which occurred in the twenties acts now more as a discouragement than a goad. Or perhaps, quite simply, we are in an interregnum; the real talent is not in poetry at the present.'[30] That was 1958 when Alvarez could find out reasons for lack of genuine poetry in England; the Alvarez of 1962 negative feedbacks is more negative, and goes on outlining the negative feedbacks one by one. The first negative feedback stopped the insights of the novelists like Melville, Dostoyevsky, Lawrence, and at times, Hardy himself, coming into the English novel. In poetry there was a reaction against the experimentation of the twenties, for the thirties poet had no time to become an expert in verse-forms; he was too politically committed to care to be difficult, inward, or experimental, although Eliot continued to influence. The negative danger did not arise as long as Auden was there. He gave the younger poets "the go-ahead because he combined an extraordinary feel for the most contemporary of contemporary idiom."[31] Auden had even set the example as to how the tradition should be made use of. In a poem called "Lurcher-loving Collier, black as night," Auden recreated Shakespeare's traditional lyric "Mistress mine where art thou roaming" in terms of the "contemporary unromantic, industrial scene."[32]

This is the ideal, Alvarez would think, a modern poet should return to. However, the followers of Auden tried to become modern at the thick end of the thirties; the experimental verse ran out of the traditional forms and the first negative feedback had injected itself into the British soil. The Auden wave was not only resisted at the beginning of the new decade; it was violently reacted against and the reaction took the form of anti-intellectualism. Auden, like Eliot, was found too hard an intellectual to be capable of dealing with extreme circumstances of emotional situations which were to be the locale of the forties poet. It was natural that the war should make poets lose confidence in social concerns, and find solutions, if any, in their own confessional verse. Dylan Thomas had talent but the public demand for the poet as blindly inspired, made him use high-blown, flamboyant language, often of high turpitude. His followers, worse even, in their attempt to sound impressive, produced verse that was devoid of meaning altogether. This was the second negative feedback in British poetry. It blocked intelligence.

"The third stage was yet another reaction: against wild,

loose emotion. The name of the reaction was Movement, and its anthology was Robert Conquest's *New Lines*."[33] Alvarez describes the Movement verse as ". . . academic-administrative verse, polite, knowledgeable, efficient, polished, and, in its quiet way, even intelligent."[34] In a satirical tone Alvarez quotes Conquest saying: "Even the editor found he could define it only in negatives."[35] For Conquest had said: "What they do have in common is, perhaps, at its lowest, little more than a negative determination to avoid bad principles." Alvarez concludes: "This, in concentrated form" is the image of the post-war Welfare State Englishman: shabby and not concerned with his appearance; poor—he has a bike, not a car; gauche but full of agnostic piety; underfed, underpaid, overtaxed, hopeless, bored, wry. This is the third negative feedback . . . ."[36]

This assemblage of negatives was examined very minutely, earlier, by Charles Tomlinson. Tomlinson, in the first instance, sees the assemblage of poets in the *New Lines* heterogeneous, a variegated lot with Enright and Davie brought there more because of their name than because of their similarity and approval of the aims and ideology of the Movement. Tomlinson finds in the poets, a desire to remain humble and close to the reader, "an unconscionable amount of self-regard, of acting up to one's mirror image of one's self. I know of no surer measure of the lack of genuineness in art."[37] For a poet genuineness towards his material can only be possible when the desire to it is inborn. In their revolt against the nets of rhetoric of Dylan Thomas, the fifties poets forgot that Wordsworth repudiated the gaudy and inane phraseology of the eighteenth century poets not so much because he wanted to come closer to the common man but because he wanted to force the language of the common man on to the creative process of his own being. The language that came out churned up this way, and the language which came out of the fifties poets use of it, makes for a vital difference. It is not exactly the common man whose speech the poet can take directly to be his own. The feeling of being close to the public does not come by organizing programmes, much less by thrusting eighteenth century poetic forms and language upon the twentieth. "Mr. Enright has here in common with a number of his fellow poets a faculty for self-congratulation, afforded by playing a conscious game with your feelings and those of your reader. Miss Jennings is so *determined* to be feminine and nice, Mr. Wain and Mr. Amis to appear bluff and human, Mr. Larkin quaint and old-maidish, or knowingly humble. . . ."[38]

In 1963, Conquest categorically denied that he ever tried to start a Movement: ". . . this unfortunate, unfavourable mutation took place about twenty or thirty years ago, and there are too many poets around with two heads. We do not really resemble each other. It is just that the ambience provides a contrast, as it were, and makes us look rather alike. The movement simply comes of assembling people who have managed not to have their genetic structure altered by this unfortunate blast."[39] Conquest recalls that *New lines* was a reaction against a certain kind of poetry which is not poetry and feelings which are not aesthetic. Describing the state of poetry, though not offering a value judgment, Conquest seems to agree with Alvarez: ". . . thirty years ago people had their theories: you were a marxist or a Freudian and all that, and you therefore had your frameworks when you were twenty, twenty-one or twenty-two, and could write poetry round that structure. Again, in the forties, you did not have to have any ballast of theories or thought at all: you could just bash away at whatever came into your head. But now it is again realized that a poem should be to some extent an intellectual structure. As well as everything else, it should have a shape, a form and sense. Yet nobody really believes any more in any great metaphysical theories, any large, all-inclusive theories."[40] If we could relate this statement of Conquest's with the negative feedbacks of Alvarez, we could be inclined to believe that poetry is gradually acquiring a synthesis of form and content. But that is the state of very recent poetry, say after the seventies. If we take into account the period between fifties and sixties, the situation must surely sound unhealthy and negative. Alvarez then next proceeds to define what he means by gentility principle: ". . . gentility is a belief that life is always more or less orderly, people always more or less polite, their emotions and habits more or less decent and more or less controllable; that God, in short, is more or less good."[41]

Such belief in an otherwise ever-changing complex of psychosomatic organism generates feelings of inertia, sterility, boredom and loss of fecundity. The creativity of poetry is sacrificed on the altars of a plurality of negative criticism, and poets, instead of being complexes of poetic organisms, become the branches of a blasted tree, hanging loosely on their stem. What is worse, the gentility principle gives the false assurance that everything is good thus giving a chance to philistines to pronounce themselves poets of an impotent age, and critics, writing unhealthy criticism ofa rotten culture, find mental satisfaction in their own small mental townships. Robert Graves got nothing but loneliness, philistinism, lewdness, insensitivity and unhappiness in his childhood, all being the result of our civilized wars and cultured hypocritical mannerisms. Robert Graves could not get spiritual solace in this culture; he developed the philosophical framework of poetic values in terms of the White Goddess. Similar was the case with George Orwell. These poets encountered the gentility principle at various social levels and at each level they were disillusioned.

Alvarez takes pains to focus our attention on the ground on which the poet stands today. This ground has a horrible past and a bleak future: "What, I suggest, has happened in the last half century is that we are gradually being made to realize that all our lives, even those of the most genteel and enislanded, are influenced profoundly by forces which have nothing to do with gentility, decency, or politeness. Theologians will call these forces evil, psychologists, perhaps, libido. Either way, they are the forces of disintegration which destroy the old standards of civilization. Their public faces are those of the world wars, of the concentration camps, of genocide, and the threat of nuclear war."[42] What shall the poet do? Obviously the poet will have to relate poetry with some form of religion of consciousness for his task has become a double one. Not only to give poetry to the public but also help it in cultural nourishment. And here again concepts like "new seriousness" and "new aestheticism" are nothing but the modern poet's search for a meditative poetry, a poetry which does not so much talk of linguistic experimentation as of aesthetic meditativeness. Perhaps European sensibility was not dissociated before T.S. Eliot made that point, and one cannot but agree with Pasternak that the bane of modern literature has been its consciousness of linguistic experimentation. The Prufrockian doubleness has created schism in the personality of the European man.

And here again we return to the point made earlier that before producing poetry we have to produce aesthetic-meditative thinking sort of persons and the poetry will take care of itself. These persons may not be the products of universities; they may be someone like Scholar Gypsy type vagrant dwellers in a modern context. If we want an example, we need only open the Bible, be it the Song of Solomon or the Vision of Ezekiel, the poetry is flowing there in streams of innocence and nosegays of beauty. The concept of the poet as seer and saint has unfortunately been replaced by a poet who reads his poems in public, creates a public image, a fame-hungry versifier, who has no sense of the cultural heritage of mankind. All this, needless to say, has thrown poetry out of the inner sacred shrine. Society does not know whether it is she who has to nourish the poet, and the poet looks askance at society for the mode he might adopt for his poems. Alvarez goes to the extent of saying that "Had Freud been born in London instead of Vienna, he would probably have finished not in psycho analysis but in criminology."[43]

At the end of his Introduction Alvarez glances at some possibilities for the poet. And the first point he makes is that great and genuine poetry cannot be written by predetermined plans or attitudinizing. In any case British society has to "drop the pretence that life, give or take a few social distinctions, is the same as ever, that gentility, decency, and all the other social totems will eventually muddle through."[44] And then comes Alvarez's vital suggestion: "What poetry needs in brief is a new seriousness. I would define this seriousness simply as the poet's ability and willingness to face the full range of his experience with his full intelligence; not to take the easy exists of either the conventional response or choking incoherence."[45] Perhaps it would not be far-fetched to suggest that whereas Conquest had even laid down specific areas open for the poet to experience and impose his frameworks, if any, upon, Alvarez had not spoken of the subject-matter a poet should adapt to. If the poet's sincerity towards the object of his experience is genuine enough, we shall not have to worry for the outcome. Moreover, Alvarez's suggestion makes no extreme statements either with regard to language or subject-matter. It is a middle way where emotions and intelligence have their own respective roles to play in the sacred act of poetic composition. The act of creation is an act of faith and the poet's confrontation with his material should be naked and without evasion. Alvarez would value discipline in new poetry, something for which he would admire Movement poets, for Freud has already destroyed the distinction between emotion and intellect. Alvarez's terms for new poetic ideology are set in no uncertain manner: "D.H. Lawrence and T.S. Eliot represent the two warring and unreconcilable poles of modern literature. The best contemporary English verse, however, shows that their influence can be creatively reconciled. In the seriousness of what I have called the new depth poetry, the openness to experience, the psychological insight and integrity of D.H. Lawrence would, ideally, combine with the technical skill and formal intelligence of T.S. Eliot. If this were to happen, we would have contemporary work which, like Coleridge's imagination, would reconcile 'a more than usual state of emotion with more than usual order.' "[46]

Alvarez considers Lawrence and Eliot the poets one can go to for two respective kinds of inspiration and guidance. He, unlike Conquest, is not very historical in his approach as to talk of relating the modern poetry with the "central traditional of English poetry." Alvarez would like to go to Lawrence and Eliot because the first faced the full range of his experience while the latter originated the forms and is the best model of formal intelligence. When these two souls shall be imbibed by the modern poet's sensibility, poetry shall not sit sullen in the eighteenth-century metaphorical homes; it shall come out in the open, having Wordsworthian spontaneity, Blakean innocence, Lawrence's insight and Eliot's formality. Conquest had made the same point while talking of proportion and reflection in poetry. Just as Alvarez, Conquest also advocated the need for foreign models: "If all British poets remained totally ignorant of and unaffected by the foreign and classical cultures, this might well produce qualms. . . ,"[47] as it would produce philis-tinism for Alvarez.

It could be noted by a perceptive reading of *New Lines* and *The New Poetry* that the background out of which the two manifestoes arise is, variation in degrees allowed, the same. Both of them talk of the weight of linguistic rigour, the poverty of subject-matter genuinely faced, and the capacity to generate seriousness and nobility; both of them point the negative aspects of British poetry and criticism. Conquest wrote that the idea that ". . . this wilful self-conscious insistence on 'tradition' of a sort should combine with an equally self-conscious insistence on experiment,"[48] has ruined English poetry. Conquest is emphasizing that the blend of tradition and contemporaneity is not achieved by an effort of will; it is assimilated gradually into our thinking compartments until it almost becomes a part of us. Alvarez is doing no more than elucidating Conquest's point when he says: "The final justification of experimentation lay, of course, beyond mere technique. The great moderns experimented not just to make it new formally, but to open poetry up to new areas of experience."[49] And here Alvarez is contradicting his own claim made earlier that recent analysis of the works of modern American poets has reduced it to "a series of techniques, gimmicks, for producing certain fashionable effects".

Excess of either techniques, or too much consciousness of tradition, will only produce a fragmented sort of poetry:

"To be cautious about experimentalism is not to urge stereotypes. Yet writing becomes non-English non-poetry when wholly imprisoned in either form of poeticism, hackneyed tradition, or experimentalist contrivance."[50] Alvarez's middle way we have already pointed to. The danger with mere experimentation was seen by Alvarez when he said that ". . . . the whole movement of English verse has been to correct the balanee experimentation has so unpredictably disturbed,"[51] and this imbalance and rigour of form was created not by Eliot but by his followers. Both the manifestoes, then, focus on the immediate needs, more or less, of the same period. They are antagonistic not in their ends but in their means; Conquest is also for a balance of formal and semantic aspect; Alvarez is also for the same. But whereas Conquest would achieve it by considerably narrowing down the range and depth poetry is capable of taking, Alvarez would impose no restrictions upon the poet's range of experience as long as it is serious and ennobles, combining, of course, the formal and the semantic equally. That was one reason, with all the stimulation and interest, even controversy *New Lines* evoked, it became, for Alvarez, a negative feedback; how Alvarez's "new seriousness" is taking shape and texture we shall now see with reference to the poets under consideration.

II

Commenting upon the Movement poets, Charles Tomlinson wrote: "The lack one experiences in I think, all Mr. Conquest's poets is their general failure to see things anew, to register any *nouveaufrisson*, . . . They show a singular want of vital awareness of the continuum outside themselves, of the mystery bodied over against them in the created universe, which they fail to experience with any degree of sharpness or to embody with any instress of sensuous depth."[52] With Charles Tomlinson, one feels, poetry is right on par with a religion of consciousness, a religion which has not hated some in its puritanical orthodoxy, or denounced others, in their unorthodox manoeuvres. It is a meta-poetry, if one would call it, where the fragmentary parts have been given a new lease of life by the sheer perception of the underlying unity of existence, a poetry, which has become aware, for the first time since 1930s, of its own sinews of strength and nerves of steel, and left far behind, questions of public taste or an obstructing involvement with language, in its search for the identity of being and consequent liberation. Tomlinson's poetry liberates, not out of, or in spite of, anything, but through its involvement with the fine and rusty filaments, the fabric, the texture of the visible and the created phenomenon; it meets the invisible at some vital point, where it becomes a consciousness and a religion. It is an experience of noumenon, of the other, and it transcends everything through everything. Even our application of terms like genuine and sincere for such poetry takes something of the purity of the nerves and bones of the poems. One feels poetry is back to its ancient golden clime; fears allayed; doubts put to rest.

A poet who had such relentless quest for the noble in life should have felt frustrated at what the Movement poets had to offer. The narrowness, parochialism, provincialism, met for the first time, their real enemy in Charles Tomlinson, who hit them hard and straight. Freud's dichotomy between emotion and intellect resolved; an alternative to two world wars found; and if a meditative verse is to be found, it is here in modern English' poetry. A new trend then, in British poetry after the Movement, is its seareh for freedom from the narrow walls of geography, which had made the entire atmosphere of poetry writing choky and suffocating. "They seldom for a moment escape beyond the suburban mental ratio which they impose on experience. A poet's sense of objectivity, however, of that which is beyond himself and beyond his mental conceit of himself, and his capacity to realize that objectivity within the artefact is the gauge of his artistry and the first prerequisite of all aesthetic genius."[53] Of the two statements of Tomlinson quoted above the important thing to emerge is the poet's ability to see *outside* himself. The incapacity to do so either results in a personal art howsoever sublime, or in a terribly limited choice of subject-matter (as Movement poetry). Eliot was successful, as Alvarez thinks because in his *The Waste Land,* he was able to combine literature and theology, and this provided him a framework which he imposed upon his intensely personal experiences: "Eliot's talk of classicism, like his use in the poem of literature and theology, was an elaborate and successful defence which forced impersonality on a deeply personal and painful subject".[54]

Conquest in 1963 had also realized that a new poem should have an intellectual structure, shape and form.[55] The slant in attitude is evident. What is more, Tomlinson's statements also restore the quality to the poet as seer for it is he who sees things anew and shows a vital awareness of the continuum outside himself. This continuum outside is God's created universe in which vitality (itself a part of God) as exhibited in the uncorrupted objects (by civilization) of phenomena, impels and forces us to search for our own centres of existences, something which Tomlinson calls "the mystery bodied over". It is a mystery in so far as we do not know it because of our voluntary separation from it. It is a challenge, therefore, to the poet, in terms of formulation of language and subject-matter, and in fact entire poetic framework. The poetry does not become abstract here. The mystery of the universe has to manifest itself with a sharpness that catches the most tangible of human experiences with "instress or sensuous depth," as Tomlinson says.

The feeling of something outside oneself gives one a sense of one's own locale in the vast universe, and the sense of one's own smallness enlarges the area of one's experience. It is then that the human consciousness takes cosmic textures and speaks in an all-time diction, all-time imagery and verse-forms which are good for once and for all (Shakespeare will serve as an example). Such poetry transcends the periodicity of time in its search for the infinite in the finite line. Alvarez's demand for the poet to encounter full range of his experience is met here, for the poet's is a conscious revolt against the "suburban mental ratio" of the Movement poets which they imposed upon their experience and thus crippled the vital nerves of the existence of the Muse. Introducing Tomlinson's collection of poems *The Necklace* (1955) Davie wrote: "These poems present analysis of human perception, how it works and how it ought to work, in a healthy personality".[56] Tomlinson himself wrote; "A little book, *The Necklace* of 1955, got me from 'wakening with the Window over Fields' to its final poem 'Fiascherino,' where the fragments of sensation seemed to knit up into a more organic whole".[57] Davie's statement could best be seen in the light of Conquest's intention of cleansing vicious taste which is generated out of indiscriminating perception of unhealthy personalities. Tomlinson's unified perception is really our central argument and point of departure from the previous poetry. Tomlinson's poems, writes Davie, build their own universe; still they are not private and do not become obscure and develop a personal mythological system. They are the products of a healthy mind and balanced nervous sensibility that has succeeded in generating its own sense of colour, texture, odour and timbre. Once we enter into this world we are renovated and refreshed. The material of the poem starts bearing the same relation to the poet that the visible phenomenon bears to its creator. The poet becomes a craftsman having power to place his images, handle his syntax, and thereby create a new poetic universe: "By arranging together pines, snow, walking feet, and a particular sort of light, or raffia, bow-strings, bows, bats, winds, bamboos, and flutes—he creates a sound, a scent, a sight, and a peculiar atmosphere compounded of these, that 'never was on sea or land.' "[58]

One of the more important aspects of Charles Tomlinson's work comes from his association with American poets. Writing about his reminiscences in America, Tomlinson wrote: "American poets, together with a painter, helped an English poet find himself."[59] And the reason was obvious enough. He went to American poets in search for poetic frameworks: ". . . one has an apparatus, so to speak, in the work of people like Stevens, like Williams, like Marianne Moore, for dealing with external world."[60] Moreover, when Tomlinson started writing, British literary scene was dominated by new apocalyptic poets and Dylan Thomas. Tomlinson could not build upon or develop their literary tradition for its negative nature became to him clear enough: "You couldn't build a solid and trustworthy poetic architecture out of the kind of diction, out of the kind of imagery which was available at that time. It simply needed something new, and for my own case I found that the Americans helped here."[61]

But this meant no surrender of identity and the American tradition was not exempt from its negative points. One was the transcendentalist concept of surrendering oneself to an impersonal reality. Tomlinson did not choose even the American idiom. He tells this clearly: "My idiom was Queen's English, deriving of course, in its poetic structure, from an American example. But 'American idiom'? I feared that when McDowell Obolensky brought out *Seeing is Believing* in the summer of 1958, he would find it uninteresting because if he read it in the light of its influences, they were clearly pre-Williams and the themes of a decidedly English and European cast."[62]

Tomlinson's eclecticism cannot but be admired. The slant towards Americanism which one comes across in his statements is generated out of the need of the time and circumstances as said earlier by Alvarez. It is, however, more important that the concept of American literature is not prior to the fact of that literature being written in English; it is secondary, and therefore, of subsidiary importance. However, Tomlinson's openness is noteworthy, and his attempts to relate the British poet to the sources of his own culture find mention elsewhere too: "MacDiarmid does not resemble Eliot technically, but like the latter he has retained in his best verse the presence of 'the mind of Europe. . .' His aim has been to resurrect the Scottish tradition that pelered out with Burns; this achievement has been to forge a Scottish verse, neither antiquarian nor provincial, but one in which a modern awareness can nourish itself on the Scottish past and that can absorb into itself Chaucer, Dunbar, Villon."[63]

What is at work in Tomlinson's sensibility is to give

post-fifties poet a ground to stand upon which was lost after World War II. Davie's *Purify of Diction* tried to find that ground in the eighteenth century, but the eighteenth century was an age which depended for its cultural and literary nourishment upon the translations from Greek and Latin.[64] It was like the world reduced thrice from the original reality being a carbon-copy of the carbon-copy. The result did not take long to unfold itself. Movement poets, in their attempt to resurrect a native tradition, could neither become antiquarian not modern, they became, without wanting it, provincial; this struck a negative note in the development of British poetry. Tomlinson is as severe as Alvarez upon this negativism: "Larkin's narrowness suits the English perfectly. They recognise their own abysmal urban landscapes, skilfully caught with just a whiff of English films *circa* 1950. The stepped-down version of human possibilities (no Renaissance, please), the joke that hesitates just on this side of nihilism, are national vices."[65]

The reasons for Tomlinson looking towards other traditions to strengthen the native one become all the more apparent here. On the contrary, the healthy practices of native tradition should be continued to be absorbed in the ever-flowing stream of poetry. Davie has been Tomlinson's tutor, and the unity of which Tomlinson talks in his *The Necklace,* became possible to achieve because of the *Purity of Diction:* "I had started to consider syntax, and it was precisely this—mediating the relation between the shapes of sentences and the way we perceive things—that broadened the style . . ."[66] It was precisely for this reason that Tomlinson assumed ironic airs on D.J. Enright's statement made in *Poets of the 1950s* that, "every poem must be its own sole freshly-created universe." Tomlinson asked: "And this forty years after 'Tradition and the Individual Talent'?"[67] Later, Tomlinson thought the whole Movement pseudo and non-literary: "I shall conclude by suggesting that *New Lines,* with its 'movement' bias, is one of the many signs of the relativity of what passes currently for literature and literary criticism. This relativity is grounded in an attitude to life, and that attitude is both widely established and rarely questioned. Its philosophy—if one can call it that—begins with a debased form of humanism which associates itself only too readily with the natural right to 'get on' and to stay on as long as possible. The 'movement' was in the first place a journalist's convenient generalisation. It is only our total relativity of standards, our want of high and objective criteria that can cause us to mistake it for a significant literary fact".[68]

Before the Movement, Tomlinson recalls, the condition was worse. The atmosphere was filled with Dylan Thomas's high-blown rhetoric, and "the problem for a young poet—at least for *this* young poet—was to get beyond it towards something a little lush. A step in this direction was made possible by the discovery of these poems of Wallace Stevens like 'Thirteen Ways of Looking at a Blackbird' . . ."[69] What is worse, G.S. Fraser's anthology *Poetry Now* falsified the whole concept of serious and genuine poetry by anthologising two hundred names. "Has *any* age produced two hundred poets at one time who, by any objective criteria, were worth anthologising?"[70]

It was this loss of objective value in literature and criticism of the forties and fifties that brought the "democratic relativity in literary standards." Literature became the battleground for establishing not the literary merit but the unliterary literary prestige. All this merely helped to "establish at large the pragmatic ethics of confusion."[71] Out of this mess, the vital question was how to emerge and find out the literary lineaments of one's own being. To Alvarez and Davie, this alarming situation calls for a new seriousness and a new aestheticism, and to Tomlinson it arouses from contemporary parochialism to a study of other traditions. In the poetry of the forties and fiftics such a situation arose because of its loss of contact either with the French poetry or with the poetry of any other tradition. On the contrary, poetry on the other side of the Atlantic grew and flourished because—"... the thing about American poets is that they realize that they simply have got to read French poetry, whereas so many English poets are so pleased with the parish pomp it doesn't seem to concern them that they ought to know what happened in French Symbolism from, say, 1870 to round about 1920: from Rimbaud up to Valery. . . it has obviously fed the American poets as well, whereas writers of my own generation were not, I think, as poets, particularly interested in that kind of thinking."[72]

The interaction among various cultural traditions and literary contexts helps one to realize one's own deficiencies without violating outlines of native identity. The loss of contact produces philistinism in cultures and wishful thinking on the part of a few egoistically pathetic figures. This, on the whole, produces literature of the sort that Tomlinson has been a witness to in the forties and the fifties. This intentness on the part of Tomlinson to strike a new note and to refurbish the native tradition we shall also notice in Ted Hughes and Thom Gunn. Tomlinson wrote on Ted Hughes that he shows "an awareness of nature, of that other England which the London-bound writer has forgotten. . . ."[73]

Coming closer to Tomlinson's own poetic universe we come across a poem in *The Necklace* (1955), "The Art of Poetry," which describes Tomlinson's own poetic process and deals with the nuances of style and tone.

At first, the mind feels bruished.
The light makes white holes through the black foliage
O mist hide everything that is not itself.

But how shall one say so?—
The fact being, that when the truth is not good enough
We exaggerate. Proportions

Matter. It is difficult to get them right.
There must be nothing
Superfluous, nothing which is not elegant
And nothing which is if it is merely that.

This green twilight has violet borders.
Yellow butterflies
Nervously transforming themselves
From scarlet to bronze flowers
Disappear as the evening appears.

The first line points to the difficulties a poet encounters while trying to apprehend the reality.[74] And then the texture of illusion which is lying like a veil over the objects of the world, which makes something or everything other than itself. This gives birth to a struggle, the tension, within the mind and soul of the poet. The next stage in the poetic process oscillates between trying to apprehend the truth (unity of experience) and virtually ending with having got something of the truth and something of the illusion (the world as fragmentary). And while this process is taking place within the mental crucible of the poet, the problem of elegance, proportion, superfluity, crops up. And the tone of the poem is set by a word or line which stands in isolation aloof: "The green twilight has violet borders." The final stanza of the poem focuses on the minutest details of the apprehended universe where yellow butterflies transplant their lineaments upon the scarlet and bronze, leaving a presence, sense of colour, smell, taste, gyrating within the poetic universe.

In his Preface to *The Necklace,* Tomlinson has written: "The conditions of the realization lay in according objects their own existence."[75] This later meets us in Tomlinson's attempt to write an absolute poem. To this view of the poem, Tomlinson had arrived at by his association with Wallace Stevens. From Williams Tomlinson learnt respect for time and place. In his Introduction to the Penguin edition of William Carlos Williams, Tomlinson quotes from Paul Rosenfeld's book on Williams *(Port of New York.* 1924), where Paul says that there is no blame laid on time, custom and environment in Williams' poetry. Williams had criticised Eliot for casting an egoistical veil over the world and for an imperiousness towards places and objects. For Williams, "place is the only reality, the true core of the universal . . ." and this is what divided him from Pound who cast an "artificial pearl" upon the native scene. Tomlinson wrote in 1949: "Two themes—sometimes related and sometimes not—which recur in my poems, are the theme of the place and that of the return," and went on to add: "But the desolation of our own urban landscape has produced no place, at all and the way into my book lies through such a stretch of unfeatured surroundings."[76]

Tomlinson's attempts have been directed to construct poems that encounter reality that is mainfest in the visible appearance of the universe but is behind them. While Tomlinson could appreciate Stevens's idea of according objects their own reality and the relationship between the observer and the observed, he is perplexed to see the narrow limits of a "poetry which stood so explicitly by a physical universe and against transcendence. . . ."[77] And this was what drew him it. Hopkins whose poetry deals with "that universe, its spaces, patterns, textures, 'a world of canon and fugue.'"[78] Tomlinson speaks of the difficulty of seizing visual appearances and making poetry out of them. In the universe that he observes the fisherman who negotiates water creates a mode of living; in the same way a poet should encounter his world or rather create one using his craft, knowledge and experience.[79] This dialectic of encountering reality at specific moments of time forms part of a writer's coming to terms with his environment—difficult and beautiful at once, "This search for forms, for patterns of order, for meaningful relationship with people and place, is the basic human act of faith."[80]

Tomlinson has succeeded in creating a universe in which the smallest of the small is observed with utmost care and minutest detail and given its due place in the existential scheme of things. As said earlier, Tomlinson's is a kind of meta-poetry that sometimes takes delight in the sheer joy of creation,[81] and sometimes catches hold of the moment when God was resting on the seventh day, having created the universe. In his poem "Variation on Paz" *(Written on Water)* we encounter a similar situation:

> . . . we feel
> Behind us the sea's force, and the blind
> Keel strikes gravel, grinding
> Towards a beach where, eye by eye,
> The incorruptible stones are our witnesses
> And we wake to what is dream and what is real
> Judged by the sun and the impartial sky

This "waking" or expanding of one's consciousness takes us into the wider horizons of a universe where we are watched not by fellow human beings in the eighteenth century style of cafe and restaurant, but "judged" by the universal powers like the sun and the sky. The contrast between the two poetic universes is obvious.

Tomlinson has considerably enlarged his vision of history and in this he is influenced by Octavio Paz, the Mexican poet. Commenting on *Written on Water,* Tomlinson wrote: "Involved in history, men are sometimes equal to it, though seldom in terms of the kind of success they seek. This is where poetry comes into its own. Octavio Paz has called it 'the *other* voice.' 'Not the voice of history or of anti-history,' as he says, 'but the voice which in history is always saying something different.' "[83]

In Shakespeare, the tragic hero often knows and pre-apprehends his own fate; he considers for a moment that he is not only equal to, but greater than, the forces that govern human destiny, the forces of history; but his own doom is predestined and therefore his rage is impotent. Macbeth's fury is a bilabial plosive of much sound but little sense. In Tomlinson the gap between human expectation and human fulfilment places man, often, in a situation which has no contexts and therefore without explanation. This brings in "the other" in his poems. "We are not only the protagonists of history," wrote Octavio Paz ". . . we are also its raw material and its victims: it can only be fulfilled at our expense. Poetry radically transforms this relationship; it can only find fulfilment at the expense of history. All its products—the hero, the assassin, the love, the allegory, the fragmentary inscription, the refrain, the oath; the involuntary exclamation on the lips of the child at play, the condemned criminal, the girl making love for the first time; the phrase born on the wind, the shred of a cry—all these, together with archaism, neologism, and quotation, will never resign themselves to dying, or to being battered against the wall. They are bent on attaining to the end, on existing to the utmost. They... wait for the poem which will rescue them and make them what they are. There can be no poetry without history, but poetry has no other mission than to transmute history. And therefore the only true revolutionary poetry is apocalyptic poetry."[84]

The attempt to hang on and cling to life even when the conditions would deny it, is the vital urge, and this urge has its sources outside the frontiers of history. "The other" was present even before the existence of Nature; Nature is an assemblage not only of the objects outside but also of human aspirations and dreams that have been and are yet to be. Every created thing is related with every other created thing in some vital way. Shapes and forms vary and create a seemingly different, and often illusory, levels of existence. Our talk of *different* traditions, literatures, cultures, is part of the same argument. The fact of death and the incident and fear of change make created things to hang on, and this unites the variegated phenomena and levels distinctions. A writer who is able to perceive this activity at work in Nature; who undertakes to transmute this vital process of history through the medium of language in poetry, is a writer who will write about the destinies of mankind through particular historical contexts. Writing on *The Shaft*, Tomlinson recalls how he has been attempting from *The Way of a World* (1969) onward, to write "principally on the theme of the polarity of nature and history, and of their interaction."[85] *The Shaft* itself is about the non-separation of history and Nature.

The tradition of apocalyptic poetry came from Blake, Coleridge and Wordsworth. Particularly, Wordsworth and Coleridge were the first to explore the nature of self and how mind and senses contribute to this discovery. Tomlinson wrote: "As my poetry is a poetry of contemplation, so it is a poetry of return to objects and to scenes long looked at and consulted for images of relationship and habitation."[86] Tomlinson's poetry is a revival of romantic poetry in a vital way, and a continuation of the Movement too, in its love for the common-place; but then, the context in which the common-place is realized as common-place in Tomlinson and in Movement are two different things. Tomlinson is for a poetry which is able to comprehend something of the Blakean innocence, something of the vital link of life without committing itself to any ideological label.

One of the important influences upon Tomlinson's use of language has been Charles Olson's essay "Projective Verse" (1950). This essay highlighted the significance of the syllable, the sense of breathing the sense and area of the operation of intelligence, and the choice of language, which, in Tomlinson's view, grew out of an interaction of Nature and history. Olson's famous criterion was: "the two halves (in poetry) are the HEAD by way of the EAR to the SYLLABLE. The HEART by way of the BREATH to the LINE." Tomlinson wrote: "'Projective Verse' (1950) looks for the writer "who will 'put himself in the open,' composing verse 'as though not the eye but the ear was to be its measurer . . . the ear, which is so close to the mind that it is the mind's, that it has the mind's speech'."[87]

It was just the kind of language Tomlinson himself was in search for. To discover the unity of life it was necessary for the poet to invent or find a language that came out of the integrated proportions of his own being. Tomlinson wanted precision in language not inertness or "energising weather." He wanted to catch secrets of time, nature, history, and the language, in any case, had to arise out of an awareness of this process. This involvement in the historical process rejected the four-stress line and the iambic pentameter. In fact each poem requires a separate language and the translation helps here. It makes one aware of the way each word works in one's own and in the other language. Tomlinson was looking for a language in which words were married to things, and both words and things were married to the intellectual ideographs. But at a certain level language *unites* the poet with the object of his perception and points to someting which is neither the language, nor the poet, nor even the process of Nature and history. As long as the dualism like "a poet encountering the language" exists, "the other" within the poet, in sheer desperation, will tear down the wretched compartments of poet's being and slip into the unknown.

Tomlinson's coming to the graphics is merely an attempt to make art say what words could not say. Commenting upon Tomlinson's graphics, Octavio Paz wrote: "Tomlinson can violate the object, observe it, leap suddenly inside it and, before it dissolves, take the snapshot. The poem is a perception of the change, a perception which includes the poet . . . But there is another frontier: that of art and poetry, which translates into sensible forms, that are at the same time archetypes, the qualitative relationships between things and men. Poetry—imagination and sensibility made language—is a crystalizing agent of phenomenon. Tomlinson's poems are crystals, produced by the combind action of his sensibility and his imaginative and verbal powers—crystals sometimes transparent, sometimes rainbow coloured. . . . The act of looking becomes a destiny and a profession of faith: seeing is believing."[88] Here, Tomlinson's verse becomes meditative, contraries become relations, relations merge into the self, and the self is lost in the unknown.

III

Tomlinson had criticised the Movement poets for their "singular want of vital awareness of the continuum outside themselves, of the mystery bodied over against them in the created universe. . . ."[89] Ted Hughes wrote: "Words are tools, learned late and laboriously and easily forgotten, with which we try to give some part of our experience a more or less permanent shape outside ourselves."[90] Tomlinson, Ted Hughes and Thom Gunn, as we shall see, are vitally related in their concern for something outside themselves. Ted Hughes is, however, different from Tomlinson in that he develops a mythological structure for his poems which reminds one of William Blake, W.B. Yeats and Eliot. Hughes leans towards a certain non-Christian premise, as Blake, Yeats, Eliot and Tomlinson do, where art does not belong to this or that school, but to the primitive cult of ritual and magic in which the ancient religion plays a very important role. This premise which acquires its own sense of form and system as it develops within the soul and psyche of the poet, not only portrays inner conflicts which are creative and concern the process of Nature, but also points forward and beyond itself to the other; and then the words lose their intentionality, become silent; it is not language which speaks; it is silence which imprints and designates and absorbs.

The influences on Hughes are not so much literary as religious and mythological. His readings of *The Tibetan Book of the Dead,* Mercia Eliade's *Shamanism;* his early acquaintance with the work of W.B. Yeats, which opened his eyes to his own system and to Indian mythology; his reading of *Myth and Religion of the North* by Turville-Petre, form part of numerous influences on the formation of his themes and ideas.

In an important essay[91] Hughes recalls that his childhood companion was a dark cliff, "my spiritual midwife at the time and my god-father ever since—or one of my god-fathers." He wrote: "From my first day, it watched. If it couldn't see me direct, a towering gloom over my pram, it watched me through a species of periscope. . . From my home near the bottom of the south-focussing slope of the valley, that cliff was both the curtain and backdrop to existence. All that happened, happened against it or under its supervision... If a man's death is held in place by a stone, my birth was fastened into place by that rock, and for my first seven years it preserved its shape and various moods into my brain . . . ."[92] It is important to recognise Hughes's early surroundings which will give us a clue to his mental formation. Hughes's life then, is set all over against this cliff and the cliff is exercising a certain hypnotic power over the poet. The underlying experience out of the relationship between the poet and the cliff seems to be one of powerful spontaneity without expression which might explode any time through the medium of Hughes's mind. Hughes further recalls: "From there the return home was a descent into the pit, and after each visit I must have returned less and less of myself to the valley. This was where the division of body and soul, for me, began."[93]

In the early years Hughes also enjoyed shooting animals, catching fish with his elder brother, which explains Hughes's celebration of the wild forces of Nature in his early volumes. Tomlinson asks: "What exactly could be the relation between the intelligence, the life of mind, and this universe of blind energies?[94]. . . Hughes once attempted to contrast man and beast when he said of his portrayal of animals: 'Each one is living the redeemed life of joy, They're in a state of energy which men only have when they have gone mad. This strength arises from their complete unity with whatever divinity they have.' "[95] Madness should not be associated with abnormality. It derives its strength from, and has its source in, the divinity within man. The madness denotes ecstasy and not blindness. The Indian concept of *shakti* would better explain what Hughes means here.[96] Tomlinson went on to conclude: "I do not know if Hughes, on reflection, would wish to equate animal energy and human madness in this way, but it is clearly a stripped-down version of man—man thrown back upon the unthinking reflexes—that fascinates him"[97] Hughes clarified: "My poems are not about violence but vitality. Animals are not violent, they're so much more completely controlled than men. So much more adapted to their environment."[98] Hughes's poetic process works in terms of perceiving analogues and discovering the archetypal significance of things. The principle of vitality in life already discovered, Hughes's perception, as it works upon the objects outside, reduces things into gyrating currents; he draws out things from their outer reality and relates them to their vital essence. Things then acquire the texture of a rhythm, and this rhythm is mad without being insane, energetic without being violent, for it celebrates the joy of creation. The advance towards Alvarez's apocalyptic poetry has been made.

Hughes's poetic process is a kind of meditational activity, whereas in yoga, the consistent looking upon the object reduces object into a quality; this quality partakes or shares something of the object and something within the perceiver, which Hughes calls the divinity; when the two are related they are part of a vital rhythm of the universe; this rhythm is Hughes's discovery, and the liberation that it gives is not theological but artistic, where the spirit derives its delight from the form and the form has its roots in the spirit. "The spiritual kind of excitement, the slightly mesmerized and quite involuntary concentration with which you make out the stirrings of a new poem in your mind, then the outline, the mass and colour and clean final form of it, the unique living reality of it in the midst of the general lifelessness, all that is too familiar to mistake. This is hunting and the poem is a new species of creature, a new specimen of the life outside your own. . . The living parts are the words, the images, the rhythms. The spirit is the life which inhabits them when they all work together."[99]

Commenting upon Wordsworth's poetry, Hughes says that things cannot be related to each other except by some concept or the other, of spirit of essence, for the greatness and even the timely significance of things doesn't essentially come from a poem's reference to many matters outside the world of the poem; it depends upon the qualities of depth, breadth, accent in the spirit of it, all in a state of intensity.[100] It is needless to say that Wordsworth had perceived unity that passeth understanding. The mind of the poet then, in the initial stages of his poetic composition, is inert, non-reactive, Locke's *tabula rasa,* where "certain memories, images, sounds, feelings, thoughts, and relationships, between these, have for some reason become luminous at the core of his mind: it is in his attempt to bring them out, without impairment, into a comparatively dark world that he makes poems. At the moment of writing, the poetry is a combination, or a resultant, of all that he is, unimpeachable evidence of itself and, indirectly, of himself, and for the time of writing he can do nothing but accept it."[101]

Memories, images, sounds, feelings, etc., are a kind of fuel to the poetic fire; and just as the heat of the sun gives life to and unites the objects of creation, so does the poetic fire give life, place and habitation to the objects of his perception. This is the world of the poem parallel and analogous to the world of God. What is important in Hughes's poetics, as also in Tomlinson's, is that the world of the poem, apart from being self-contained to ensure stability, should also point forward to a world beyond, outside, where the poem should lose its existence in the improbable, the unknown, the mystery that is our existence wherefrom, and consequently, the poet can bring it back to life again by giving each word, image, sound, symbol, tone, its due, in the scheme of verbal structure: "The result should be a free poem of sorts where grammar, sentence structure, etc., are all sacrificed in an attempt to break fresh and accurate perceptions and words out of the reality of the subject chosen."[102]

The moments that have elapsed within the diacritical marks of the past are like the unextinguished fire, whereupon the present reacts, sometimes in its attempt to quash it; sometimes to derive life, inspiration and guidance from it. The whole world is then an imaginative body, very much in the Blakean sense; the poet brings back to life the neglected, the forbidden, which vitally connects itself with such apocalyptic concepts as "the old Adam, with volcanoes, world-endings, monstrous outrages, etc."[103] The qualities which Hughes admires in Keith Douglas's work are his own: "Pictures of things no longer interest him much: he wants their substance, their nature, and their consequences in life . . . his mind is whole, as if united by action, and he produces poetry that is both original and adult."[104]

The quest for substance, nature and consequences, develops into an artistic obsession and leads Hughes into the world of myth. This obsession has its roots in a certain sexual dilemma, as in the case of Shakespeare, and the world of myth, ritual, magic and symbol that Shakespeare enacts, is simply an elucidation and amanifestation of this sexual instinct.[105] As remarked earlier, Hughes's poetic imagination works by a psychology of association, ". . . poetic imagination is determined finally by a state of negotiation. . ."[106] and this negotiation makes Shakespeare relate his own psychic conflicts with events in the history of Elizabethan England. Poets whose minds operate within the mythic realm, work by a certain process of "empsychosis." In this state the mind appropriates certain qualities on to itself and imposes them upon the objects of its perception. The artist's thinking becomes mythic and the world appears as a play of myth, allegory, symbol and ritual. This is the vital "spirit" of Hughes, the creative potency, that reduces the visible phenomenon into parables.[107]

A poet either develops into history outward, *i.e.,* the society, the contemporary events, or inwards into the world of imagination and spirit. Organizing the inner world is a far more difficult task than putting into order the outer; and the difficulty of a poet who enters both the inner and the outer worlds, can well be imagined. "The ideal aspect of Yeats's development is that he managed to develop his poetry both outwardly into history and the common imagery of everyday life at the same time as he developed it inwardly in a sort of close parallel. . . His mythology is history, pretty well, and his history is as he said 'the story of a soul.' "[108]

Hughes has developed upon the concept of Nature as Mother earlier developed by Robert Graves. He even applies this concept on to Mary and Elizabeth enlarging them to archetypal proportions. This concept is found in Orphic, Hindu and Pagan mythologies. What may turn out to be the most remarkable contribution of Hughes twenty or thirty years hence, is his work upon translation of poems of every nation evolving a common poetics. Hughes's going to pre-Christian religions and cults is symptomatic of the same instinct—to find a world culture and a world language.[109] This concept of Mother-Nature, Hughes enlarges in his "Note" to *A Choice of Shakespeare's Verse:* "The Queen of England was already, automatically. the representative of the old goddess—the real deity of Medieval England, the Celtic pre-Christian goddess, with her tail wound round those still very much alive pre-Christian and non-Christian worlds. That goddess had been naturalised into the old Catholicism as Mother Mary and Satan. . . the fusion of the two in one person happened all the more naturally in that the Isis behind the virgin Mary and the Celtic goddess behind medieval England had originally been one."[110]

It is the same mythopoeic instinct and imagination of Hughes that associates Blake's poem on The Tiger with the upsurge of French revolution, and his own poem on Jaguar as first, aliteral description of Jaguar, then an invocation to the goddess, developing into a kind of incantation, and finally, the loss of this verbal detail into the elememal forms of nature. Hughes describes the structure of myths that is operative in all great literatures, even in his own poem *Crow:*"... it's the whole procedure and practice of becoming and performing as a witch-doctor, a medicine man, among primitive peoples. The individual is summoned by certain dreams. The same dreams all over the world. A spirit summons him . . . usually an animal or a woman. If he refuses, he dies . . . or somebody near him dies. If he accepts, he then prepares himself for the job. . . Once fully-fledged he can enter trance at will and go to the spirit world. . . he goes to get something badly needed, a cure, an answer, some sort of divine intervention in the community's affairs. Now this flight to the spirit world he experiences as a dream. . . and that dream is the basis of the hero story."[111]

Hughes tells us that to take part in a world lived by our ancestors one hundred and fifty million years ago is like a blood-transfusion which refreshes and renews us.[112]

We have seen then, Hughes's first attempts in his boyhood, to enjoy in the sheer vitality of life outside; contrast the vitality of natural life with that of the animals; establish a context for man in this world with the help of myth and symbol, and finally, view this whole activity as man's attempts to come to terms not only with his environment but with God who created man and his environment, although the word God is not very frequent in Hughes. ". . . How things are between man and his idea of the Divinity determines everything in his life, the quality and connectedness of every feeling and thought, and the meaning of every action."[113] Poetry here becomes meta-poetry in its effort "to regain his genuine self," which has been "man's principal occupation. . . ."[114]

This reality is subtle, tender, immeasurable in terms of

rational discourse or any verbal poetic device, and this complicates the task of the poet. Hughes wrote of Douglas's language: "He is a renovator of language. It is not that he uses words in jolting combinations, or with titanic extravagance, or curious precision. His triumph lies in the way he renews the simplicity of ordinary talk, and he does this by infusing every word with a burning exploratory freshness of mind—partly impatience, partly exhilaration at speaking the forbidden thing, partly sheer casual ease of penetration."[115] With Hughes the case was a little different because of his entirely visionary quest relating to an entirely different subject-matter. Precisely because of this, words often failed to convey for Hughes what his vision wanted to unfold. Words become fleeting shadows for as Hughes says no word could capture the flight of the crow. Hughes's is a concern with energies—energies from all over body, heart and brain; these things concern and try to solidify Hughes's principal subject which is to "celebrate the pure solidity of my illusion of the world."[116] Although Hughes agreed with Ekbert Faas that metre, rhyme and rhythm always do not accommodate what he would wish to,[117] he described his central method of composition thus: "The way I do this, as I believe, is by using something like the method of a musical composer. I might say that I might turn every combatant into a bit of music, then resolve the whole uproar into as formal and balanced a figure of melody and rhythm as I can. When all the words are hearing each other clearly, and every stress is feeling every other stress, and all are contented—the poem is finished."[118]

IV

From the "myth of the middle-brow poet with blood and guts, as a 'Left-Bank, ironside lumberjack', with a taste for Heming-way and Sartre,"[119] in 1957, Gunn was recognised as "a metaphysical poet in any sense you like"[120] in 1958, and again in 1961, as "not in any ordinary sense of the word a religious poet, but he is (both in the ordinary and to some degree in the literary sense of the word) a metaphysical poet."[121] Gunn figured in Robert Conquest's anthology *New Lines* (1956). In 1952 or 1953, Gunn recalls, he met Wain who came to Cambridge to deliver a lecture, and this got him into the Movement anthology. However, Gunn says that he "never subscribed to any programme."[122] Gunn and Hughes in the 1950s were thought to be so much alike that they won a common epithet: Ted-Gunn, in their concern for toughness and violence. Ted Hughes made one of the most important statements, disagreeing with all the negative-feedbacks that British poetry had been subject to since 1930: "We have settled for the minimum practical energy and illumination—anything bigger introduces problems. . . That is the psychological stupidity, the ineptitude, of the rigidly rationalist outlook—it's a form of hubris, and we're paying the traditional price. If you refuse the energy, you are living a kind of death. "[123]

This was the new creed and the statement of Thom Gunn had further strengthened it: "I'm trying to show (in 'Innocence, *Sense of Movement)* how the celebration of energy can lead one to a kind of commitment where one finds that energy is not just in a vacuum; it is very often destroying the energy of other people . . . I suppose this is one of the main problems of being alive; how can one show the most oneself, whatever you call it without destroying the most in other people, infringing on the most in other people and possibly destroying them. Often in quite quiet ways without actually killing them."[124] Hughes's and Gunn's concern with energy in itself makes them in some sense metaphysical. The vital problem is of course the direction this energy should take in the scheme of poetic formulation. To be sure then, in the first instance, Gunn is not celebrating the wildness of energy for its own sake, as was the case with, Hughes. The much talked about "toughs" on motor-cycles in Gunn's poem do not refer to themselves but something beyond them; and their exquisitely human dilemma of having no destination speaks volumes of Sartrian existentialism. The influences on Gunn are wide in range—Donne, Pound, Eliot, Yeats, Auden, Keats, Stevens, Robert Bly, Gary Snyder, Alexander Pope, and, of course, Shakespeare. But as Gunn would put it, none in particular has influenced him and references in his poems can be found to Italian painting, Californian scenes and characters, Greek mythology, French literature and philosophy. Gunn insists on finding his own voice: "what I want is the kind of voice that can speak about anything at all, that can deal with the perceptions and concerns as they come up."[125]

The Poet's Tongue, edited by W.H. Auden and John Garrett, which Gunn read during his school days, defined poetry as "memorable speech," which is "still the only workable definition I've come across . . ."[126] In this anthology Gunn read poems by Donne and Auden both of whom influenced his early writing. Gunn said on his inclusion in the Movement anthology: ". . . I was told I was writing like Empson before I'd actually read any of Empson's poetry. I think this was because I was imitating Donne and Auden at the same time: I suppose a combination of Donne and Auden comes out as something like Empson."[127] One more idea of Gunn's poetic creed comes out of his early writing a poem on a peony:

O peony you smell
Like the heavenly nectar Hebe split
On luxurious Olympus.

The references to Greek myths are obviously in imitation of Keats who also lived in Hampstead. Reacting to Keats's poem "I stood tiptoe upon a little hill" Gunn said, "why, it could be Hampstead Heath,"[128] Gunn's celebration of energy then, begins with the natural surroundings he was in. At seventeen, he read Meredith, and the poem whose meter and subject-matter excited Gunn was "Love in the Valley," which began:

Under yonder beechtree, single in the greensward,
Couched with her arms beneath her golden head,

Gunn wanted something even more strongly felt and experienced to attach his feelings "to something outside of me,"[129] a concept already met in Tomlinson and Hughes:

"What trite adolescent dreams of being toved by a demonic hero are behind *Wuthering Heights,* what visions of being a dashing young soldier annihilating enemies in battle and breaking hearts in the drawing room are behind Stendhal's novels? Fantasy must always precede fictions, and fictions are as necessary as reality to literature. Love poetry started as the fantasies of troubadours, who by definition had to love at a distance. You can't get the girl you want, so you create a fantasy about her so complete that it can give you some temporary satisfaction. Later I had for a while a theory of poetry as 'loot,' a prize grabbed from the outside world and taken permanently into the poet's possession. But of course it is not taken, it continues out there in the world living its own independent existence, stepping from the tubetrain at a later stop, and coolly unaware of all the furore it is causing."[130]

The key words are reality and fiction. And the discovery of this vital principle in arts leads Gunn to myth, ritual and magic. Gunn wrote on his book *Moly* in 1971, that Moly is the name of a herb by eating which Odysseus will be free from the witchery of Circe who has turned sailors into pigs. This ancient myth Gunn uses in a present context: "Magic is not completely separate from ordinary processes: it works by strengthening an impulse in us, even if that impulse in us is something we didn't recognise as being there . . . We all have in us the germs of the brutal, greedy, and dull. And we can all avoid becoming pigs, though to do so we must be wily and self-aware. Moly can help us to know our own potential for change: even though we are in the power of Circe or Time. . ."[131] This gives an answer to those who hold that Gunn celebrates violence for its own sake. Other concepts round which Gunn's poetics revolves are: will, poem as action and exploration, and the two selves in man. In a poem "To Yvor Winters, 1955," Gunn wrote:

You keep both Rule and Energy in view,
Much power in each, most in the balance two:
Ferocity existing in the fence
Built by an exercised intelligence.

Gunn also prefaced *My Sad Captains* with a quotation from Shakespeare's *Troilus and Cressida:* "The will is infinite and the execution confined, the desire is boundless and the act a slave to limit." This 'will' fulfills Alvarez's criterion of a poet who faces the full range of his experience, as motor-cyclists in Gunn's poem do. As opposed to this in Larkin the protagonist never takes the risk for some unknown horror.[132] The problem of giving some direction to this will which is a combination of the intellectual and the visionary, takes Gunn to write poems about the divided self: "A Plan of Self Subjection." Gunn's poems then, concern themselves with exploration than solution. He does not find any sense in such platitudes as a writer has created "a world of his own" "We might answer that we do not want any world but the one we live in, and that what we demand of a poet is a few good poems about it."[133] The poet is the person who acts through his poems; explores a world in them of a "particular kind of experience or concept or emotion."[134] Just as Hughes went on to show the use of violence in various poets as a continuous tradition, so does Gunn say:

I think of all the toughs through history
And thank heaven they lived continually.

Poems in Gunn's *Jack Straw's Castle* become more brooding in nature. Gunn wrote: "The design in this collection connects such matters as self-destructiveness, solipsism in the aspects both of freedom and improvement, the strategies of inconsistency and self-rescue. . ."[135] And finally the attention centres on the man himself, in his latest collection *The Passages of Joy*. Gunn recalls that the theme of the book is the channelled and unchannelled, ". . . after all the nine channels with their nine holes through which we get most of our physical joys."[136] The original idea of the nine seems to have been derived by Gunn either from Young's *Night Thoughts* or Blake's *The Four Zoas,* or even Blake's "The Book of Urizen," where Los shapes Urizen in nine ages.[137]

In Gunn, if one might say so, the use of myth has been

given a more human context. Gunn does not agree with Eliot or Bly or Williams that form in itself can reflect the modern life. Even meter is an instrument of poetic will, and when form reflects life, it sounds childish, as in B.B. Cummings.[138] Gunn believes that by writing in syllabics he can achieve certain effects which are not possible by the use of meter. Gunn had published *My Sad Captains* (1961) in two parts: "The first half is the culmination of my old style—metrical, rational, but may be starting to get a little more humane. The second half consists of a taking up of that humane impulse in a series of syllabic poems which were something new in my work. Syllabics are really only a way of teaching myself to write free verse."[139]

Syllabics has helped Gunn record casual perceptions more easily, while in traditional verse, he felt that the emotion is rather taut, a "clenched" kind of emotion. About diction Gunn thinks that we cannot talk now in terms of natural or poetic diction for Wordsworth and Pound have won their battles. Now, formal and informal sort of diction is more relevant and both can be used profitably. However, it is the unity of diction, form, subject and tone, that produces a good poem: "Yet I feel much about the split in my work between the two kinds of poems I write, the metrically intense and syllabically casual. Each excludes too much of the other. The poem I want to write, in fact, is one in which the qualities of each co-exist: it would be a kind of equivalent in poetry to the best of Isherwood for example, the passage about the liner in *The World in the Evening* or the first two pages to the second 'Berlin Diary' in *Goodbye to Berlin*, where the particularity of the things described does not diminish the intensity of their implications and where the language is plain, unornamented, and eloquent."[140]

V

With Charles Tomlinson, Ted Hughes and Thom Gunn, the break with the Movement poetry is complete. The new trends and tendencies that have emerged in these writers concern both the width of range, depth of experience, perfection in craftsmanship, and objectivity in style. Unornamented and simpler parts of melody, it is proved, do not necessarily come from the subject-matter concerning man within the social set-up and his manners; it comes from the treatment of subject howsoever deep and uncommon. The poets, therefore, freely go into the realms their imaginations lead them to, experimenting with poetic forms and techniques, as well as borrowing them from other traditions where demands for novelty press. The new poetry is a down-right rejection of the Movement poetics and the return to the world of myth, symbol, magic and ritual, is enlightening and refreshing. Hughes wrote: "If you refuse the energy, you are living a kind of death. If you accept the energy, it destroys you. What is the alternative?"[141] It was precisely here that the Movement poets faltered and were caught in a dilemma; and the best way to them seemed to nurse the disgruntled body of their Muse in, sometimes, the conservative eighteenth century homes, and, sometimes, in the Victorian and Georgian arguments who celebrated a decadent romantic creed. Hughes gave the answer: "To accept the energy, and find methods of turning it to good, of keeping it under control-rituals, the machinery of religion. The old method is the only one."[142] And yet it is not the Elizabethan times thrusted upon twentieth century as eighteenth century was thrusted upon twentieth by the Movementeers. Eliot's objectivity, Williams's sonority, and Olson's music through ear to the mind, still live in the poems and poetic theories of these poets. These poets have fully exploited the best available knowledge of European, American and Oriental traditions either with reference to subject-matter or technique. What is more, they have again related art with the idea of a creator, Tomlinson and Hughes in particular. The seriousness of new poetry makes it almost an incantatory kind of verse where the poet's concerns are not with the provincialism of man in society, but man in the universe, faced with the existential predicaments—problems of life, death, unity and diversity of existence. These problems are best handled by the tools of myth and symbol, whether classical or oriental. The new attitude to poem is both that of an artifact and a gateway to new experience; both coalesce and co-exist. Where the effects of free verse are needed, poets use it as candidly as they use traditional metrics when situations and effects demand.

Although Larkin has also said that ". . . it certainly never occurred to me that I had anything in common with Thorn Gunn, or Donald Davie. . . and in fact I wasn't mentioned at the beginning."[143] But this is what makes Larkin a typical Movementeer and he surely does not have anything in common with later Davie and Gunn. Tomlinson, Hughes, and Gunn, are, on the other hand, poets who are shadowed earlier by Conquest's and Enright's anthologies; and their seriousness did not start after Alvarez's call in *The New Poetry*. It was the need of time and the pressure of circumstances that gave recognition to Movement first. But poets who do not fit in a prevalent milieu are rejected by it; when they create their own milieu, the milieu accepts them. This process of death and renewal is analogous to the poetic process of all great art.

Notes and References

1. It is significant that these poets had shot into prominence simultaneously as the Movement poets during the fifties. But the immediate climate of public opinion denied immediate recognition of their poetic creed.
2. R. Conquest, *New Lines*, p. xii.
3. In the sequence of action and reaction which make up for the movement in history, Dylan Thomas had also reacted against the poetry of social commitment of the thirties, and his rhetorical use of diction and style, may find its own justification. C.H. Sisson says: "Looking back over the half-century, as well as one can at this distance, one sees that the real inventiveness was mainly before 1925. In this period the poetry was corrected and improved by the canons of prose. By the thirties an ideological overlay has spoiled the outline. By the forties, a twentieth century version of Lord Chesterfield's lesson in poetics is creeping back: 'Prose, as you know, is the language of common conversation; it is what

you, and everybody speaks and writes. . . But poetry is a more noble way of expressing one's thoughts.' The dog returns to his vomit. *English Poetry 1900-1950: An Assessment* (London: Rupert Hart-Davis, 1971), pp. 263-64.

4. A. Alvarez, ed., *The New Poetry* (Penguin: Harmondsworth, 1962), p. 17.
5. *Ibid.*
6. John Wain, "English Poetry: The Immediate Situation," *op. cit.*, p. 358.
7. "The war-time 'romantic' will be with us, I imagine, throughout our lives, just as there are still people who learned to write verse in 1910 and are still writing it in the same way in 1957." Wain, *Ibid.*, p. 366.
8. Wain, *Ibid.*, p. 372.
9. *New Lines*, I, p. xiv.
10. Donald Davie, "Views," *Listener*, May 10, 1973, p. 611.
11. Conquest in "Context," *London Magazine*, Vol. 1 (Feb. 1962), No. 11, p. 34.
12. *Ibid.*
13. *New Lines*, I, p. xv.
14. "Remembering the Movement," in Barry Alpert, ed., *The Poa in the Imaginary Museum*, p. 73.
15. *Ibid.*, pp. 74-75.
16. "After the Tranquilized Fifties" by C.B. Cox and A.R. Jones, in *Critical Quarterly*, Vol. 6 (1964), p. 120.
17. "Larkin often makes the point that for him withdrawal from life is necessary for the preservation of the self, though in poems such as 'Dockery and Son,' 'Self's the Man' and 'Send no Money' he explores with subtlety his own doubts and the heavy price he has had to pay." *Ibid.*
18. " . . . Americans coming to poetry at the beginning of this century had almost nothing to go on, not even a properly substantiated poetic language from which to develop and differ." Alvarez, *The Shaping Spirit* (London: Chatto and Windus, 1967), p. 164.
19. *Ibid.*, p. 165.

20. *Ibid.*, p. 169.
21. Anthony Thwaite, "The Two Poetries," in D. Abse, ed., *Poetry Dimension*, 2 (1964), p. 149.
22. Charles Tomlinson, "Poetry Today" in Boris Ford, ed., *The Modern Age* (Penguin: Harmondsworth, 1973), pp. 471-72.
23. *The New Poetry*, p. 17.
24. *The Shaping Spirit*, p. 191.
25. *Ibid.*
26. "Four Conversations," *London Magazine*, Vol. 4 (1964), No.8.
27. Boris Ford, ed., *The Modern Age*, p. 472.
28. Quoted by Davie in *The Poet in the Imaginary Museum*, p. 48.
29. For non-Christian elements in English poetry see Denis Saurat, Literature and the Occult Tradition.
30. *The Shaping Spirit*, p. 189.
31. Alvarez, *The New Poetry*, p. 18.
32. *Ibid.*
33. *Ibid.*, p. 19.
34. *Ibid.*
35. *Ibid.*
36. *Ibid*, p. 20.
37. Charless Tomlinson, "The Middlebrow Muse," *Essays in Criticism*, Vol. VII (April 1957), No. 2, p. 213.
38. *Ibid.*, p. 212.
39. Robert Conquest interviewed by Morrish in Peter Orr, ed., *The Poet Speaks: Interviews with Contemporary Poets* (London: Routledge & Kegan Paul, 1967), p. 49.
40. *Ibid.*, p. 46.
41. Alvarez, *The New Poetry*, p. 21.
42. *Ibid.*, p. 22.
43. *Ibid.*, p. 23.
44. *Ibid.*
45. *Ibid.*, p. 24.
46. *Ibid.*, p. 28

47. *New Lines,* II, p. xxiv.
48. *Ibid.,* p. xvii.
49. *The New Poetry,* p. 17.
50. *New Lines,* II, p. xxviii.
51. *The New Poetry,* p. 17.
52. Tomlinson, "The Middlebrow Muse," p. 215.
53. Ibid.
54. *The New Poetry,* p. 24.
55. Conquest in Peter Orr, ed., *The Poet Speaks,* p. 46.
56. Tomlinson, *The Necklace* (London: Oxford University Press, 1966), p. xvi.
57. Tomlinson in *Poetry Book Society Bulletin,* No. 97, Summer 1978.
58. Davie's Introduction to Tomlinson's *The Necklace,* p. xiii.
59. Charles Tomlinson, "Foreword" in *Some Americans: A Personal Record* (California: California University Press, 1981).
60. Tomilnson in Peter Orr, ed., *The Poet Speaks,* p. 250.
61. *Ibid.,* p. 252.
62. *Some Americans,* "Foreword" by Tomlinson, *op. cit.,* pp. 20-21.
63. Tomlinson, "Poetry Today," in B. Ford, ed., *The Modern Age,* p. 472.
64. The point has been made in Chapter I that in spite of translating Homer and Virgil, eighteenth century could not produce one epic poet.
65. Tomlinson, "Poetry Today," p. 479.
66. Tomlinson in *Poetry Book Society Bulletin,* No. 97 (Summer 1978).
67. Tomlinson, "The Middlebrow Muse," p. 214.
68. *Ibid.,* p. 216.
69. *Poetry Book Society Bulletin,* No. 97 (Summer 1978).
70. Tomilnson, "The Middlebrow Muse, p. 217.
71. *Ibid.*
72. Tomlinson in Peter Orr, ed., *The Poet Speaks,* p. 252.

73. Tomlinson, "Poetry Today," p. 484.
74. It can be recalled that Movement poets shrank from forging their link with the object of their experience, what Alvarez calls facing the full range of their experience.
75. "Author's Preface," in Tomlinson, *The Necklace.*
76. *Poetry Book Society Bulletin,* No. 82 (Autumn 1974).
77. "Author's Preface," Tomlinson, *The Necklace.*
78. *Ibid.*
79. Tomlinson on *Written on Water* in *Poetry Book Society Bulletin,* No. 75 (Christmas 1972).
80. *Ibid.*
81. "Some of these poems (in *Written on Water)* speak of the sheer delight in a universe that flows." *Ibid.*
82. Tomlinson has carried the tradition of Movement poetry in his own poems. Davie remarks: "Tomlinson's morality is sternly traditional, classical, almost Augustan." Introduction to Tomlinson's *The Necklace,* p. xvi.
83. *Poetry Book Society Bulletin,* No. 75 (Christmas 1972).
84. Charles Tomlinson. ed., *Octavio Paz: Selected Poems* (Penguin, 1979), p. 15.
85. *Poetry Book Society Bulletin,* No. 96 (Spring 1978).
86. *Ibid.,* No. 82 (Autumn 1974).
87. Charles Tomlinson, ed., *William Carlos Williams* (Penguin, 1972), p. 213.
88. Octavio Paz, "Black and White: The Graphics of Charles Tomlinson," *Poetry Nation,* 5 (1975).
89. Tomlinson, "The Middlebrow Muse," p. 215.
90. Ted Hughes, *Poetry in the Making: An Anthology of Poems and Programmes from Listening and Writing* (London: Faber, 1967), p. 119.
91. "The Rock" in G. Summerfield, ed., *Worlds: Seven Modern Poets* (Penguin, 1974).
92. *Ibid.,* p. 122.
93. *Ibid.,* p. 126.
94. Tomlinson, "Poetry Today," in Boris Ford, ed., *The Modern Age,* p. 485.

95. *Manchester Guardian,* March 23, 1965.

96. Compare also Blake's picture of Albion rising upon the Rock of Ages.

97. Tomlinson, "Poetry Today," p. 485.

98. *The Guardian* March 23, 1965, p. 9.

99. Ted Hughes, *Poetry in the Making,* p. 17.

100. Hughes selected passages from Shakespeare "for poetic intensity, length and completeness . . . that might surprise some readers." See his *A Choice of Shakespeare's Verse,* p. 181.

101. "Context," *London Magazine, op. cit.,* p. 45.

102. Hughes, *Poetry in the Making,* p. 23.

103. *Ibid.,* p. 51.

104. Ted Hughes, ed., *Selected Poems: Keith Douglas* (London: Faber, 1964), p. 12.

105. See p. 181 in Ted Hughes, ed., *A Choice of Shakespeare's Verse.*

106. *Ibid,* p. 184.

107. See "Context," *London Magazine, op. cit,* p. 45: " . . . all this infatuation with infancy and innocence, what did these have to do with the great issues of the time? Nothing whatsoever, till the spirit that worked through Wordsworth and Coleridge and Blake chose them for its parables:" Ted Hughes.

108. "Ted Hughes and Crow," *London Magazine,* Vol. 10 (January 1971), No. 10, p. 15.

109. See p. 16, *Ibid.,* where Hughes talks of his knowledge of philosophy. Compare also Hughes's attempts at arriving at world-culture with William Blake's All-Religions-Are-One Thesis.

110. p. 180.

111. "Ted Hughes and Crow," *op. cit.,* p. 17.

112. *Poetry in the Making,* p. 76.

113. Hughes, A *Choice of Shakespeare's Verse,* pp. 184-85.

114. Hughes, *Poetry in the Making,* p. 124.

115. Hughes, *Selected Poems: Keith Douglas, op. cit.,* pp. 12-13.

116. "The Rock" in G. Summerfield, ed., *Worlds: Seven Modern Poets* p. 126.

117. See *London Magazine,* Vol. 10 (Jan. 1971), No. 10, pp. 19-20.
118. "The Rock," *op. cit.,* p, 127.
119. "Charles Tomlinson, "The Middlebrow Muse," p. 210.
120. Frank Kermode's review of A *Sense of Movement in Listen,* Vol. 2 (Spring 1958), No. 4, p. 17.
121. "G.S. Fraser, "The Poetry of Thorn *Gunn," Critical Quarterly,* Vol. 3 (Winter 1961), No. 4, p. 366.
122. "Four Conversations," *London Magazine, op. cit.,* p. 70.
123. "Ted Hughes and Crow," *op. cit.,* p. 10.
124. "Four Conversations," *op. cit.,* p. 67.
125. *Poetry Book Society Bulletin,* No. 90 (Autumn 1976).
126. Thom *Gunn* in "My Suburban Muse," in G. Summerfield, ed., *Worlds: Seven Modern Poets,* p. 58.
127. "Four Conversations," *op. cit.,* p. 59.
128. "My Suburban Muse," *op. cit.,* p. 59.
129. *Ibid.,* p. 61.
130. *Ibid.*
131. *Poetry Book Society Bulletin,* No. 68 (Spring 1971).
132. See p. 360 in *Critical Quarterly,* Vol. 3 (Winter 1961), No. 4, G.S. Fraser's article, "The Poetry of Thom Gunn."
133. "Three Poets," review by Thorn Gunn in *Listen,* Vol. 3 (Winter 1958), No. 1.
134. *Ibid.*
135. *Poetry Book Society Bulletin,* No. 90 (Autumn 1976).
136. *Ibid.,* No. 113 (Summer 1982).
137. The idea also occurs in *Atharava Veda,* 10. 8. 43: "A lotus with nine gates enveloped by three strands/In it is a being strange, possessed of self:/That is that knowers of Brahma know."
138. "Four Conversations," p. 64.
139. Autobiographical note written for Faber & Faber, 1972.
140. "Context," *London Magazine,* p. 40.
141. "Ted Hughes and Crow," p. 10.
142. *Ibid.*
143. "Four Conversations," p. 72.

3

Journey Round the Pool of Desire

The first section of the chapter will introduce *Crow* (1970); the second will focus on the character of Crow while analysing the poems. The third section will deal with images in *Crow,* while the final section will be a criticism on ideas from *Crow.*

I

"The trickster hero may perhaps be the source of a literature, naive and picaresque at first, then extremely refined and consciously artistic. The trickster god, on the other hand, is the transpersonal source of a particular life-style and way of experiencing the world. There is, firstly, the known experience of the world, based on the assumption that man stands there alone and self-dependent, endowed with a consciousness which is receptive only to sense impressions that can be evaluated scientifically. For that type of experience, however. which expresses itself not scientifically but mythologically, there is no such assumption. Rather, it is open to the possibility of a suprasensual guide and psychopomp, capable of affording impressions of another kind: impressions grounded in sense experience, which do not contradict the observations and findings of science, and which yet transcend the scientific view of the world". (Paul Radin, *The Trickster,* pp. 189-90.

Ted Hughes's meeting with American sculptor, engraver, and publisher, Leonard Baskin, in 1957, was the cause of the origination of the idea of *Crow,* a long narrative poem published in 1970.[1] *Crow* is a poem which borders upon the mythic,[2] and elements of myth, ritual, and symbol, might have entered this poem and Hughes's poetry in general, from Hughes's reading of such books as *Myth and Religion of the North;*[3] *Shamanism;*[4] *Literature Among the Primitives: The Primitive Reader;*[5] *The Otter's Tale;*[6] *Folk Tales of Japan, Folk Tales of Israel;*[7] *Folk Tales of Chile, Hindoo Fairy Legends, The Glass Man and the Golden Bird, The Black Money;*[8] Paul Radin's *The Trickster*[9] and his collection of *African Folk Tales and Sculpture,*[10] among his other books; R.H. Chamberlain's collection of Ainu tales,[11] and, of course, *The Golden Bough* of J.G. Frazer and books by Joseph Campbell. Poetry, however, is neither anthropology nor myth. Hughes, conscious of his poem being read as an exercise in comparative religion and mythology, wrote to Keith Sagar: "My main concern was to produce something with the minimum cultural accretions of the museum sort—sometimes autochthonous and complete in itself, as it might be invented after the holocaust and demolition of all libraries, where essential things spring again—if at all—only from their seeds in nature—and are not lugged around or hoarded as preserved harvest from the past. So the comparative religion/ mythology background was irrelevant to me, except as I could forget it. If I couldn't find it again original in *Crow,* I wasn't interested to make a trophy of it."[12] *Crow* combines the elements of comedy and romance, and its structure is a parody of the structure of the myth jof eternal return. The protagonist also parodies hero as saviour figure found in religions and mythology

The poem is a nightmare of God.[13] In 1975, Hughes gave two readings of *Crow.* Gifford and Roberts note that two different styles of story-telling could be distinguished. They have also noted Hughes's own version of *Crow* story which is as follows: "After having created the world God has a nightmare in the form of a voice and a Hand which ridicules the (creation and particularly God's masterpiece, Man. God claims that his crcation has been a complete success and a debate ensues which is interrupted by a message from the world that Man wants God to take life back. God challenges the nightmare to do better and the Nightmare's response is to create Crow. 'God, who regards Crow as a poor competitor for his creation, shows him round the universe and sets him various challenges and ordeals, in the course of which Crow becomes more intelligent and resourceful. The universe is one in which all history is happening simultaneously, so Crow is able to move from one era to another, from the beginning of the world to the end. He observes and is occasionally implicated in various aspects of the creation. During his adventures he begins to wonder who his own creator is and he encounters various female figures who are avatars of his creator, but he never recognises her and always bungles the situation."[14]

All myths, before they take account of other details of life, deal with the origin or birth of the world: "Myth, then, is always an account of a 'creation.' "[15] In his 1970 interview, Hughes said: "The story is not really relevant to the poems as they stand. Maybe I'll finish the story someday and publish it separately. I think the poems have a life a little aside from it. The story brought me to the poems, and it was of course the story of Crow, created by God's nightmare's attempt to improve on man."[16]

II

Crow is written in ironic mode having both the elements of comedy and romance in its structure. Ted Hughes himself put a note on the dust-jacket that the book "contains the passages of verse from about the first two-thirds of what was to have been an epic folk-tale".[17] We could even call *Crow* a modern romance.[18] "Modern romance," writes Campbell, "like Greek tragedy, celebrates the mystery of dismemberment, which is life in time. The happy ending is justly scorned as a misrepresentation; for the world, as we know it, as we have seen it, yields but one ending: death, disintegration, dismemberment, and the crucifixion of our heart with the passing of the forms that we loved."[19] The dream-motif of the poem we have pointed out earlier. In *London Magazine* interview (1971), Hughes had said that once the shaman has entered trance in his magic flight, he goes to the spirit world ". . . he goes to get something badly needed, a cure, an answer, some sort of divine intervention in the community's affairs. Now this flight to the spirit world he experiences as a dream. . . and that dream is the basis of the hero story."[20] In *Crow,* thc Crow as protagonist is produced by God's Nightmare, and the function he has to perform is to improve upon man.

The first occurrence of Crow in Hughes is in a dialogue from *Eat Crow* (1964). The Crow and the man are ascribed thc following qualities by Hughes:

"SHE: A crow is a sign of life. Even though it sits motionless.

MORGAN: And a man, lying alone, among stones, with a rifle, lying limply in a waterless land, in a grey desert of tumbled stone, with one bullet, a man dryer than a lizard, is a sign of life. Even though he does not move.

SHE: The crow watches the man.

MORGAN: Between the crow and the man, across three hundred years of primeval stone, a horrible connection has found its way. Now these two can never separate. The stones are in their usual trance, rapt in the circles of galactic dust. They hear nothing of the song silence these two sing together, these two silent living ones, alone with each other in the stone land. . . . The furnace roars in the silent man, and the crow glitters, in the early grey light, molten bronze and phosphors settling in his darkness, set out to cool, fresh from the furnace. The crow ruffles.

SHE: The crow is composed of terrible black voice. He is neither stone nor light. But voice that can hardly utter. He looks this way and that. The forms of the stones, the fractures of heavenly accident, the resolute quality of light, hold the crow anaesthetized, every hour in more skilled patience, resigned to the superior stamina of the empty horizon, limber and watchful.

MORGAN: The laws are still with the living.

SHE: The crow arrived before dawn, smelling the man, and settling to watch at extreme range.

MORGAN: And when he saw the crow, in the blue thinning light, the man gave thanks to the studded, baleful pallor of the heavens, and to this strange-faced company of stones. His prayer has produced not quails and not manna. A crow has come up from the maker of the world.

SHE: The crow watches the man."[21]

The images of stone, pallor of heavens, Craw's watching the man, and the overall situation of the dialogue have been assimilated into the plot of *Crow.*

Accounting for the sources of crow in mythology, Keith Sagar says that "The Crow is the most intelligent of birds, the most widely distributed, and the most omnivorous. . . Eskimo legened tells us that in the beginning the raven was the only creature and the world was, like him, black... Hughes's mythology of crow is deeply rooted in such legends".[22] Sagar also draws our attention to the god of healing, Cronos, Saturn, Aesculapius, and Apollo, who was a Crow-figure.[23] Hirschberg says about the genesis of Crow: "The precarious, lovely yet resilient figure of Crow owed its genesis to the portrayal of the Raven as Trickster in the myths of the North American Indians, particularly those of the Haida and the Tlingit on the North-West coast."[24] Crow, however, like the Wolf, the Bear, and other animals, is the medium of a shaman for his magic flight and journey underground or above.[25] There are two kinds of shamans—black and white. The white ones have contacts with gods; it is they who constitute characteristics of a quest-hero, who yield to the demands not only of comic complication but also of comic resolution. Such shamans are yogis and tantrics. The black shamans, on the contrary, have contacts with "evil spirits" and often descend to the underworld. Their costumes, along with their purposes, differ.[26] This shaman is anti quest-hero and celebrates dismemberment. The result is not comedy but "modern romance" of perpetual death, dismemberment, and concurrence of life-cycles with no apocalypse. Similarly, in a later Tlingit myth, there are two kinds of tricksters—the one who transforms the world, the other who acts like a fool.[27]

However, the comparison of raven with crow is based on an equation of functions and neither Hirschberg, nor Keith Sagar, nor Terry Gifford and Neil Roberts, have located the actual source of the crow myth. Among the Gros Ventre tribe of northern Montana, the creation myth runs: "The people before the present people were wild...Nixant (the Father or God-figure) did not like the way they lived and died. He thought, 'I will make a new world'. He had the chief pipe. He went outdoors and hung the pipe on three sticks. He picked up four buffalo-chips. One he put under each of the sticks on which the pipe hung, and one he took for his own seat. He said, 'I will sing three times and shout three times. After I have done these things, I will kick the earth, and water will come out of the cracks. There will be a heavy rain. There will be water over all the earth! . . . The water came out, and it rained for days, and over all the earth was water. By means of the buffalo-chips he and the pipe floated . . . He floated wherever the wind took him. For days he drifted thus. Above him the Crow flew about. All the other birds and animals were drowned. The Crow became tired. It flew about crying, 'My father, I am becoming tired. I want rest.' Three times it said this. After it had said so three times, Nixant said, 'Alight on the pipe and rest.' Repeatedly the Crow cried to him, and each time was allowed to alight on the pipe. Nixant became tired sitting in one position. . . After he had cried a long time, he began to unwrap the chief pipe. The pipe contained all animals. He selected those with a long breath to dive through the water. . . Meanwhile the Crow did not alight, but flew about crying for rest. . . the Crow had become very tired. Then Nixant, when he had scraped the earth into his hand, began to sing. After he had sung three times, he shouted three times. Then he said, 'I will throw this little dust that I have in my hand into the water. Little by little let there be enough to make a strip of land large enough for me.' . . After he had made the land, there was no water anywhere. He went about with his pipe and with the Crow: These were all that there was to be seen in the world. . . He tried to think how he could get water. He shed tears. . . when he stopped crying, a large river was flowing. Thus he made rivers and streams. He became tired of being alone with the Crow and the pipe. He decided to make persons and animals. . ."[28]

The myth tells that the Crow and his creator have existed from the beginning. The reason for Hughes choosing Crow as his protagonist, therefore, should be clear enough. Throughout the passage quoted, the Crow is doing only two things: either he feels restless and keeps on flying, or he alights. In any case he is at the mercy of his creator whom he calls his Father. In the 1975 narration of the Crow story, Hughes had said that "God, who regards Crow as a poor competitor for his creation, shows him round the universe and sets him various challenges and ordeals."[29] These ordeals the Crow goes through, in the passage quoted, in his flight from one place to another, because God has no place to give him to rest. That Crow's basic search is to find the rest, in both Hughes and Montana creation myth, is part of our central argument. "The various female figures,"[30] of whom Hughes talks, are in fact rivers and streams in the passage, which were created by the tears of God. And moreover, the fact that God was tired of Crow, and *therefore* created persons and animals, is what instigates Crow in Hughes's poem to become a demiurge and hold comparison with his maker. A perceptive reading of the passage will reveal its similarity in narrative outline with the story of *Crow.*

The challenge of Crow to his maker nullifies God's labour for regeneration and apocalypse and Crow succeeds in promoting the dynamics of cosmogonic round. The quest-hero opens our eyes to a new world, the symbol for which is often the "virtuous sword," while the symbol for cosmogonic cycle is;. "the scepter of dominion, or the book of law". "The characteristic structure of the first is the winning of the bride[31]—the bride is life. The adventure of the scene is the going to the Yather—the father is the invisible unknown,"[32] something which. Crow does in Hughes's poem.

The beginning of the passage quoted from Montana myth does not resemble the beginning of Hughes's poem. For this we have to go to another Crow myth. *Crow* begins:

> Black was the without eye
> Black the within tongue
> Black was the heart
> Black the liver, black the lungs

The Tlingit Raven cycle begins: "At the beginning of things there was no daylight and the world lay in darkness."[33] Madam Blavatsky, in her monumental study on comparative mythology and religion, *The Secret Doctrine*, has shown that most creation myths do not begin from the beginning. This is equally true of "Two Legends" with which Hughes's poem begins. The oxymoron is implicit in the first two sections of the opening poem because it is not the chaotic, pre-existential blackness of non-entity, but the blackness which is shrouded upon the eye, tongue, heart, liver, lung, etc.—limbs of Crow that lie potent in the blackness of the egg.[34] The moon and the sun already existed before the birth of this egg and by alternating their course upon egg's surface, they start the process of life. The emptiness of the poem points us back to "Stations" (' *Wodwo)* I where, "In the great Emptiness you sit complacent,/Blackbird in wet snow." This is existential emptiness or the loss of meaning in creation.

This emptiness, in psychological terms, is the lapse of superconsciousness (where creation stands in an imaginative relationship with its creator) into unconsciousness (lapse frow imagination to inertia), and therefore, from the egg is produced· not some hermaphroditic being, as in most mythologies, but Crow, the most apt symbol for this degeneration. "Indeed, the lapse of superconsciousness into the state of unconsciousness is precisely the meaning of the biblical image of the Fall."[35] What is suggested, therefore, is that the hero of *Crow* is already born, and the two poems ("Two Legends" and "Lineage") are not an exercise in creation but attempts to bring protagonist into the realization of his physical self. In the trickster cycle also, Paul Radin remarks: "Considering the crude primitivity of the trickster cycle, it would not be surprising if one saw in this myth simply the reflection of an earlier, rudimentary stage of consciousness, which is what the trickster obviously seems to be."[36]

The emphasis on "never, never, never," which begot Crow, is part of the argument that Crow is a reasoning negative. The style of the "Lineage" is "the Old Testament style of genealogy" as noted by Hirschberg.[37] However, this style is common to most of the creation hymns or cosmogonic emanations. The Maoris creation hymn, for example, begins:

From the conception the increase,
From the increase the thought,
From the thought the remembrance,
From the remembrance the consciousness,
From the consciousness the desire.[38]

Crow's first cry is the cry for blood, grubs, crusts. It is the hunger, and Radin believes that the earliest Trickster cycle would have begun with "an account of a nondescript person obsessed by hunger, by an uncontrollable urge to wander. . . ."[39] After the first two poems in *Crow,* the rest of the poems are songs of Crow in the nature of apocryphal hymns. These songs form part of the quest of the protagonist of modern romance. Crow's first realization in the world he finds himself in is death. Crow asks eighteen questions and answers to all fail to transcend the finality of death. Before death and world become synonymous, Crow asks: "But who is stronger than death?" and the answer is an explosion of Crow's ego: *Me, evidently.* Paul Radin remarks about the trickster hero: ". . . what is so astonishing is the powers of resistance which enable the 'core' to survive these changes. My own observations confirm Emerson's definition of the hero: 'the hero is he who is immovably centred.' "[40]

The Crow is enmeshed by now ("A Kill") in his own psychological unconscious and this poem in particular, as *Crow* in general, has something of the unconscious horror which Macbeth feels before murdering Duncan. Macbeth can feel the presence of knife without it being actually present. In such conditions of "empsychosis" things lose their thinginess and become mental states. Crow's own limbs nave become the sepulchres of his broken relationship with himself and his environment, and the horror is generated not by one's misunderstanding of the world one is in, but by one's misunderstanding of one's own self:

> Flagged lame with legs
> Shot through the head with balled brains
> Shot blind with eyes
> Nailed down by his own ribs

Crow is a demiurge and appropriates the qualities of Blake's Urizen, Shelley's, or Hughes's own Prometheus. He tries to become the counterpart of such distinguished predecessors as Ishvara, Brahma, Prajapati, Vasudeva, Adam Kadmon, etc., who created the world.[41] Not realizing his limitations and the one-sidedness of his powers, Crow tries to parallel God by performing acts of heroism and valour. "The perennially childlike quality of romance is marked by its extraordinary persistent nostalgia, its search for some kind of imaginative golden age in time or space,"[42] and while the ego of the protagonist stretches his instinct for survival beyond an imaginable point (Crow, stronger than death), the protagonist's doom and defeat is foreshadowed in this very survival.

The Crow of "Crow and Mamma" is a Crow who is separated from other created objects and organic relationships. Glancing through the portholes of creation, Crow

> . . . saw the stars millions of miles away
> And saw the future and the universe
>
> Opening and opening
> And kept on and slept and at last
> Crashed on the moon and awoke and crawled out

Dismemberment and quest is the basic characteristic of

the hero of romance. The dismemberment is the result of disintegrated perception arising out of disintegrated personality. Perception is an act of self-identification, Blake believed, and the time the perceiver and the perceived become separate, perception becomes memory and generates spectres. In the lines quoted above, the Crow is not "willing" to see anything which would have put him in a proper relationship with stars and other objects of the universe; the objects fall back involuntarily upon the mind of an impotent quest-hero, and since the mind does not know what to do with them, relapses into an inertia or sleep. Craw's mother, in the meantime, dies.

In the Winnebago Hare cycle, after the Hare is born, his mother dies: "The immaculate conception of the hero, Hare, who is born in seven months and whose mother dies upon his birth . . . is reared by his grandmother."[43] The reason for mother's death is the independent nature of the son, as Hirschberg also thinks.[44] The impulse to "govern" all created things in Crow, is the basis of Oedipus story, and Oedipus's nature to copulate with his mother (desire to see mother as wife) is part of the same argument—that all mothers are part of Mother Nature, and the basis of civilization, as the burden of history, has been to score a victory over the Mother.[45]

"The Door" explains the mother image in terms of "earthen wall" within the bounds of which every creature lives:

All are rooted in earth, or eat earth, earthy,
Thickening the wall.

Crow's flight over the wall and his entrance into the earth through a black doorway is reminiscent of Satan alighting upon the earth, and Hirschberg compares Crow with Satan holding him responsible for mortal sin and sexual awareness.[46] Craw's flight also reminds of Milton's descent from the heavens of Albion and his entrance into the mundane egg in Blake's poem *Milton.* Milton, however, comes for the regeneration of Ololon, his sixfold emanation.

In "A Childish Prank," Crow tries to parallel God's act of creation by trying to infuse soul in the bodies of man and woman. The laughing of Crow is another milestone in his increasing amount of stupidity.[47] The worm may refer to the serpent who lived in the garden of Eden, and he (worm), being bitten by Crow and stuffed into man and woman, goes to show that Crow, like Prometheus, has succeeded in stealing a march over his creator (God sleeps), and confirms our belief that he is a buffoon.[48] The hero of romance is associated with "spring, dawn, order, fertility, vigour, and youth,"[49] says Northrop Frye, but because *Crow* is a parody of true romance and the quest-theme, and is written in the ironic mode, all the above images have got only an inverted significance in Hughes's poem. Crow is in fact associated with blackness, "confusion, sterility, moribund life,"[50] qualities which belong in romance to the enemy of the hero. Even the instinct for survival over death in Crow has become his curse, and here he invites comparison with Tennyson's Tithonus. Tithonus, however, longed for death for his liberation; for Crow the concept of liberation does not exist. This poem is not so much a parody of the biblical story of Adam and Eve;[51] it is more likely that Hughes is parodying here the Blackfoot myth of Winnebago Hare cycle which describes an Old Man and an Old Woman, who try to share between them, functions to create and run the universe.[52]

Crow shows signs of physcial development and God tries to teach him the first, and perhaps the only, lesson:

> God tried to teach Crow how to talk.
> 'Love', said God. 'Say, Love.'
> Crow gaped, and the white shark crashed into the sea
> And went rolling downwards, discovering its own death.

God tries thrice but fails. The crookedness of Crow comes to the fore when man and woman try to separate themselves from each other. Crow feels "guilty" (for he has a conscience) and flies. God curses and weeps for the universal damage has been done. Compare these qualities of trickster with Crow: ". . . never wholly subdued, ruled by lust and hunger, for ever running into pain and injury, cunning and stupid in action. Disorder belongs to the totality of life, and the spirit of this disorder is the trickster."[53]

The title "Crow Alights" reminds us of God's granting request to repeated cries of Crow for rest in the Montana myth.[54] Crow's flight, parodying quest-journey, takes him to sea, mountains, stars, forests, all of whom, Crow thinks, are "virus" of God. The virus adds horror to the guilty conscience of Crow, and he begins to search for a place which is *not* made by God. As each of Crow's actions becomes an exercise in unrelatedness due to the loss of the sense of discrimination, each line of the second half of the poem stands, as if, in terror of isolation:

> Crow blinked. He blinked. Nothing faded.
> He stared at the evidence.

Radin's remarks that the trickster is "in many respects stupider than the animals, and gets into one ridiculous scrape after another. Although he is not really evil he does the most atrocious things from sheer unconsciousnes and unrelatedness,"[55] holds true of Crow in every respect. The death image of "Crow Alights" is taken to the next poem "That Moment." The image of cigarette is common to both poems; the twice used phrase "closed forever" and the word "abandoned" in the latter poem, lead us to a sense of vacuity without aim, relations without contraries.

"Crow Tyrannosaurus" is yet another attempt of Crow to understand God's creation. The discoveries are nothing new. Mourning and lament, death-struggles, sorrow on sorrow of cat, dog as a filterbag and man as a walking Abattoir, lead Crow to ask the vital question:

> Crow thought. 'Alas
> Alas ought I
> To stop eating
> And try to become the light?'

It would be more than clear from Crow's utterance that

he has got a human conscience and asks human questions. But the limitation of his own nature does not allow his development from inertia to imagination. The conclusion he draws concerning the problem of survival is to become deaf to others' cries ('the ear's deafness') and eat and do all that is necessary for survival ('eye's roundness'). In other words Crow is trying to become neutral, a detached observer of nature, always trying to to return the unconscious of his primeval blackness. Instead of taking his journey forward, he circumambulates and returns to himself, like Blake's Urizen, caught in wheels within wheels. The dog who disgests so many lives in the poem, is a symbol of worldly delusion. In *Mahabharata,* when Krishna leads all Pandavas to heaven, Yudhisthira, the eldest, is refused entry because his dog accompanied him.

"Crow's Account of the Battle" relates the battle of history which man has fought in the past and will continue to fight in the future. Man has created numbers, theories, scripture, physics, etc., to escape into death only. Many trickster myths are a satire upon social customs and foibles of man.[56] Many lines in the poem run, without any punctuation marks, one after the other, and full stops come only at the end of comparatively long stanzas. This gives a sense of freedom to the movement, and an equally efficacious selection of words beginning or ending with "t" or "d" sounds, has succeeded in evoking the tumult and cry of war. But the consolation does not lie in an end to inhuman war; it lies in its continuation:

> And when the smokes cleared it became clear
> This had happened too often before
> And was going to happen too often in future
> And happened too easily

After this, fifteen lines without punctuation emphasize futility, uncertainty, and meaninglessness of our existence. "So the survivors stayed" puts to an end the question of peace as man's understanding is enmeshed in the cumbrous and tyrannical wheels of cosmogonic round; the hero returns to where he started from, making apocalpyse an idealised nostalgia. The hero of modern romance does not show outer development. The boundary lines of the world are given and defined; the hero may take flight from one place to another (Crow), or he may go on creating his own world, here and now. Paul Radin says: "I must confess that I have not been able to discover, either in the Winnebago trickster stories or in any other archaic narrative or its dramatic representation, any such thing as the 'inner development of the hero.'"[57] Crow comes now to the metaphysical question as to why "The Black Beast" should exist. The poem begins and ends with this question asked eleven times by Crow. When Crow gets no answer his wrath kills a frog, roasts earth into a clinker; the silence of space decamps and the vacuum, caused by Crow's breaking of relations, inflinges itself upon him. In a terrific bid to escape through, Crow flies past the stars questioning "where is it? Where is the Black Beast," never searching it within himself. Crow's ego has blocked the gates of his understanding and perception. He is in a state of unconsciousness and does not know that he is an answer to question he is asking others.

In "Crow Communes," Crow wants to discuss with God the problem of creation. This leaves God snoring and agape. The problem of death and evil, taken by "A Grin" and in "Crow Communes" is again taken by Crow in "Crow's Account of St. George." Hirschberg rightly thinks that "the Crow's account of St. George is a reversal of the archetype of the conquering hero who vanquishes chaos, evil and temptations, after having conquered elements of weakness within himself."[58] St. Georege, the patron saint of Christianity, thinks that the mystery of creation is explainable in terms of numbers and other human systems of knowledge. By coalescing words with a comparatively new origin ('refrigerates') with words having metaphysical signification ('emptiness'), Hughes succeeds in evoking a sense of the ludicrous. And then

. . . The great stones fall open.

With the faintest breath
He melts cephalopods and sorts raw numbers
Out of their dregs.

Creatures which stare at St. George while he is busy in the exercise of numbers, are a demon, a bird-head, whose relationship with the patron-saint seems to be a relationship of innocent creatures with a sinner:

He smashes the egg-shell object to a blood-rag,
A lumping sprawl, he tramples the bubbling mess.
The shark-face is screaming in the doorway
Opening its fangs.

St. George is also a symbol of modern spirit of enquiry and analysis. Modern man has left nothing for silence to speak for itself. It has bifurcated, dissected, and the exuberance of nature (in Blakean sense) is nature methodized (Alexander Pope). But the climax is yet to come. Our pseudo St. George snatches a sword (and 'sword,' as said earlier, is a weapon associated with the conquering hero), and murders his own wife and children:

He stands trousered in blood and log-splits
The lolling body, bifurcates it
Top to bottom, . . .

The dramatic ending of this poem reminds us of Browning's poem "Porphyria's Lover," and St. George too, like the lover, seems to be a psychological case, though in a different context. Keith Sagar says that for the murder "The immediate source was a Japanese folk-tale about a Samurai whose professional pride and militancy ossifies into madness in which he kills his wife and children."[59]

Crow poems are so arranged as to show a progression in meaning. We come now to "The Battle of Osfrontalis," a poem in which "words" have discovered Crow, and are all out to attack him. "Osfrontalis" is the part of the head associated with higher thought processes. Again, the technique of juxtaposing words in common use ('Life Insurance Policies') with words having serious meaning, produces ludicrous effect. The best way to escape, Crow thinks, is to feign dead. The humour in this poem verges from sardonic to pure ridicule—

Words come with Aladdin's lamp—
He sold it and bought a pie.

The whole poem is arranged in two-line sequences; the first line attacks Crow, in the second line, Crow plays some trick and escapes. At last, words retreat thinking Crow "the skull of a dead jester." It might be remarked here that critics who quote[60] the following passage from Paul Radin that trickster's ". . . hunger, his sex, his wandering, these appertain neither to the gods nor to man. They belong to another realm, materially and spiritually, and that is why neither the gods nor the man know precisely what to do with them,"[61] do not emphasize the essentially human implication of Hughes's Crow. Crow, before he is the trickster figure, having his source in American Indian myth, is Hughes's persona, and voices Hughes's concerns, and his own sense of the understanding of the world. *Crow* is not myth; it has its source in myth. And the difference between myth and poetry is as clear as that the myth is not poetry and poetry is not myth.

"Crow's Theology" makes Crow sensible enough to think that there is a God who loves him. This directs our attention to the long passage quoted from Paul Radin on the origin of Crow myth,[62] where Crow would have died but for the mercy of God. God's love seems to have answered for Crow, the question of death, on personal level. But Crow's typically human sensibility drives him to think of stones, shot-pellets, who also exist. Does God also love them? And

Crow realized there were two Gods—
One of them much bigger than the other
Loving his enemies

This is Hughes's rejection of the God of conventional Christianity.

The messengers of a technological age are capable of singing only a "Criminal Ballad" instead of the ballad of God. The protagonist of this poem is a man who invites comparison with the poem on St. George, the poem is a study of contraries in relations and celebrates the theme of unrelatedness and disintegration. The protagonist is at a loss to behave properly with his wife, children and even himself.

> . . . when he walked in his garden and saw his children
> Bouncing among the dogs and balls
> He could not hear their silly songs and the barking
> For machine guns
> And he could not even turn towards the house
> Because the woman of complete pain rolling in flame
> Was calling to him all the time
> From the empty goldfish pond

The man in this poem is in total enmity with his environment; at last he runs along the road into the woods, and weeps till his weeping changes into laughter, a typical Blakean proverb from *The Marriage of Heaven and Hell,* where the excess of joy weeps, excess of sorrow laughs. Excess of sorrow gives knowledge of true nature of things (therefore 'laughter'), while excess of joy attaches one into the complexity of relationships, and clouds one's understanding of true nature of things (therefore 'weeping').

"Crow on the Beach" reminds of trickster's flight in the Winnebago Hare cycle where we come across sentences like "After that he (trickster) walked down a slope and finally came to a lake,"[63] or "Again trickster started out walking along aimlessly."[64] Whenever Crow looks at the universe, horror and wonder have become central to his perception. Crow sees shingle explode; the smell of the whale's den, and the gulping of the crab's last prayer, alter Crow's sensibility to the point of metaphysical realization of "something fleeting." There are a number of poems where the Crow is juxtaposed with the sea, but the sea always remains a mystery, with its ogrish cry and convulsion. The poem ends in the same ambivalence and confusion of environment Crow is in: "What could be hurting so much?"

"Oedipus Crow" relates vitally to the Oedipus story not in its oft-celebrated "Oedipus-complex" aspect,[65] but in its equation of Craw's pride, arrogance and lameness, with that of Oedipus. When Mummies storm into his torn insides, he vomits empty and flies. Then he survives ordeal of the grave-stone by bitting through it and rejects what the water-spirits in the happy valley have for him. This ego-centric act of Crow is paralleled by the attempt of death to impoverish him:

> One-legged, gutless and brainless, the rag of himself—
> And held him up with a laugh, only just alive.

The Crow is maimed, both physically and mentally, and his desperate search for permanence leaves him scuttling across; the floors of silent seas:

> Crow dangled from his one claw—corrected.
> A warning.

In many poems Hughes has given value-judgments upon Crow and "Crow's Vanity" is one such poem. The progression in theme is clear enough. This poem also relates to William Blake's "The Song of Los" where religions and history are considered as man's unsuccessful attempt to catch the joys of eternity: ". . . Churches, Hospitals, Castles, Palaces,/Like nets & gins & traps to catch the Joys of Eternity." Crow, in Hughes's poem, is also trying to understand the nature of his creator through the objects of creation. The "evil mirror" is another name for the world, and history appears to Crow' as:

> Mistings of civilizations towers gardens
> Battles he wiped the glass but there came
> Mistings of sky-scrappers webs of cities

The emphasis in Blake's poem is, however, on God who

is to be understood by man; in Hughes poem "misting civilizations" supplement the primary idea of God, and Crow fails to understand his environment, nothing to say of his understanding the creator of this environment.

"A Horrible Religious Error" relates to error not of God but of Crow who ate the serpent. The serpent is addressed as "The sphynx" of the final act who throws riddles for human beings, never solving them. Nevertheless, it was God's will that he existed, and man and woman, who are probably Adam and Eve, kneel and accept God's decree. But Crow, just as formerly, when he infused soul in the sleeping man and woman, again tries to steal a march over God's design, grabs the serpent by the slack-skin nape, beats the hell out of it, and eats it. Hirschberg says that "the special twist here is that Crow is able to deal with evil far more ably than a virtually impotent God."[66] Hirschberg is pretty sure that Hughes is dealing with the biblical serpent and therefore makes the above statement.

"In Laughter" is full of technological imagery—cars, steamer, aircraft, and a host of other images follow in a cataloguing fashion, all created by Crow. The main thing to be commented upon in this poem is the laughter itself. Hirschberg says that "Laughter itself is a deliberate obliviousness to the destructive consequences of violent action."[67] The objection to this obliviousness is that it is not "deliberate" but natural. Laughter comes when the perceiver has not only detached himself from the object of his perception, but when the object permits the perceiver to laugh at itself because of its sheer aimlessness in what it considers to be aim, and meaninglessness in what it considers to be meaning. This is an existential paradox and laughter comes from a person who is able to see this eternal round from a position of aloofness and isolation. But, this is psychological interpretation. Compare this account of trickster from Ogala theology. Paul Radin says: "In this myth he (trickster) is represented as being punished by the supreme deity for having brought shame and ridicule upon other gods and is condemned to go to the world and remain there without friends, is condemned to the fate that all mankind will hate him. To this he is represented as responding with a long and loud laugh, and as telling the supreme deity that he had forgotten the birds and other animals; that he would dwell with them . . . and that on earth he would enjoy himself and make fools of mankind" (*The Trickster,* p. 165). The laughter and character-traits of Crow from this account are clear enough.

"Conjuring in Heaven" seems to be a satirical parody of the Upanishadic saying which means that the world was perfect; from the perfect was deduced the perfect; what remained was the perfect.[68] In the course of fourteen lines in the poem, "nothing" is used nine times. Why is it not used eight or ten times is clear enough—that all the nine gates of the body are closed. The parody in the poem will become clear if we contrast the mystical signification of "nothing" with the nothingness, chaos, blackness of the poem out of which Crow is made.

The title of "Crow Goes Hunting" may well be taken as a parody of the traditional preparation of a shaman going on his journey. Crow's decision to "try words" is a reversal of the situation we encountered in "The Battle of Osfrontalis." Crow tries words—not with a view to communicate and understand them and others, but to dominate over them. The poem is a struggle for supremacy between Hare and Crow, while the style parodies the style of genealogical narration. Crow orders words to kill the Hare. The Hare changes into a bunker, the bunker into starlings, starlings change into cloudburst, cloudburst changes into a reservoir, reservoir into an earthquake, and earthquake again into an Hare. Crow is left gazing in admiration. In the trickster cycles Hare is described as "the typical culture-hero"[69] and his task is to make the earth habitable for man. In the Winnebago Hare cycle, the Hare is not only the expert hunter, but his mother was a human being, and he "was sent by Earthmaker to teach the people on earth a better life."[70] In the poem, Hare serves as a contrast to Crow in his motives and functions. Hare might also be taken as a higher form of the consciousness of crow.

I have pointed out that Crow partakes of the qualities of a shaman in his impersonating aspect, *i.e.*, his capacity to imagine himself as wolf, bear, etc.[71] In certain episodes, the trickster "gets his head caught inside the skull of an elk, and the next episode shows how he overcomes this condition by imprisoning the head of a hawk inside his own rectum."[72] The point to be driven home is that the owl is Crow's own antagonistic self. "Owl's Song" sings of the destruction of egoes, pretences, appearances, knowledge—something Crow is yet to learn. "Crow's Undersong" deals with the theme of Mother Nature. Her account is taken from birth into puberty, and as she grows, she expands and stays, "Even after life even among the bones". Her association with wheels in the next stanza is but an elaboration of her nature—of running the wheel of the universe, the cosmogonic round; her expression is in the form of furs, rainbows, and the line "She has come amorous it is all she has come for" states Hughes's central belief.

In "Dawn's Rose" Crow has renewed himself but his cry, compared with an old woman's mouth, new-born baby's grieving, remains desolate. We are movmg in a world which ends where it began—the redness of dawn's rose and the redness of star of blood. "Crow's Playmates" tries to solve the problem of desolation. The power of creating something which is given to the trickster, the Crow does not possess; and whenever he attempts creation, created objects retract upon him, and make miserable Crow's own existence. In the poem, gods of mountain and river, which Crow created, tear free and attack Crow. Crow is left lonelier than ever. Hirschberg compares Crow with Zeus who attacked Chronos, his father, and ruled over the universe.[73]

The juxtaposition of absurd with serious, high with low, is best seen in "Crowego." Crow is a trickster hero or rather a parody of him. But this does not satisfy him; he wants to become Ulysses, Hercules, Beowulf. Crow commits an error by strangling Dejanira, the wife of Hercules, who killed her husband. Craw's killing of her proves him stronger than Hercules. The gold melting out of Hercules's body after his cremation at AEtna becomes an electrode in Craw's brain. And in spite of his association with three heroes Crow could not become heroic.

So he gazes into the quag of the past
Like a gypsy into the crystal of the future,

Crow's ego and self-closed nature is best illustrated by lines like "His wings are the stiff back of his only book/ Himself the only page—of solid ink."

"The Smile" expands the theme of "A Grin," and becomes in the end apocalyptic. It originated under the groan of the forest (event associated with the creation of the world) and it ran through the earth and the sky. The conflict in the poem is between the people in their masks and appearances, and the unbridled, unchained smile, whom rust of civilization could not cover; it outflanked all. The smile is that portion in every human being which constitutes his essential individuality; but somehow, man has always tried to hide it because of the social set-up. Man has been made civilized to the point of de-humanization.

And there was the unlucky person's eye
Pinned under its brow
Widening for the darkness behind it
Which kept right on getting wide, darker
As if the soul were not working

The smile relates very vitally to Wordsworthian argument of man's loss of contact with nature or his environment which is Hughes's primary theme. To this sick man in the poem, the smile raises from his torn roots, touches his legs, alters his eyes, and mends evetything till the man is restored fully to his natural habitat.

In many of *Crow* poems the role of Crow is similar to the role of Tiersias in Eliot's *The Waste Land*. In "Crow Improvises," Crow relates how the man whom the smile (environment) restored to his senses, mounts on his adventurous quest for dominance (as opposed to understanding) over nature (smile) and murders her in the process. This man in the poem, imposes self-directed, artificial, conclusions upon the world of nature and its rhythm. No wonder then, each time he attempts, loses either some part of his mask or of his physical body. At last when tired–

. . . he took his birth-sneeze in one hand
And his death-chill in the other
And let the spark scour him to ashes.

Hirschberg compares this man with Osiris, Attic, and Perzival figures, waiting to be healed.[74] Crow's helplessness and agony at the state of this man is understandable in "Crow's Battle Fury." In trickster cycles, the "trickster contains within itself the promise of differentiation, the promise of god and man,"[75] and in the poem under consideration, Crow shows such a promise though with a difference. Crow laughs in order to come to the realization of the alarming situation: "On the earth's blue bulge/Trembling its tambourine." Remembering the painted masks and the looming of the balloons:

Of the pinpricked dead
He rolls on the ground helpless.

The gravity and horror of the situation is measured in terms of the increase in swelling and displacement of man's limbs:

His heels double to the front,
His lips life off his cheekbone,
His heart and his liver fly in his throat,

The death of this man has left for Crow nobody to rule over. The man provided shelter to Crow's ego. Crow simply fails to extend the gravity of the diseased man (vegetation myth figure) in terms of some universal loss. Instead, he advances "a step,/ and a step," and a step," to eat what is left of the man. Keith Sagar draws our attention that lines

13-18 of the poem are from *The Tain,* and compares Crow's battle fury with Cuchulain: "Cuchulain's madness was his belief that he could impose his will upon the world by sheer strength and energy such as cannot be in this world."[76]

It is natural that we shall now have "Crow Blacker than Ever." This poem celebrates disgust and disintegration in which Crow "turns the idea of Christian redemption upside down."[77] The poem also misplaces the hierarchy of celestial bodies—God, heaven, man (Adam) and Eve. Crow nails heaven and earth together for Crow only knows how to nail things which are incongruous; earlier he had nailed Worm, the Son of God, into sleeping man and woman. The inchoate, unproportioned act of voluntary intersection results in the creaking of the joint, and the poem's lines, at more than usual distance from each other, consisting no more than a single word, impinge upon, and scatter the sense of disintegration:

The agony
Grew
Crow
Grinned
Crying: 'This is my Creation,'

"Revenge Fable" picks up the argument of "The Smile." The person of this poem, in order to understand his mother (Nature), arms and equips himself with numbers, equations and laws, like St. George earlier, and calls them truth. Man cannot think anybody higher than himself, and so the possibility of his "truth" being certified by a higher reality does not exist. Not content with all this, the man "investigated," "incriminated" and "penalized" his mother for no visible offence of hers. Bulldozers, detergents, requisitions, rifles, whisky, and above all the knife, mock man's sense of victory and localize the outlines of his identity in a world which simply could not be understood by the timidity of the science of hydrodynamics; the victorious man's head is fallen like a leaf at the end of the poem.

This man is a projection, not only of every man of Crow's

universe in "A Bedtime Story," but of every object which suffers from hypochondriasis, common both to Crow and his creation. The fragmentation of this man is highlighted, and the truth emphasized, that atomic precision is no answer to the imaginative wholeness of man. The perceiver and the perceived are not in harmony, and in the poem, when the man perceives, what he gets in return is not the object but its reflection.[78] His sense of hearing, seeing, his face, legs, are gone as a result of punishment for his attempted murder of his mother (Nature) in the previous poem. While Tiersias's blindness is a symbol of knowledge and intuition, this man is really blind, both physically and metaphorically. He tries so many things in the poem, but the impossibility of gain complicates his sense of compulsion to live within self-imposed conclusions. These conclusions become the nightmares of his debilitated existence, and the wish to write an autobiography, results in the breakdown of his nerves. In sheer exhaustion he says, "I give up," and creation fails again. Creation is the name of the balance between man and nature. Crow (and man), can destroy it; he cannot supplement or replace it.

The tragic point in the thematic progression of *Crow* is that the protagonist does not show signs of *mental* development, and the failure of creation does not make Crow look beyond and outside of himself; it instigates him into yet another exercise of self-impotency—"Crow's Song of Himself." This poem is again a recreation of the inverted version of Christian concepts ofcreation, fall, and redemption. We know that there were only two creatures in the world in the beginning.[79] When God was "tired of being alone with the Crow,. . . He decided to make persons and the animals."[80] In the poem God makes so many things out of Crow, gold, diamond, alcohol, etc., and finally man and woman. But somehow God was not happy with His creation, and Crow, seizing upon the opportunity, attacked man and woman.

Just as Urizen, in Blake's *The Four Zoas,* having already rebelled against God, goes on creating one world after another, in terrific sense of loss of proportion, and finally wonders at the horror of his own creation, so too, Crow, in "Crow Sickened" winds the world "like a ball of wool,"[81] but since the last end is tied round his own finger, he cannot escape. Even death cannot kill Crow, for God made Crow the redeemer, and Crow we have seen, survives death and even redemption. For the first time Crow asks the long-awaited question: "Where is this somebody who has made me under?" In romance, the protagonist always searches, through the course of the poem, his father: "Where the goal of the hero's effort is the discovery of the unknown father, the basic symbolism remains that of the tests and the self-revealing way."[82] The hero, who is blessed by his father, returns after his journey and strikes the theme of integration. A hero like Crow, who tries to prick holes in his own Father, ends in disaster.[83]

From one angle many poems in *Crow* are based upon the archetype of cosmogonic round. "Song for a Phallus," for instance, which recreates the Oedipus story, begins with Oedipus struck in his Mummy's belly and ends with his being curled up inside the belly again. There is nothing new in Hughes's version of Oedipus story except two variations: first when Oedipus's father ties Oedipus's legs, and throws him before the cat, Oedipus survives;[84] the second concerns the sphynx riddle. Sphynx used to kill everybody who could not answer riddles. In Hughes, Oedipus kills the sphynx saying "The answers aren't in me, he cried/Maybe your guts have got'em." From beginning to the end, Oedipus remains a rebel figure indulging in attempts to murder his father, sphynx, and tearing apart his mother like a melon. But the tragic irony in Oedipus's life is that he remains an incestuous figure, like the true trickster, who is unbridled in his sexuality. Oedipus's nature confronts that of Crow at a vital point; Oedipus wants to become a hero by desiring to subdue his father and mother, without having real heroic qualities. The poem is written in the ballad form, and at the end of each stanza, "Mamma Mamma" does not become so much a rhythm for song, as the continuous cries of a child whose physical victory over his parents is subdued by his moral defeat.

"Apple Tragedy" extends the argument of "Childish Prank." God squeezes the apple while the serpent drinks the juice. Adam and Eve accept the serpent as their God; the serpent seizes the opportunity and copulates with Eve, while the latter cries "Rape! Rape!" (Refer also to stories in Greek mythology where the serpent would emerge from the sea to take away the maidens, see Joseph Campbell, *Primitive Mythology,* p. 101). Adam smashes a chair on the serpent's head, and even though God is well pleased with Adam's act, ". . . everything goes to hell." The poem begins with a reversal of Genesis story when we find the serpent resting on the seventh day and not God. God is no more than a servant of serpent in the poem, and His pleasure at Adam smashing a chair upon serpent's head, while it speaks of his feebleness before evil, also bespeaks of his contradictory nature, which created a serpent first, and then became afraid of its evil nature, to eradicate which He could do nothing.

Crow is the kind of creature whom words cannot kill nor the rays of the sun. This is because the origin of Crow as trickster is as old as that of the sun and the rock,[85] and apart from being a "reflection of an earlier, rudimentary stage of consciousness,"[86] Crow is also "'Cosmic' being of *divine-animal* nature."[87] The sun burns everything in the poem probably with a view to renewing the cycle, but in Crow, it finds a creature made of different substance; we know that Crow can survive death, and the lines "Against which it (sun) raged and charred. And rages and chars," while they give us a sense of continuity of the activity of burning in the past and into the present, confront in Crow a being who is both inside and outside the time-space barrier. All created things exist at a certain level of consciousness, as distinct from the unconsciousness of supermundane creatures or objects like the rock and the sun. But when one can go into the unconsciousness of his previous births like the Crow, one also transcends limitations conscious existence is subject to. Crow's (trickster's) "longevity could also be explained by the strength and vitality of the state of consciousness described in the myth. . . ."[88]

Precisely because sea's unconscious existence ("Crow and the Sea") is higher and larger than Crow's own, Crow utterly fails to communicate and understand the mystery underlying sea's existence. Craw's tricks of ignoring the sea, talking to it, sympathizing with it, and healing it, simply do not work. It is this meaninglessness, non-responsiveness of sea which is characteristic of all lives, including that of Crow, and therefore, man's adjustment with his environment is a perennial problem ever insoluble.

The quest of Crow to get hold of something permanent in a world of fleeting realities is the theme of "Truth Kills Everybody." The sea in this poem appears as Proteus, the sea-god (a humanised version of sea and therefore more meaningful?). The phrase "he (Crow) held it" occurs in the poem no less than ten times; Craw's attempts to hold all things that appear, is a desperate quest of the hero-figure to get at the meaning of the mystery of existence; but the held things anticlimax Crow's relentless quest-theme with a sharp repulsion and retraction by banging in upon him and blasting him to nothing. Crow holds Proteus, then Achilles, son of sea-goddess Thetis, and then a staring shark, ". . . naked power line, 200 volts." He attempts to befriend and understand these primeval, mythic nature-creatures, and by doing so Crow is trying to return back to the forces that produced him. Hughes has said: "Any form of violence—any form of vehement activity—invokes the bigger energy, the elemental power circuit of the Universe."[89]

The source of "Crow and Stone" is the following story from the Raven cycle of the Tlingit: "There then lived in a house at the head of Nass river a being called Raven-at-the-head-of-Nass (Nascaki-yel) . . . .First of all beings Nascakiyel created Heron as a very tall and very wise man and after him the Raven, who was also a very good and very wise man at that time. Raven came into being in this wise. His first mother had many children, but they all died young, and she cried over them continually. . . By and by Heron came to her and said, 'What is it that you are crying about all the time?' She answered, 'I am always losing my children.

I cannot bring them up: Then he said, 'Go down on the beach when the tide is lowest, get a small, smooth stone, and put it into the fire. When it is red hot swallow it. Do not be afraid.' She said 'All right.' Then she followed Heron's directions and gave birth to Raven. Therefore Raven's name was really It-CAK, the name of a very hard rock, and he was hence called TAqlik-ic (Hammer-father). This is why Raven was so tough and could not easily be killed."[90] The stone in the poem which is called the "champion of the globe," because of its hardness and strength, is at enmity with Crow. The Crow, on the contrary, who is as hard as the rock, is an advancement on the featureless stone stage in the development of his consciousness. Moreover, Crow was born when his mother swallowed the stone. This deliberate impingement of forms, human or animal, upon the formlessness of nature, is the theme of the poem. But Crow has far outwitted the stone, his source of birth, and this relates to the belief that trickster's mother dies at the time of his birth. Moreover, "If men had come from the rock there would be no death,"[91] tells the same Tlingit story. This explains Craw's mastery over death. But the universe Crow finds himself in, is not to be measured in terms of victory or defeat; and what perplexes Crow and makes him helpless, is its stillness, nothingness, a world whose argument is a treacherous one—everything is nothing and nothing is everything—something which is too much for Crow to understand and swallow.

"Fragment of an Ancient Tablet" expounds the mother-image in archetypal terms of heaven and earth, good and evil, etc. The ambivalence of the tablet is a paradox for the quest-hero who wants to understand it in so simple terms as either this or that. Hirschberg thinks that the title refers to the emerald tablet of Hermes Trismegistus.[92] "Notes for a Little Play" depicts the world at the time of apocalypse. The sun is a giver of life only from a distance. In the poem it has violated the limit of this distance and burnt everything except "two strange items" which are the masculine and the feminine principles. Surrounded by the all round darkness and holocaust these male and female grip each other to establish a pattern over formless nature. They start dancing to set the cosmogonic round moving again. But they suffer from fear, and fear is aroused by a sense of purposelessness, which is howling, always, from the back-door, over the life of these people. "They do not know what else to do." And this leads them to celebrate a marriage, which is an act and exercise in disintegration, for neither the sun, nor-God or any guest, are participants. The rift between man and his environment has begun from the beginning. That is Crow's-principal burden.

These male and female meet us in the form of Adam and Eve in the "Snake Hymn," a poem which celebrates their love, and the "Love Song" further elaborates the theme under discussion. In the later poem the lovers are trying to inject their limbs violently, into each other; the love has become a battle-ground for the supremacy of will. In *tantra,* the male tantric, who is the seeking self, copulates with the *bhairvi* (woman), who is the answering self; when *bhairvi* is excited, she also behaves like the male, and the repetition of this act infuses each into the other; their union is supposed to correspond with the union of Shiva and *Shakti,* of *Prakriti* and *Purusha,* and what we get as a result is a being who is both male and female, *ardhanarishwara.* In Hughes's poem:

> In their entwined sleep they exchanged arms and legs
> In their dreams their brains took each other hostage
> In the morning they wore each other's face

The poem does not have a single punctuation mark depicting nature's trance in love.

"Glimpse" has its source in the following Tlingit myth we referred to earlier: "Nas-Caki-Yel (creator-figure) tried to make human beings out of a rock and out of a leaf at the same time, but the rock was slow while the leaf was very quick. Therefore human beings came from the leaf. Then he showed a leaf to the human beings and said, 'You see this leaf. You are to be like it. When it falls off the branch and rots there is nothing left of it.' That is why there is death in the world. If man had come from the rock there would be no death."[93] In the poem the touch of a leaf guillotines Crow's throat because the birth from leaves entail, death. We already know that Crow is born of rock and therefore is beyond death. This is what makes him a god. But the idea of a god is an ironic reversal[94] of the power and potentiality a god enjoys, in Crow's context.

Crow is a "King of Carrion," and his problem is not to attain immortality but to understand death—a fact deliberately adhered to in many poems. Perhaps Crow's death would have given him the possibility of his renewal and regeneration; but he is born of a substance which stagnates, deadens, and makes a hell in heaven's despite:

> The empty world, from which the last cry
> Flapped hugely, hopelessly away
> Into the blindness and dumbness and deafness of the gulf
> Returning, shrunk, silent
> To reign over silence

It is strange and ironical that in Crow we encounter a being who is born of nothingness, who eats nothing, who rules over nothing; nothing can cause him death, nothing can rule over him—this array of "nothings" has made Crow a pseudotrickster, who, though asks intelligent questions, presents human situations, nevertheless, never gives us the perception of a "divine being and as a true transformer of the world. . ."[95] a trait which is part of trickster's essential nature.

"Two Eskimo Songs"[93] account for man's history and relationship with nature from the earliest times. The first part "Fleeing from Eternity" describes how nature has been the source of everything for man, and man, though humanizing her by giving her eyes, mouth, etc., has totally failed to understand her. The man stupidly laughs in the poem at the song of nature while nature feels cheated. In the second poem "How Water Began to Play," water expresses seven times its desire to live, but is refused every time by the sun, the tree, the flowers, etc. Seven times may refer to the theosophical seven worlds up to which existence is possible within time. At last the water wants to die, but death, likewise, is also not granted to it for water is eternal. While this is a clear depiction of Crow's own dilemma, it is also an answer to his problem. The water at last has shown humility (as opposed to Crow's ego), and it is by showing humility and appreciation of other's viewpoint that he has found its true place in its relation to other created objects. It could as well have flooded everything and destroyed, as Tharmas does in *The Four Zoas.* The water, at last, in Hughes's poem, has not only found its place, it has discovered its outlines of identity as well "utterly clear."

"Littleblood" ends *Crow* by further giving us a glimpse of the world of the king of Carrion. The littleblood is hiding itself from every other created thing—mountains, stars, but its own life depends upon sucking the blood of those it is hiding from. Its wisdom and its terribleness (which do not go together) depict well Crow's nature and that of his world, and the poem ends with poet's mock-epic invocation (reversing the traditional epic invocation at the beginning of the poem) of the littleblood who is asked by the poet to "Sit on my finger, sing in my ear, O littleblood."

III

In his Introduction to *Leonard Baskin Catalogue* (1962), Ted Hughes wrote: "In our time, the heroic struggle is not to become a hero but to remain a living creature simply. . . the particular misery and disaster of our time are, uniquely, the perfect conditions for the purest and most intense manifestation of the spirit, the Angel, the ghost of ashes, the survivor of the Creation. . . ."[97] While this gives us a clue to the character and structure of *Crow,* the passage relates vitally to Hughes's view of the modern man's existence in a world whose imaginative spontaneity has become a nightmare in broad day light, chiefly because of "rational" techniques of discovering the truth, in a spirit of scientific enquiry, investigation and analysis: "The scientific Spirit was born of the common hunt for the nourishing morsel, nursed by the benign search for objective truth, schooled in the pedagogic idolatry of the objective fact, graduated through oldmaid specialized research, losing eyes, ears, smell, taste, touch, nerves and blood, adapting to the sensibility of electronic gadgets and the argument of numbers, to become a machine of senility, a pseudo-automaton in the House of the Mathematical Absolute. So it outs humanity from man and he dedicates his life to the laws of the electron in vacuo, a literal self-sacrifice, and soon, by bigotry and the especially rabid evangelism of the inhuman, a literal world-sacrifice, as we all too truly now fear."[98]

The dismemberment of hero's body is Hughes's primary theme in *Crow* and *Gaudete.* What the above passage means, then, is that Hughes finds himself in a world where a traditional heaven above and a underworld below the earth have reversed their respective positions; the underworld has identified itself with existence upon earth, while heaven has permanently changed its lineaments with those of hell. And because our existence upon earth has become hellish, the need for Crow to go to the traditional underworld is simply underscored. The earth *has become* the underworld and this further outscores the need for a redeeming messiah-figure, who is simply laid impotent and ineffective in a world where man bas broken his relationship with nature, nay, lost it. The world is, therefore, a continuously tantalizing panorama of sepulchres and tombstones in Hughes's vision, where each human being, because of the crime with himself and with nature he has committed, fails to account, either for the birth of the messiah-figure, or for a consequent redemption. In *Gaudete,* Nicholas Lumb, a clergyman, tries to become the father of messiah-figure; while his project ends mid-way in fiasco, he has also to undergo punishment in the form of death, wrought by cuckolded husbands of ladies Lumb had made pregnant. While this is a mockery of messiah-figure, and perhaps of physicists who are trying to produce. Neitzschian super-man in a test-tube, who is no more than a symbol of man's displacement of personal sin; this also outlines Hughes's metaphorical expolitation of traditional heaven, hell and underworld in the immediate present, unchanging, carcass-like, where man has become a caricature of his human-divine self, and the reality of meaning has disappeared into the imbecilic confusion of total senselessness.

Our hero in *Crow,* and Mr. Lumb in *Gaudete,* obstruct, contradict, and frustrate, possibilities of human regeneration. Crow's heroism is his own cowardice, his cowardice his own defeat. As Frye says: ". . . every typical character in romance tends to have his moral opposite confronting him, . . ."[99] so in *Crow,* Crow is always reproaching, invalidating, rejecting, and frustrating, the schematic design of a God who is responsible for *His* creation. Crow's desire to supplement his own world (thinking it a better one), is the cause of the whole malady. The waste land of Crow's world, therefore, never changes into a city or a garden, as it does, for example, in the form of Golgonooza in Blake, or garden in Thom Gunn. Crow's world is an excruciatingly painful, horrible, and torturing world of perversions; it is a monument of folly where nature has written a permanent "No" to regeneration; earth has become an existential hell, while heaven has turned its back and disappeared beyond the outlines of identity.

Parody dominates in demonic imagery along with the idea of an inscrutable fate which is always dormant. "Under the world where Earthmaker lives, there is another world just like hand of this world, he, Trickster, is in charge."[100] This is the world which speaks in the images of serpent, the womb-door, blackness, Mother-Nature, among others, which we shall now take consideration of. The blackness which we encounter especially in "Two Legends," "Crow Blacker than Ever" or "The Black Beast," refers both to the environmental blackness (and this supplements traditional 'darkness') as in the first poem, and to the metaphysical blackness, as in later two poems. We have referred to the source of this blackness in the Raven cycle on the Tlingit: "At the beginning of things there was no daylight and the world lay in blackness."[101] This blackness later, in the same myth, is as: "All of the beings

Nas-caki-yel had created, however, existed in darkness."[102] This blackness or darkness with which Hughes begins *Crow*, is common to Christian tradition and certain trickster myths. Hughes, however, interpolates Charistian concept of blackness *ex nihilo*, with non-Christian myth of egg as the symbol of creation:

> Black is the earth-globe, one inch under,
> An egg of blackness
> Where sun and moon alternate their weathers
> To hatch a crow.

This egg is common to Greek, Syrian, Egyptian, Indian and Finnish traditions. But at the time of the bursting of this eggshell,[103] in the mythological traditions above, we have the birth of a giant-being, often hermaphroditic, who is the progenitor of the human race. In Hughes, the parody of these mythological traditions only produces an infantile Crow, a tiny creature, trying to account for the untiny task of creation. Crow is also called a "black rainbow;" rainbow among the Hawaii island people, is a medium through which their hero-figure climbs up to heaven, and performs the act of redemption. Rainbow is also a road by which a shaman reaches the realm of spirits.[104] In the poem, however, even the rainbow has been parodied, and Crow, in spite of continuous flying over emptiness, never reaches his father-figure.

Crow is in molecular tension of ego with his creator and in "A Childish Prank" he bites the Worm, "God's only son:"

> Crow laughed.
> He bit the Worm, God's only son,
> Into two writhing halves.

In Oglala theology, where the trickster is called "Iktom, *i.e.* Spider, was the first-born son of the Rock and a being called the Winged One."[105] Radin quotes from J.R. Walker's paper,[106] the Spider-Worm son of God as saying; "I am a god and the son of a god. My father, the Rock, is the oldest of the gods."[107]

"Womb door" that we encounter in "Examination at the Womb-door," is obviously taken from *Bardo Thodol* of *The Tibetan Book of the Dead.* The image is also common to certain tantric traditions[108] and occurs in the *Gita* too. Krishna says; "The great Brahm is my womb. In it I place my foetus; and from it is the production of all nature. The great is the womb of all those various forms which are conceived in every natural womb, and I am the father who soweth the seed."[109] Here nature (Brahm) is imagined as a womb, and God (male principle) as the father who puts the seed. In Hughes's poem the implication of womb-door is that entrance into it (birth) results in death—a fact which is stated no less than sixteen times in the poem, and therefore, Crow escapes this fact by refusing ('examination') entry into it, thus becoming stronger than death, But does he regenerate himself by doing so? or does he transform the world he is the hero of? Crow supplements his mental cunningness to God's benevolent design, and death which is necessary for renewal, by not being entered into, complicates Crow's victory over death which is already a defeat.

The serpent is the source of evil and Crow even ate it once ("A Horrible Religious Error"). The serpent with tail in its mouth is a perfect symbol of fall. In Hughes, the serpent is depicted to be more powerful than God ('So on the seventh day/ The serpent rested,' "Apple Tragedy"), and while God is always afraid of him, Crow never quite succeeds in eradicating this menace, for by shedding its skin it renews itself. In "Snake Hymn" the snake has become the blood of Adam and evil is firmly implanted. In the Bible serpent is also referred to as the Covering Cherub (water as chaos) and Leviathan. One of the reasons for Crow not succeeding to kill finally the serpent may be, that the Crow is made out of blackness. Accounts of creation, as for example Mesopotamian, which precede Biblical account, tell us of the creation of the world after the hero has killed the sea-monster or the serpent who personified the chaotic blackness;[110] in

Crow, Crow parodies messiah-figure, and thereby lets evil perpetuate.

IV

Crow is the king of a world of contradictory principles which has failed to account for or explain the ambiguity of creation. It was but apt for Hughes to choose Crow as his symbol for this world. The issues *Crow* raises are of a metaphysical nature and concern the dilemma Western man has been caught in since the days of Plato. Reviewing Max Nicholson's *The Environmental Revolution*,[111] Hughes wrote: "The fundamental guiding ideas of our Western Civilization are against Conservatism. They derive from Reformed Christianity and from Old Testament Puritanism . . . They are based on the assumption that the earth is a heap of raw materials given to man by God for his exclusive profit and use . . . By the skin of her teeth, woman escaped the same role. The subtly apotheosised misogny of Reformed Christianity is proportionate to the fanatic rejection of Nature—and the result has been to exile man from Mother Nature—from both inner and outer nature. The story of the mind exiled from Nature is the story of Western Man. It is the story of his progressively more desperate search for mechanical and rational and symbolical securities, which will substitute for the spirit—confidence of the Nature he has lost. The basic myth for the id al Westerner's life is the Quest. The Quest for a marriage in the soul or physical reconquest. The lost life must be captured somehow. It is the story of spiritual romanticism and heroic technological progress. It is a story of decline. When something abandons Nature, or is abandoned by Nature, it has lost touch with its creator, and is called an evolutionary dead-end. According to this, our Civilization is an evolutionary error."[112] In the same year, in the *London Magazine* interview, Hughes again said: "When Christianity kicked the devil out of Job what they actually kicked out was Nature . . . and Nature became the devil."[113]

The Book of Job portrays man's existential dilemma in terms of his relationship with God and Satan two extreme poles of existence, with man himself in between at the mercy of both. We know from *The Book of Job* that Job was a good, honest, pious, moral, virtuous person within the context of a theocratic state. But Satan, because he is jealous of Job's happiness, instigates God to test Job's loyalty to Him. God gives Satan full freedom and Job undergoes one torture after another. Job remains loyal throughout though his typically Western man's habit of intellectually asking for an explanation of God's benevolence, and his sense of self-pride, are much too evident. Job thinks that this God is a weak God who has allowed Satan to inflict pain and misery upon him. He demands death from God but that is not granted. Satan inflicts Job from head to foot, and when Job's wife advises Job to reject both God and Satan, and die, Job dismisses her saying that a God who gives good will also give evil, and we have to accept both. Job's wife, who, by Western theologians has often been described as a second Eve,[114] disappears from the scene, castigated and rejected by her husband. Job is restored in the end by God, and lives for another hundred years or so. Job's story tells us about the triumph of a person who already suffers from a sense of personal loss. His triumph is, therefore, not his triumph but the triumph of orthodoxy[115] and a certain patriarchic, theocratic polity.[116] Such sacrifices of individual identity for the seeming cause of the State are found elsewhere too.[117] When the individual loses his freedom of meeting God naked and alone, and is caught by the inescapable knot of Mosaic legalism,[118] theocracy murders the sensitive human vitals, and man, before he is able to bloom like a flower in spring, hangs crucified in the empty portals of his own lost identity.

Perhaps the East and the West would not have differed so much in their approaches had Christianity not mocked at the Pagan and Greek Nature-deities, and imbibed the worth imbibing influences it was open to in its formative stages. Plato developed his own ideal *Republic* where emphasis fell upon rationality and submission (loss) of personal identity to the State. The poor poet was thought to be no more than a liar by wise Plato, who spoke out of his senses because inspiration was a horrible religious error. When religion becomes Establishment, God is confined within the priestly legalism and, instead of talking to the man straight, He talks to him through His guardians and protectors. What Hughes is attacking in *Crow* is this separation of Western man from Nature. In *Gaudete* also, Mr. Lumb fails to make Nature his wife and when the poem ends he is seen singing hymns for the female deity. An examination of Hughes's poems on nature[119] in *Crow* has already shown how man has insulted, humiliated, exploited, and subjected nature for his selfish ends, and then deserted her like Job deserting his wife: "Christianity deposes Mother Nature, . . ."[120] On the other hand, man's attempt to understand nature and explain her in rational terms (like St. George) by creating numbers, theorems, and calling them truth ("Revenge Fable") are blatant lies, and an insult to man's naked dignity.

The problem of evil that we encounter in *Crow* arises from the same basic Christian dilemma of a good God having created an evil world whose origin is Satanic. After Job's wife is gone from the scene, Job explains to his three friends the omnipotence of God; Job attributes the dichotomous existence of good and evil to a God who is beyond human comprehension. When good and evil become two fixed moral absolutes in a world where everything is relative and changing, God remains not a God; He becomes a trickster.[121] That the serpent is more powerful than God is encountered in poems like "A Horrible Religious Error" and "Apple Tragedy" where Genesis story is put upside down. The problem of calling a good God impotent is rooted in man's separation from nature; when this nature becomes objective, independent, it appears to man in the form of a serpent and evil, and an entity, which should have been made part and parcel of human experience, remains isolated and becomes a battleground not for its understanding by man, but for man's "supremacy" over it. This unfortunate and debilitating pseudo rationalism of the Western man has dehydrated the tenderness of the vitals of his mind. Modern physicists' "'rationality' has evaporated in an astonished watchfulness and the struggle to keep a grasp on the human dimension of things . . . They've landed themselves, and us, in a delicately balanced, purely electrical Creation . . . For a purely electrical Creation is one without walls, where everything, being an electrical power, can have an electrical effect on every other thing, and where electrical effects are vital effects."[122]

The attempt to supplement and improve upon (like Crow) God's universe is the biggest instance of Satanic holiness. Man has to learn qualities of submission, humility, love (which Crow fails to learn) which gave Job victory over Satan. The simple doctrine that humility is more powerful than ego should not be forgotten. Jesus loved even his murderers, because love is more powerful than ideas of murder. What we get if we go prior to the Genesis story in the Bible, as Hughes does, is a complex of cultures flourishing upon one common idea of a vegetation god who is born, grows, becomes old, and, dies. What else is Christian idea of the birth of Jesus, his death, and consequent resurrection, based upon?" . . . the Angel of Life is also, in spite of itself, to its own horror, the Angel of Death . . . 'The Hanged Man' is not dead: it is the Angel, shattered by death, dispersed to the Universe, re-assembled by joy, that here takes up a position in which it is equal to the whole of its past and the whole of its future."[123]

When we supplement the concept of a static God sitting alert on His chair after having created the universe into good and evil elements, with the concept of a God who is cyclic in nature and who exists not apart from, or in spite of, nature, but because of His perfectly balanced relationship with her, we get good and evil transfigured as spectacles of encyclopaedic vision of history which is ever on the move. Genesis creation myth imposes a vertical, stagnant fixity of realities (God, Satan, Adam, Eve) upon the cyclic rhythm of nature, and thereby fails to clarify its position upon Nature.[124] Myths of vegetation gods, on the contrary, are clearly based upon a balanced relationship of the human with natural world, and include nature as part of its own (and God's own) dynamic process of birth, growth, decay, death, and renewal (redemption). The identity of god never dies; it renews itself and thereby sublimates. Hughes told Fass that his original idea was to make Hagen the hero of *Gaudete:* "So Hagen would discover everything through Garten, his little foxy character and general knockabout, who through his spying sets everyting going . . . So I was vaguely thinking of that kind of balance for a while. The balance also between German/Scandinavian, and ancient Britain/Celtic, between puritanical suppressive and Catholic woman worshipping."[125]

Hagen's task in *Gaudete,* then, would have been to strike a balance between male and female principles. When this balance is achieved, man shall understand the "need" for God; God will become, not the school-master of human souls, herding his children to attend the class, but an object of love and veneration. Crow is crooked we know, and in "Crow's Theology" even this anti-God, anti-love, creature confesses that ". . . God loved him/Otherwise, he would have dropped dead." Hughes is clearly for dropping the God of good and evil in favour of a God who absorbs these and transcends both:

> Crow realized there were two Gods—
> One of them much bigger than the other
> Loving his enemies

How else do we account for the victory of Job over Satan? Humility, love, loyalty, after all, are more powerful than any tricks of seduction Satan is capable of showing. God, Satan, Job's wife, therefore, are not residents of a geographical locality or hypothetical figures of a theorem; they are part of Job's own being. The drama of Job is not a detail of political or even religious warfare, but the fact of a reality that everyone of us experiences at some time or the other. Even in "A Battle of Osfrontalis," what is remarkable about Crow is his passivity, but his passivity, unlike Job's, is not self-surrender to a higher reality; it is his "trick" to escape the attack of words which would draw him in a network of relations with other objects and make him "equal" to them.

Hughes, therefore, very justly changes the concept of static God with a God who is immanent in every created object: "Not Godlessness, but the imminence of a God altogether different from what dogmatic Christianity has ever imagined. A God of absences and negative attributes, quite comfortless. A God is whose creation the camps and modern physics are equally at home. But this God has the one Almightiness that matters: He is the Truth."[126] As for the balance between the male and the female principles, "Love Song" is the best poem in *Crow.* The poem was presented by Hughes at Ilkley as Crow's answer to the question "who paid most, him or her?" and was followed by "Bride and Groom" which concluded:

She stitches his body here and there
with steely purple silk
He oils the delicate cogs of her mouth

She inlays with deep-cut scrolls the nape of his neck
He sinks into place the inside of her thighs

So, gasping with joy, with cries of wonderment
Like two gods of mud
Sprawling in the dirt, but within infinite care
They bring each other to perfection.[127]

Notes and References

1. The edition to be used here is Ted Hughes, *Crow: From the Life and Songs of the Crow* (London: Faber, 1970). For a picture of Crow, see Keith Sagar's book on Hughes. Hughes had also written an Introduction to *Loonard Baskin Catalogue* (1962).
2. Gifford and Roberts, after arguing that myth cannot be viewed apart from its social context, ask: "Is there, then, an impossible contradiction in calling Crow 'mythic'?" See their *Ted Hughes: A Critical Study,* p. 125.
3. E.O.G. Turville-Petre, *Myth and Religion of the North: The Religion of Ancient Scandinavia* (London: Weidenfeld and Nicolson, 1964); review by Hughes in *The Listener,* March 19, 1964.
4. M. Eliade, *Shamanism: Archaic Techniques of Ecstasy* (London:

Routledge and Kegan Paul, 1964); review by Hughes in *The Listener*, October 29, 1964.

5. By John Greenway; review by Hughes in *New York Review of Books*, December 9, 1965.
6. By Gavin Maxwell; review by Hughes in *New Statesman*, May 18, 1962.
7. Review by Hughes in *The Listener*, December 12, 1963.
8. Review by Hughes in *New Statesman*, May 24, 1968.
9. Paul Radin, *The Trickster: A Study in American Indian Mythology* (New York: Schocken Books, 1956).
10. See Ekbert Fass, *Ted Hughes: The Unaccommodated Universe* (Santa Barbara: Black Sparrow Press, 1980), pp. 176-77.
11. Ibid.
12. *The Art of Ted Hughes*, p. 107.
13. The dream setting of poems is found in Langland's *Piers the Ploughman*, Young's *Night Thoughts*, Blake's *The Four Zoas*, among others. In Indian tradition, God, having created the Vedas, fell asleep. The demons came and stole the Vedas. The Australian totemic myths "tell, how, in the 'Dream Time' (*alcheringa*)-*that* is, in mythical time -these Supernatural. Beings made their appearance on earth and set out on long journeys, stopping now and again to change the landscape or to produce certain animals and plants, and finally vanished underground". See Eliade, *Myth and Reality*, *op.* cit., p. 14.
14. Gifford and Roberts, *Ted Hughes: A Critical Study*, p. 116.
15. M. Eliade, *Myth and Reality*, p. 6.
16. "Ted Hughes and Crow," in E. Fass, *op. cit.*, p. 206.
17. Quoted in Gifford and Roberts, *Ted Hughes: A Critical Study*, p. 115.
18. Since Hughes has said that he will complete *Crow* story someday and publish it separately, our conclusions on formal structure are only tentative.
19. *Hero with a Thousand Faces*, pp. 25-26.
20. Vol. 10 (Jan. 1971), No. 10, p, 17. In "Logos" *(Wodwo)*, the nightmare description runs: 'Creation convulses in nightmare. And awaking/Suddenly tastes the nightmare moving/Still in its mouth/And spits it kicking out, with a swinish cry—/

Which is God's first cry.' In the Indian tradition, one of the ten incarnations of God is swine. The context in which it is used in Hughes, however, is entirely different. In Indian tradition swine is a hero figure.

21. Quoted in Keith Sagar, *The Art of Ted Hughes,* pp. 101-02.
22. *Ibid.,* p. 105.
23. *Ibid.,* p. 106.
24. S. Hirschberg, *Myth in the Poetry of Ted Hughes* (Dublin: Wolfhound Press, 1981), p. 69.
25. See pp. 89, 106, 232, 389, in Eliade, *Shamanism.*
26. *Ibid.,* pp. 184-85.
27. Sec Paul Radin, *The Trickster,* p. 160. The tradition of Clown in drama is part of Trickster myth.
28. Paul Radin, *The Trickster,* pp. 160-61. Crow is also an American Indian tribe. For the creation myth of Crow of Montana tribe, for example, see R.H. Lowie, "Myths and Traditions of the Crow Indians," *Ibid.,* p. 162n. See also Eliade, *Shamanism,* pp. 102n, 335n. Crow is also a Siouan tribe. See Radin, *Ibid.,* p. 121.
29. See quotation no. 70. For the idea of trickster's constant flying from one place to another, see Winnebago trickster cycle in Paul Radin, *The Trickster,* pp. 4-53.
30. *Ibid.*
31. The problem which Hughes raises in *Gaudete.* The archetype for bride symbolism can be traced to the Song of Songs in the Bible, which symbolises a marriage between the king, a symbol of nation, and the land, which is nation's bride. Blake exploited this symbolism in *Jerusalem,* where Jerusalem, a city and a bride, is in possession of Babylon the Whore and tribes like Amalkites and Cannanites. Jesus is the groom who is to secure this bride by releasing her from captivity into the religion of imaginative ideal union. In *Gaudete,* Mr. Lumb fails to understand even the task he has to carry; he becomes impatient, and longs for ordinary life. The bride (female nature) remains without a groom. The poem ends with Mr. Lumb singing hymns in praise of female divinity.
32. J. Campbell, *Hero with a Thousand Faces,* p. 345.
33. Radin, *The Trickster,* p. 158.

34. Cf. "The Green Wolf" where the "old brains, old bowels, old bodies" wait to be recreated. Ted Hughes, *Wodwo,* p. 40.
35. J. Campbell, *Hero with a Thousand Faces,* p. 259.
36. *The Trickster,* p. 201.
37. *Myth in the Poetry of Ted Hughes,* p. 128.
38. Campbell, *Hero with a Thousand Faces,* p. 273.
39. *The Trickster,* p. 165.
40. *Ibid.,* p. 185.
41. See Charles Eliot, *Hinduism and Buddhism* (London: Routledge, 1954), Vol I, p. 444.
42. Northrop Frye, *Anatomy of Criticism* (New Jersey: Princeton University Press, 1973), p. 186.
43. Paul Radin, *The Trickster,* p. 130. The mother of Buddha, another hero-figure, Maya, also dies at the time of the birth of Buddha. When Krishna was born he was also separated from his real mother and taken to his step-mother.
44. *Myth in the Poetry of Ted Hughes,* p. 74.
45. The metaphysical implication of this concept can be found in the *Gita* where nature as Mother loves her son (man), while the son, in spite of this love, feels enchained, and tries to break the bond of motherly relationship.
46. *Myth in the Poetry of Ted Hughes.* p. 75.
47. Crow's laughter is a parody of God's laughing. In the *Mahabharata,* when Krishna has killed either Kansa, the demon, or Kalia, the thousand-headed monster (snake), He emerges from the waters in a laughing posture. Laughing is a condition of soul and is born out of man's divine innocence.
48. One of the qualities of a trickster is his buffoonery. See Radin, *The Trickster,* p. 184.
49. *Anatomy of Criticism,* p. 188.
50. *Ibid.,* p. 187.
51. ". . . in 'A Childish Prank,' Hughes inverts the Garden of Eden myth by presenting human sexuality bequeathed to Adam and Eve by a Satanic Crow for his own amusement while God lethargically dozes." Hirschberg, *Myth in the Poetry of Ted Hughes,* p. 127.

52. See P. Radin, *The Trickster,* p. 127.
53. *Ibid.,* p. 185.
54. Refer to quotation No. 82.
55. *The Trickster,* p. 203.
56. For Wakdjunkaga cycle as satire see P. Radin, *The Trickster,* pp. 151-154.
57. *Ibid.,* p. 184.
58. *Myth in the Poetry of Ted Hughes,* p. 85.
59. *The Art of Ted Hughes,* p. 122.
60. See, for example, Gifford and Roberts, *Ted Hughes: A Critical Study,* p. 120.
61. *The Trickster,* p. 168.
62. Refer to quotation no. 82.
63. Radin, *The Trickster,* p. 19.
64. *Ibid.,* p. 20.
65. "Sexuality" is one of the basic attributes of the character of the trickster. See Radin, *The Trickster,* p. 165. Hughes's Crow completely bypasses this aspect of trickster's character.
66. *Myth in the Poetry of Ted Hughes,* p. 95.
67. *Ibid.,* p. 97.
68. Pūrna midah pūrna midam purnāt pūrna mudachyate. Purnasya pūrnamādāya pūrna mewavasisyte.

    This saying occurs in *Isavasyopanishad* as it does before most of the Upanishads which begin with this invocation. It means: "That is perfect. This is perfect. From perfect is produced perfect. When perfect is added to perfect, what comes is perfect. When perfect is deduced from perfect, what remains is perfect."
69. Radin, *The Trickster,* p. 166.
70. *Ibid.,* p. 91.
71. *Ibid.,* Radin says: "There is something of the trickster in the character of the shaman...". This statement could be true in its reverse: too. See p. 196.
72. *Ibid.,* p. 203.
73. *Myth in the Poetry of Ted Hughes,* p. 104.
74. *Ibid.,* p. 108.

75. Radin, *The Trickster,* p. 168.

76. Keith Sagar, *The Art of Ted Hughes,* p. 134.

77. S. Hirschberg, *Myth in the Poetry of Ted Hughes,* p. 109.

78. Blake had developed this idea in terms of Imagination and Memory.

79. Refer to quotation No. 82.

80. *Ibid.*

81. Cf. Blake's "The Everlasting Gospel" where he calls Jewish religion 'The Pharisaic Worldly Ball.' Cf. also the metaphor with vegetable world appearing like a sandal on Milton's left foot in William Blake's *Milton,* I.21, 12-14. In Hughes, the 'ball of Wool' reverses back upon the creator in ironic reversal; in Blake the sandal is a metaphor of purification.

82. J. Campbdl, *Hero with a Thousand Faces,* pp. 346-47.

83. In religious history we find Mohammad as the figure of the hero as tyrant, but this tyrannical nature is part of his larger design—to teach people that there is but one God, one Father and not many. Crow as hero is a wholesale mockery of such figures.

84. Hirschberg draws our attention to a Jegend where Oedipus survives. *Myth in the Poetry of Ted Hughes,* p. 114.

85. Radin, *The Trickster,* p. 164.

86. *Ibid.,* p. 201.

87. *Ibid.,* p. 204.

88. *Ibid.,* p. 205

89. "Ted Hughes and Crow," *London Magazine, op. cit.,* p. 9.

90. Radin, *The Trickster,* pp. 158-59.

91. *Ibid.,* p. 159.

92. *Myth in the Poetry of Ted Hughes,* p. 121.

93. Radin, *The Trickster,* p. 159.

94. Cf. Tharmas in Blake's *The Four Zoas,* where, after having-destroyed everything by his control over the waters, he asks himself: 'Is this to be a god? I would rather be a man.'

95. Radin, *The Trickster,* p. 160.

96. For the source of Eskimo legend, Hirschberg refers to E.M. Weyer, *The Eskimos* (Harnden, Conn: Archon Books, 1969), pp. 446-47, 226-27. See his *Myth in the Poetry of Ted Hughes*, p. 124.

97. E. Fass, *T. Hughes: The Unaccommodated Universe*, p. 167.

98. Ibid.

99. N. Frye, *Anatomy of Criticism*, p. 195.

100. Radin, *The Trickster*, p. 53.

101. *Ibid.*, p. 158.

102. *Ibid.*, p. 159.

103. For a detailed consideration of the egg myth, with reference to Blake, see my *The Chariot of Fire*, pp. 109-13.

104. See M. Eliade, *Shamanism*, pp. 78, 118.

105. Radin, *The Trickster*, p. 165.

106. "Oglala Sun Dance," *Anthropological Papers* of the American Museum of Natural History, Vol. XVI, Part II (New York, 1917), pp. 166-67.

107. Radin, *The Trickster*, p. 165.

108. Hughes says that "the special weirdness and power of all things Tibetan in occult and magical circles springs direct from *shamanism*, not the Buddhism." *London Magazine interview, op. cit.*, p. 17. Shamanism, in fact, is a form of tantra, concerning flight and return, and its practice among the Tibetan lamas, Buddhist tantrics, and Indian Yogis is contemporaneous. It is difficult to locate its date of origin. Buddhism as an organised religion begins with Buddha not the tantric practices associated with Buddhism; they antidate Buddha's birth who himself was preceded by twenty-five Buddhas, he being the twenty-sixth. There is a broad agreement among scholars that shamanism etymologically comes from Sanskrit and Pali words 'Sramana-Shaman.' See M. Eliade, *Shamanism*, p. 495 if. 'Sramana' (n) comes from the verb 'Srama' in Sanskrit, which means to practise austerities; 'Sramana' means one who mortifies his flesh, especially the Buddhist and Jain mendicants. The term is applied to Buddha himself. See A.A. Macdonell, *A Practical Sanskrit Dictionary* (London: OUP, 1924), p. 320.

109. Charles Wilkins, *The Bhagvat-Geeta or Dialogues of Kreeshna and Arjoon* (London, 1785), p. 107. The writing of the *Gita* and

the birth of Buddhism as an organised religion are more or less contemporaneous. The tantric practices predate both. In the history of Hinduism, Buddhism is not considered a separate religion but part of it. The occurrence of the womb image, therefore, is common not to Buddhism or Shamanism but to certain tantric practices and sects, *e.g., Malinivijaya Svacchanda,* and *Kularnava,* etc., whose period is roughly 1000 B.C. to 500 A.D. The theory goes that Aryans, who came from the Middle East, composed the Vedas, while Dravidians, the original inhabitants of India, composed the tantra. Tantra, however, was continued in an oral and practical form, and written down only after the Vedas. Unlike the *Yoga-Sutras* of Patanjali, tantra texts are scattered and no formal codification exists.

110. In one of the Indian accounts of creation, earth is shown resting upon the muzzle of the snake. In *Mahabharata,* Krishna, the child-god and hero-figure, kills Kalia, the thousand-headed serpent, and restores confidence among people. Here, too, Krishna fights with the serpent under the sea, and after subjugating the serpent and the waters, emerges upon the sea's surface sounding his flute.

111. In *Your Environment,* 1 (Summer 1970), 3, pp. 81-83.

112. E. Fass, *Ted Hughes: The Unaccommodated Universe,* p. 186.

113. "Ted Hughes and Crow," *London Magazine, op. cit.,* p. 8.

114. See "Introductory Essay: Joband Trickster," by Stanley Diamond in P. Radin, *The Trickster,* p. xvi.

115. *Ibid.,* p. xx.

116. *Ibid.*

117. In the Indian tradition a similar situation occurs. Rama, the eldest son of King Dasaratha, rules over his kingdom, Ayodhya, after the completion of his fourteen years in exile. He is the king of the most ideal republic upon the earth imaginable. But one day a washerman informs Rama that Ravana, the demon and king of Lanka, has violated Sita, Rama's wife, while Rama was away hunting in the forest. Rama, believing the responsible citizen of the state, castigates Sita from the kingly palace into the forest. Sita, who was the daughter of earth, disappears in the earth. When Rama realizes his mistake it is too late for him.

118. "When the modern mediumistic artist looks into his crystal,

he sees always the same thing. He sees the last nightmare of mental disintegration and spiritual emptiness under the super-ego of Moses, in its original or in some Totalitarian form. . ." Ted Hughes in his review of *The Environmental Revolution,* Fass, *op. cit.,* p. 186.

119. "Crow and Mama," "The Door," "Criminal Ballad," "Crow's Undersong," "The Smile," "Revenge Fable," etc.

120. Hughes's review of *The Environmental Revolution* in Fass, *Ted Hughes: The Unaccommodated Universe,* p. 187.

121. P. Radin, *The Trickster,* p. xvii.

122. "Superstitions (1964)" in Fass, *op. cit.,* p. 172.

123. "Leonard Baskin (1962)," *Ibid.,* p. 166.

124. In the *Gita,* for example, Krishna declares that creation does not take place on *Prakriti's* own accord; it is not fortuitous but willed by God. God is the male while *Prakriti* is the female principle. Their union produces the world. The balance between God and Nature extends to the balance between man and nature.

125. E. Fass, *Ted Hughes: The Unaccommodated Universe,* p. 215.

126. "Janos Pilinszky (1976)," *Ibid.* p. 193.

127. Quoted in Gifford and Roberts, *Ted Hughes: A Critical Study,* p. 117.

4

Self's Cryptic Metaphors

The first section of the chapter will introduce Thom Gunn's *Moly* (1971) and comment upon aspects necessary for an understanding of the poem. The second section will discuss *Moly* poems.

I

In *Moly* (1971) the human self, which is a complex combination of man-woman, reason-passion, etc., is viewed in its relation to Nature and its forces, which imprison as well as liberate. There are two kinds of transformations taking place in the poem: one is the transformation brought about by Circe who turns sailors into pigs; with this assumption the poem begins. The other transformation is based upon the myth of Hermes who gave Odysseus the Moly herb by eating which Odysseus became a proof against Circe's powers and also saved his sailors. The mythical framework of the poem Gunn makes clear by prefacing *Moly* with the following quotation: "When I (Odysseus) was near the house of Circe, met Hermes in the likeness of a young man, the down just showing on his face. He came up to me and took my hand, saying: 'where are you going, alone, and ignorant of the way? Your men are shut up in Circe's sites, like wild boars in their lairs. But take heart, I will protect you and help you. Here is a herb, one of great virtue: keep it about you when you go to Circe's house.' As he spoke he pulled the herb out of the ground and showed it to me. The root was black, the flower was as white as milk; the gods call it Moly."[1]

Gunn's preoccupation with man as adventurer and archetype of the hero-figure is as old as motor-cyclists in "On the Move" (*The Sense of Movement*). Gunn has said that "Many a poet since Pound has liked to see himself as Odysseus, an explorer and adventurer who lives experience through, in detail, and yet can always extract himself from it."[2] *Moly*, however, comees very close to another of Gunn's narrative poem, "Misan-thropos" (*Touch*), which also deals with the basic human problem of the bifurcation of the self. The tradition of poems dealing with man's divided self especially got emphasis after the two world wars. The division in the mind of man results because of man's misunderstanding, either of environment or of himself; the problem of re-adjustment complicates the existence of the protagonist. Man is "aware of blood-powers and earth-powers that he does not fully understand, but they are sometimes very kind to him, because he has recognised them and respected them. Their kindness most often takes the form of showing him' the full range of possibilities when in a time of danger or despair there has seemed only one, and that a destructive one, availabie."[3]

Thomas R. Whitaker, in his "Foreword" to Merle E. Brown's *Double Lyric,* says that "shaping the work of Geoffrey Hill, and to some extent that of Thom Gunn, John Silkin, and Charles Tomlinson, is a tensely judgmental inner dialogue that often seems to have generated two opposed but mutually inclusive centres of speaking and listening in the same poem."[4] Merle Brown's study of modern English poetry in this light is laudable. It is, however, clear that divisiveness has been an inescapable quality of the personality of man in crises, whether in life or in art. Shakespeare's heroes, when speaking their soliloquies, Browning's dramatic monologues, and, of course, T.S. Eliot's "The Love Song of J. Alfred Prufrock" will illustrate the point. A perceptive reading of the poem will make the structure of "Misanthropos" clear. The first poem, "The Last Man" will show where do we stand: history has played its game; civilization stands ruined, and therefore, the last man has become self-contained like birds waiting is to go upon the final hill—the reduction of man to a stage out of which he raised monuments of civilization. The cycle of history is based upon the cycle of nature, and winds that bury seeds underneath the ground also bring them back to life. "Misanthropos" ends with an awareness of a larger community within the protagonist's self who is called upon to discover the immeasurable and make it a sharable part of human experience. Merle Brown remarks: "Now Gunn, in 'Misanthropos,' is working with just this moment of transition in the external course and recourse of nations, the moment of decadence as it turns into the moment of innocence."[5]

Moly also begins with everything in the grip of Circe, the witch, and the theme of division in the soul of the protagonist is consistently elaborated upon. Then the hero encounters Hermes and the process of transformation towards innocence begins. Nature becomes not an objective counterpart to human will; it becomes its subject, while the protagonist becomes its master. It can be argued that the structure of most works of literature, or that of human thinking, depends upon a threefold combination of the principles of original disharmony (or harmony), climax of crises (or climax of harmony), and the resultant harmony (or disharmony), which later develops into the genre concepts of tragedy, comedy, etc. This idea could even be elaborated upon in terms of rhythms of nature (Vegetation myth) or the rhythms of history (cyclic theory) It would not be far-fetched to suggest that the protagonist of *Moly* is a hero-figure, and that the vocabulary, images and rhythms, through which his figure is materialised, and gets meaning in the poem, are internal referents to his psychological states; they do not very much relate to the traditional hero's journey outward, and his consequent fight and victory over the demons. Gunn recalls that "Proust and Stendhal as well as Shakespeare and Donne had taught me to watch for the inconsistencies of the psyche."[6]

Moly was written after the poet had taken the drug LSD. Thus, on the personal level, Odysseus's eating of the Moly herb parallels with poet's taking of LSD. This has a bearing upon the concept of persona in the poem who is ever shifting his multiple selves within the larger concept of his total personality. In 1965, Gunn was in San Francisco and he found that it was the time of Beatles and of LSD: "These were the fullest years of my life, crowded with discovery both inner and outer, as we moved between ecstasy and understanding. It is no longer fashionable to praise LSD, but I have no doubt at all that it has been of the utmost importance to me, both as a man and as a poet. I learned from it, for example, a lot of information about myself that I had somehow blocked from my own view. And almost all of the poems that were to be in my next book, *Moly,* written between 1965 and 1970, have in some way however indirect to do with it."[7]

In the second chapter, while discussing Gunn's, Hughes's and Tomlinson's poetics, I focussed on their common concern for the "other" in poetry and a desire to transcend ego-boundaries. I have related this to the meditational activity of the poet as yogi or seer, who can concentrate his energy on vital points of consciousness, and imagine himself as a composite of different selves, one after or over the other, or all at once. Hughes's interest in Shamanism is part of the same argument. Just as a shaman impersonates himself in a boar, bear, etc, so does the poet change himself into something small or something bigger than himself. Shamans and many other practitioners of the occult art take drugs to induce states of hypothetical ecstasy.[8] Gunn also says: "The acid trip is unstructured, it opens you up to countless possibilities, you hanker after the infinite."[9]

To this is also related Eliot's argument of impersonality in poetry which Gunn very much liked: ". . . I have found usable modes in the work of other poets, and I have tried to invent some myself. Moreover, it has not been of primary interest to develop a unique poetic personality, and I rejoice in Eliot's. lovely remark that art is the escape from personality."[10] Gunn has also praised American poet Robert Duncan, for adventuring into the unknown in his poetry, "where you may find yourself using limbs and organs you didn't know you possessed."[11] Gunn owed Robert Duncan, to some extent, his concept of poetic persona. In his essay "Homosexuality in Robert Duncan's Poetry," Gunn remarks: "Most homosexual writers until at least the 1960s dealt with autobiographical and personal material only indirectly. One method was for a poet to address his work to an unspecified 'you,' giving an occasional ambiguous hint about what was really going on to those in the know only. (This is what Auden did, and what I was to do later.) Another method was to 'translate' either to change the gender of a character into its opposite, in a play or novel, or by a less conscious procedure to do what Duncan admitted doing in earlier poems: in the past, he said in *Politics,* he had 'tried to sell (homosexual feelings) disguised, for instance, as conflicts rising from mystical sources."[12]

In *Moly,* the protagonist's Upper portion is that of a human being, and the lower that of an animal. But he is constantly changing the complexes of his identity, in the poem, with characters like Justin, Phaedra, the Sand Man, and Tom-Dobbin. Homosexuality, as referred to above, makes an artist conscious of his other self, and the method of indirect narration culminates in the creation of a fictitious persona. In *Moly,* Gunn has also changed the gender of his protagonist by making him both male and female, man and animal—a being who is on a quest for self-completion. Referring to one of his earlier poems, "Carnal Knowledge," Gunn said: "Now anyone aware that I am homosexual is likely to misread the whole poem, inferring that the thing 'known' is that the speaker would prefer to be in bed with a man. But that would be a serious misreading, or at least a serious misplacement of emphasis. The poem, actually addressed to a fusion of two completely different girls, is not saying anything as clear-cut as that."[13] The quotation is given to emphasize that the poet or the events of his life are not to be read in the poetic persona, however deeply involved the poet might be in the artifice of his creation.

Because of the dominating presence and figure of Circe in *Moly,* the atmosphere of the poem is grounded in a certain dreaminess, supernatural witchery, of which magic is an essential part; in a certain environment of illusion, and the poem might well be taken as a movement from illusion to reality. Gunn wrote: "Magic is not completely separate from ordinary processes; it works by strengthening or inhibiting an impulse in us, even if that impulse is something we didn't recognise as being there."[14] About the merger of different selves in the protagonist of *Moly,* we refer to the following statement by Gunn: "The prototype of the experience of shifting identities is to be found in the dream, in which a friend may merge into one's cousin, who may in turn merge into some well-known political figure. Much of Duncan's poetry, particularly what he published from 1960 onward, has been based on dream work. And by acknowledging the dream-basis to so much of his writing, he gives a peculiar rightness and strength to the associationistic procedure. One person melts into another in the poem as he did in the dream, but never arbitrarily, because there is a rationale to the order of the most random seeming dream, even though it may elude the dreamer."[15]

The associationistic procedure in itself is more coherent than any conscious design, and Gunn has exploited in *Moly* with a remarkable success, by taking the drug himself and going into the unconscious. The "I" in *Moly,* therefore, refers to the protagonist and not to the poet. In the fifties, Gunn was also developing his theory of "pose," derived from various sources—Donne, Shakespeare, Yeats, and Sartre. Gunn explained his theory thus: ". . .everyone plays a part, whether he knows it or not, so he might as well deliberately design a part, or a series of parts, for himself. Only a psychopath or a very good actor is in danger of *becoming* his part, however, so one who is neither is left in an interesting place somewhere in between the starting point—the bare undefined and undirected self, if he ever existed—and the chosen part. This is a place rich in tensions between the achieved and the unachieved."[16]

At Cambridge, Gunn also came in contact with Tony White, a student and an actor, and the romantic-existentialist character of *Moly* and its protagonist, may owe something to Tony White's influence.[17] I have remarked that there are two kinds of transformations taking place in *Moly,* and therefore, the "I" as imprisoned and ignorant, is to be distinguished from the "I" as liberated and moving towards liberation (knowledge). The "I" is a participator in events—physical, mental, spiritual, and this participation makes events part of "I's" being. This is not true of the narrator in the poems of James Merrill who "was most comfortable as an almost anonymous observer. . .,"[18] or Conrad's Marlowe in *Lord Jim,* and Tiresias in Eliot's *The Waste Land,* who are detached observers or reporters of the scene around them.

II

"Rites of Passage," with which *Moly* begins, is a poem of four stanzas of six lines each; each line has a four-stress pattern and the rhyme scheme of each stanza is abcabc. The protagonist is a satyr as the bright horns in his hair indicate. The first line of the poem tells that 'something is taking place;" the ignorance of what is taking place makes the speaker somewhat helpless. Circe has already turned the speaker into a satyr and satyr's invocation of Father to see the transformation of his being—

—Skin that was damp and fair

Is barklike and, feel, rough is an indication of change from a state of composedness and design to a state of featurelessness. The speaker has already become a paradox and a dilemma in the second stanza. Although he has acquired freedom to rear, break loose, and neigh, the sense of incompletion underscores the validity of freedom, for it imprisons instead of liberating. There is a certain hymn-like quality in the implorations of the speaker to the Father though Gunn has not used hymn meter to make his poem hymn.[19] The last two lines of the second stanza "And next I make my way/Adventuring through your garden" make the garden a playground for the witchery of Circe where the identities of sailors are lost; the garden image also reminds .of the garden of Eden, and the fall of Adam (and Eve) is by no means ambiguous in the image of satyr, for he is both male and female. The garden is also the place where the Father lives; the speaker, therefore, adventures through the garden to attain self-completion. Recalling his life in 1965, and his experiences with LSD, Gunn gave San Francisco's Golden Gate Park a poetic colouring:

> The first field of a glistening continent
> Each found by trusting Eden in the human.[20]

The Father figure in the poem is not a symbol of tyranny as Alan Bold thinks.[21]

Each of the first three lines of the third stanza ends with a period and extends speaker's implorations to the Father. The verse movement well mimes the wandering in the garden with emphasis on vividness and clarity of detail. The final stanza introduces two new figures, the Old Man and the speaker's mother. The note or pre-determination is struck by lines—

> All planned before my birth
> For you, Old Man, no other,

The Old Man and mother figures may refer to the primal male and female That the birth of the speaker took place because of the Old Man, enforces the idea of the continuity of life where the son becomes the medium for the realization of his father's dreams and completes father's and his own incomplete personality. In his article on Gary Snyder, Gunn referred to the fertility magic: ". . . Often in Snyder, as in the. Pound of Canto 47, we find the rituals of the life-cycle presented without pedantry or patronage.. ."[22] The mother may also refer to Circe, and the speaker has two-fold tasks before him. One, to absorb the father-figure into his own being; the other, to make Circe, now in her role of mother as demonic nature, his wife. The title of the poem reminds of rituals that were generally performed when heroes went on their journey; it gives a magical character to the poem.

The second poem describes the "Nightmare of Beasthood" into which Circe has turned all sailors. The dream motif of the poem, referred to earlier, helps various identities merge into each other, and shift within the total framework of the identity of the protagonist. Moly is the name of the herb and the hero in the poem searches it. The poem is remarkable for juxtaposition of the images of the underworld or of unconscious, and tight and clear rhythmic units. The poem is written in couplets. The first line, generally, can easily be divided into two parts of two stress each. While the poem's first part summarises the entire environment, the second part localises the activity and focusses attention on the particular—the speaker —who snorts and struggles to wake, only to see and wonder at the beasthood skin Circe has made him to cover himself in.

The next three couplets are to be taken as a sequence one after the other. The speaker is no ordinary beast; he is. many beasts in one:

> Leathery toad that ruts for days on end,
> On cringing dribbling dog, man's servile friend.
>
> Or Cat that prettily pounces on its meat,
> Tortures it hours, then does not care to eat:
>
> Parrot, moth, shark, wolf, crocodile, ass, flea.
> What germs, what jostling mobs there were in me.

Gunn has learnt to approach his subject directly, and the language he moulds his experience in, does not subscribe to any abstract ideological label; it approaches the facts of experience, things to be said. The respect for particulars, the given reality, localised in time and place, Gunn learnt from Williams: "He (Williams) was in love with the bare fact of the external world, its thinginess; and the love mastered him for a life time."[23]

The use of rhyme, accompanied by repeated reading, gives a certain incantatory character to the line which is not very true in case of blank verse or unrhymed lines. The images of leathery toad, dog cringing and dribbling, and not caring to eat, and cat torturing its meat for hours, very well portray the degenerating transformation that has taken place. Moreover, they succeed in evoking mental states of disfigured lineaments—things losing their shapes, colours, textures, in an encompassing world of engrossing beastliness. Circe has wrought havoc by reducing civilization to the stage of dinosaurs and other creatures of the underworld. The first line of the third couplet, above, uses as many as seven nouns, and the extension of stress pattern from four to seven, emphatically delineates the widening isolation of the protagonist from the real identity, ". . . I am gross-grey, gross, flap-eared." The only human feature left in the speaker is the "pale-lashed eyes." The rhyming words "feature," "creature," side well with the verb "tear" used twice, in creating identical sound effect. The horribleness of the hero by this time is appalling for he can even eat a man which in reality he himself is. But then comes a sudden flash of memory:

> Oh a man's flesh already is in mine.
> Hand and foot poised for risk. Buried in swine.

The remembrance of his former self drives the protagonist to search for Moly the herb, and he invokes the powers like the traditional hero, before the search begins:

> Direct me gods, whose changes are all holy,
> To where it flickers deep in grass, the moly:

Hughes had remarked in *London Magazine* intervie v (1971)

that Eliot and Yeats dealt with the last phase of Christian civilization. The same remark may apply on Hughes and Gunn as well. The protagonist in *Moly* very well resembles Yeats's beast in "The Second Coming" who "slouches towards Bethlehem." The idea of the last phase is clearly born out of the sense of disgust with the present. While it presents the original archetype of the second coming of Christ, poets have also found their personal solutions. Thus' Gunn often echoes a dialogue between the last man left in the world, probably upon the hill, and the new man taking his place to start the cycle afresh. Merle Brown even says that "Gunn's shifting from poem to poem between the last man as objectively third person and as subjectively first person can be explained in no other way."[24] The Old Man of the "Rites of Passage" and the speaker in the poem under consideration are arguments in the same dialectical process.

"For Signs" relates the experiences of the half-man half-animal creature. Michael Schmidt says that " 'For Signs' is an obscurely powerful poem in which metamorphoses are experienced but no specific meaning limits them. They are not arbitrary—apparently-but the poem exists unparaphrasably in them."[25] The poem is divided into three sections. The first section which consists of one stanza of six lines, with each line having four stress, might be taken an epigraph to the rest of the poem. The metaphor implicit in the stanza, and in the poem, is that of death and rebirth as cyclic rhythm.

Gunn had obviously learnt the principles of imagist poetry from Yvor Winters and Williams. The stanza introduces a number of supple and incisive images in each line while the final line strikes the key to the meaning:

In front of me, the palings of a fence
Throw shadows hard as board across the weeds;
The cracked enamel of a chicken bowl
Gleams like another moon; each clump of reeds
Is split with darkness and yet bristles whole.
The field survives, but with a difference.

Obviously, this kind of poetry is in direct antithesis to the poetry of direct statement where the poet *tells* of his intentions. The images are suggestive, yet they do not develop into symbols. How then do we discover the meaning? Gunn has said that in imagism "meaning is to be found in the words themselves. . ."[26] There are two sets of images in the stanza, intertwined and inseparable: one having association with the metaphor of death, the other suggesting the metaphor of life.

The image of the shadows of the palings of a fence suggests a certain break in the continuity of life (metaphor of death), while the comparison of this image with board across the weeds, resuscitates the dying rhythm of life for weeds have the potential of sprouting again. This process of death and rebirth is carried on to the next set of images. On the one hand, the enamel of a chicken-bowl is cracked (metaphor of death); on the other, it gleams like another moon (metaphor of life). The third image of the stanza exploits the death and life metaphor in terms of the darkness of the reeds and their bristling. The earth is a silent witness to the changing death and life rhythms. The four-stress beat of the lines captures well this cyclic movement of nature. History does not stand as a proof for man's sanity. Man has violated all the sacred sanctuaries of his mind, and his attempt at recreating the field and its observer, draw the protagonist in the poem into emptiness. The acts of desire for shapliness and yearning for freedom, are balanced by an outcome of impotency, where the mind and energies of the protagonist retreat and run away from the slum of history. The incapacity to master and recreate the past in terms of an acceptable present compel the speaker to dream. By this time the moon has already completed a cycle, passing through all the twelve signs of the zodiac. In a flashback, the protagonist recapitulates his own life in terms of a cycle:

> . . . the real is shattered and combined,
> Until the moon comes back into that sign
> It stood in at my birth-hour;. . .

As the poem develops into narrative, the images become less concentrated and more mobile, capturing the ebb and flow of the cosmic movement. After a jolting dose of emptiness the observer returns to the field[27] and encounters someone who is gazing upward from the grass. He is the dream mentor, one who gives meaning to the void and emptiness of dream. His staring makes the protagonist look inward into himself, and the; reply comes from within that he (the speaker) too has passed through the cindered passages of the decaying rhythm of nature. The last section of the poem views the moon's journey in terms of a cycle. Sometimes the moon is reduced into the small dimensions of a seed, and sometimes, it is swollen "again" above the air. There is no punctuation mark in between the lines of the last two stanzas, except in the final line of the last stanza. This facilitates the portrayal of moon's journey without any obtrusion. The metaphor of sun and light is implicit throughout *Moly,* as noticed by Alan Bold too,[28] and even the coldness of the moon burns because it keeps the rhythms of life alive.

"Justin" is a poem of two stanzas of eight lines each with first line rhyming with the third and the second with the fourth. The stress pattern of lines is the usual four beat which is reduced to three in the second stanza. The first person narrator is missing; the protagonist narrates objectively what he sees. The poem dramatises nature cycle in terms of two human figures, Justin and the lady he is waiting for. Justin is an autumn figure who is waiting for the lady (spring) in a small park. The lamp-light's little world parallels with Justin's own which is clasped round by the sweet rot and dark of autumn. This dark is further elaborated in the poem in terms of decay of Justin's personality to the elemental level:

His live flesh like onion-skin
From finger-bones where it had held,
And saw the muscle fray within,
Peeling from joints that bunched and swelled.

The argument of the poem advances by analogy, and the fraying of Justin's muscles, and the peeling of his joints of the body, catches vital changes and convulsions in nature towards the end of one cycle. The tragic phase in the protagonist's life is emphasized by focussing on the contrast between the changes in nature and the changelessness in Justin's own life. Autumn season is not only a symbol of death; it is also a symbol of the renewal of life, something which does not take place in the life of Justin. His waitings for the lady develop into a heavy load of debt, and the abstract concept of the lady which never changes into living bones and flesh of reality, dwindles Justin's pain, longing and debt of waitings, into self-torturing morbidity and negativism. Justin, and the lady he is waiting for, are part of the protagonist of the poem who is waiting for self-completion. But the lady who does not come and frustrates waiting, is an image of Circe by analogy, and unless the protagonist masters Circe's powers of witchery, the possibility of his making Circe part of his own being is remote. This explains lady's absence and frustration she is causing to Justin.

The overall sense of dryness, death, and dissatisfaction, is carried over in "Phaedra in the Farm House", a poem of six "Stanzas of six lines each. The line has three stress pattern and the punctuation varies according to the thought movement of the poem. The protagonist returns to the first person narration. About William Carlos Williams, Gunn said that "In 'Dog Injured in the Street' and 'The Drunk and the Sailor'. . . poems 'which twenty years before would merely have implied Williams as onlooker, the subject is Williams himself so much involved in what he witnesses that he as good as participates in it."[29] This is true of Gunn as well, and through the medium he is exploring his own self for he regards art as self-expression and exploration. The protagonist hears the clanking of the slow-rolling churns over the flags which wakes him from his sleep. The negative tone of the poem is set by a heaviness in the atmosphere which chokes. The speaker says, "Aches me," and then as if to dwindle speaker's sense of nostalgia, the next sentence in the same line follows: "The room returns". The fourth line of the first stanza has two short sentences which are the direct expression of frustration, pain, gloom, and inertia, that the speaker feels, induced by the dull environment of his locale. The next two lines are a detail of exposition, and the two commas that come one after the other, "I hurt, I wake, . . ." give us a sense of heavy, restless sense of breathing of the protagonist, so reduced by a particular moment. "The cold dead end of night."

The first line of the second stanza, which introduces a father and his son, has two sentences with no verb or connective in between, which enforces upon us that the father and the son are two separate individuals in spite of their kinship. The relationship of the speaker to the father and the son is not clearly known, though the protagonist cooks food for the two and sleeps with one. The sense of ritual for preparation of disintegration is implicit from the third stanza. The activity of "rabbitting" by a certain "you" just come from the stable, strengthens the belief that it is the end of a cycle, which is what spelling the news means. In the fourth stanza the cycle of the day has returned back, the same dull round as Blake called it, from the morning (first stanza) to the night (second stanza); and again, from evening (third stanza) to the night (fourth stanza). The personality of "you" is the focal point for changes that are taking place in nature and in the mind of man. Playing of cards, and later, the protagonist's dealing in a grown man's fate, immediately remind us of clairvoyant lady in Eliot's *The Waste Land*. The "you" is not playing well and the dismemberment of his body can clearly be seen:

I smell the oil-lamp's jet,
The parlour's polished smell,
Then you—soap, ghost of sweat,
Tractor oil, and the yeards.

The dismemberment is from the reality of an identifiable structure (you's personality) to its dissolution in flowing, featureless, "ghost of sweat" and "tractor oil".

The fifth stanza makes "you" almost a mysterious figure:

Your quick grin never speaks:
I study you for hints
—Hints from those scrubbed boy-cheeks?
I deal a grown man's fate.

The loss of speech is a sign of felessness, and hints for which the protagonist studies "you" are the hints which foretell that

The chimney will be split,
And that waistcoat be blood.

The image of churning used in the first stanza returns in the last stanza too. Churning implies not only the churning of the mill; it also implies the churning of the world by nature for world's continual renewal. The milk not only refers to the blood which flows through all life; Gunn has also described the flower of the Moly herb "as white as Milk." The milk going sour and the churns waiting in the mud, are, therefore, images of degeneration which have disappeared in the mud they rose from.

The protagonist's reduction to "The Sand Man" from "Churns wait on in mud" is logical enough. The poem is in the third person, with the usual "I" absent. It has six stanzas of four lines each, with first line rhyming with the third, second with the fourth. The poem may also be taken as a description of San Francisco. Gunn tells us about *Moly* that "it could be as a history of San Francisco from 1965-9, or as a personal memoir of myself during those years."[30] This suggestion is strengthened by the images of the first stanza:

Tourists in summer, looking at the view,
The Bay, the Gate, the Bridge,
From sands that, yearly, city trucks renew,
Descry him at the postcard's edge.

Recalling his experiences in San Francisco, Gunn has written: "Golden Gate Park, the scene of so many mass trips and rock concerts, seemed like 'The first field of a glistening continent/Each found by trusting Eden in the human.' We tripped also at home, on rooftops, at beaches and ranches, some went to the opera loaded on acid, others tried it as passengers on gliders,. . ."[31] Gunn has also told us that ". . . if you write consistently about what is most important to you, you do end up with an organic consistency to a collection of poetry written within a certain span of time."[32] The images in the stanza quoted, of tourists, the bay and the accompanying sand, clearly parallel the images in Gunn's own account of the scene at San Francisco.

However, the focal point of this geographical detail is the sand man who is seen at the edge of the postcard. The gathering of the crowds (tourists in Gunn's poem) by the bay or sea-shore, is part of vegetation myth, when people immerse the image of the corn god, signifying the end of a cycle. The suggestion of the sand man as a protean god (Isis or Osiris), is, by no means, ambiguous in the poem. The ripening of corn is well paralleled by the white hairs of the old man, and the ripeness of his years in terms of the maturity of the cycle, is. depicted in terms of old man's personal character traits:

> . . . who hauls up lengths of wood
> And lies beside his fire
> Motionless on his side, or gumming food,
> Without a thought, or much desire.

While the lines remind us of Pope's lines "Happy the man whose wish and care/A few paternal acres bound," the ease of the movement, generated out of the rhythmic arrangement of verbal units, slackens the tension mostly seen in the early stages of the life or nature cycle. Usually, the first two lines of every stanza form a single sentence with the second line being a subordinate clause which generally provides additional information. The desireless, motionless sand man has scored victory over many a disgruntling moment of his life. Though the outer environment damaged his consciousness, yet he managed to recover the basic human innocence. But as the cycle comes to an end, the sand man must identify himself with the real texture of his being:

Bare to the trunks, the body on the ground
Is sun-stained, ribbed, and lean:
And slowly in the sand rolls round and round
In patient reperformed routine.

The absorption of the sand man in the sand is effected through the reduction of his body's parts: "sun-stained, ribbed, and lean." The next stanza compares the sand man with the sandflies who are able to perfect themselves during the tide. The protean godfigure in the myth obviously does not die. His image, which is immersed in the river, or reduced to the ground, lives there at the elemental level, only to resuscitate itself next spring. The sand man

Dispersing with the sands
He feels a dry cool multiplicity
Gliding his body, feet and hands.

As the sand man disperses the fragments of his being, he develops into many selves and his motionless posture (second stanza) is re-enlivened by the joy of "cool multiplicity," which again glides his body, feet, and hands. The sand which in the first stanza was renewed by the city trucks is now renewed by reinvigorated sand man himself.

It is natural that in a renewed cycle the position of the female should be reassessed. "Apartment Cats" both elaborates and is a comment upon Circe's nature. The cat image for girls again takes us to Eliot's Prufrock poem. Gunn's poem is a poem of three stanzas of six lines each with varying rhyme scheme. At the beginning of the new cycle, the girls as female principle, wake in the first stanza, and in the second stanza, awakening borders on awareness. The metaphor which is dominantly explicit in the poem, is suggested through the girls. Although cats rub the leg of the speaker while one sniffs round his shoe, we are told that this activity is being carried on by girls. Gunn has remarked in his article on William Carlos Williams, that "Between image and statement there is, of course, metaphor. . ."[33] This applies to the poem under consideration very well. The other cat rolls on the floor in ease with her stomach exposed.

The ease of the first stanza slowly develops into tension in the remaining two stanzas while the first person narrator completely withdraws. Each line of the second stanza stands by itself in broken relationship with any other line. The corridor is the scene of activity, and as the cats re-enact their play known as *Ben Hur,* they slowly develop into tension. Their noses twitch, eyes get wild, bodies become tense, and the prudence seen in the first stanza disappears.

Now, more awake, they re-enact Ben Hur
Along the corridor,
Wheel, gallop; as they do,
Their noses twitching still,
Their eyes get wild, their bodies tense,
Their usual prudence seemingly withdraws.

The relationship among the cats develops from good to bad (second stanza) and from bad to worse (third stanza). Cats wrestle with each other, their minds have lost understanding (blind hug), though their sense of self-defence is very much alive:

If either, though, feel claws,
She abruptly rises, knowing well
How to stalk off in wise indifference.

The poem emphasizes the unpredictability, cleverness, and blindness of the female principle in nature, and these qualities apply on Circe as well, whose analogy the girls and cats are.

"Three" is a poem which deals with the theme of the repossession of innocence. In an article, "Writing a Poem,"[34] Gunn tells us: ". . . one day I was walking on a hill going down to the Pacific, which it met at a narrow, partly-sheltered beach. I came to the beach from some bushes and was confronted by a naked family—father, mother and small son. The son rushed up to me very excited, shouting 'hi there, hi there' in his shrill voice, . . . I mentioned it to some friends that evening and to others the next day, and the day after that I realized that I wanted to write a poem about the naked family. . . When I saw the naked family I didn't know why they satisfied me so much. . . Certainly their appearance was more than a pat embodiment of innocence and its repossession . . ."[35]

The poem's narrative is advanced through accurately observed images which form the descriptive detail of the poem:

> All three are bare,
> The father towels himself by two grey boulders
> Long body, then long hair,
> Matted like rainy bracken, to his shoulders.

This objective description of father's lineaments is juxtaposed with the image of the Pacific in the second stanza, whose cold live sinews tug at each limb of the father. There is an air of immeasurable contentment brought about in father by the confident and self-assuring touch of the sea-waves. The last two lines of the second stanza show how tiny a creature man is against the world of nature, though the latter works, not in opposition, but for the benefit of man, and is the medium for man's transformation. Gunn sounds almost Wordsworthian here. The mother, nearby, reclines Upon the stones as if they were the earth's bones. The closeness of body's limbs with the objects at the sea-beach borders on inter-penetration. The nakedness is not only physical, it is also metaphorical. The mother is

Stripped white where clothes have been,
To the heat that sponsors all heat, from the sky.

The human response to the call of nature is very vital throughout the poem. It gives transubstantiation to human beings as the Eucharistic bread and wine are supposed to change into Christ's body and blood.

The soothing and transforming effects of sea's environment upon the father and the mother are identical though there is no noticeable difference on their son who is brown all over, rapt in endless play. The son's age of three years is vitally related to the title of the poem as we shall presently see. There is a difference between the innocence of parents which is achieved in and through the experience of the world, and the innocence of the child, who is yet to enter the experimental realm of the world. This child has to learn the nakedness of the parents:

> He still leaves it
> And comes back to that pebble-warmed recess
> In which the parents sit,
> At watch, who had to learn their nakedness.

Gunn said of Williams's poem "Spring and All," though his remark is not meant for this poem only, that "A perfect accuracy of description, by means of which the world is both mastered and lived in, becomes thus a moral perception."[36] The last line of "Three" is an instance of the case in point. The number three may also be the symbol of the life-death-life cycle. While the father and the mother are advancing towards death after having lived life, it is their son who has to reflect their hard-won innocence in his life which is ahead of him. The son's age of three, therefore, not only means life and death; it also means renewal of death into life. Innocence is a victory over the fact of experience, and the child, who is to survive his parents, has to enlarge, widen, and deepen, his relationship with the environment he is in.

"Words" is a poem in which the "I" is both a spectator

and a participator in the phenomenal world of light, shadow and growth. The figure of the poet as artist is very much present in the poem, and the reality he is trying to sketch on the page through the medium of words, is fleeting and changing. Gunn believed that poetry should exist in the tension between the truth of experience and the artifice of art. The poet's faithfulness to the observed detail, without circumlocution and rhetoric, Gunn has learnt from Winters, Gary Snyder, and his praise of Fulk Grevile, Hardy and Duncan, is based upon the belief in the principle of direct, cool and exact description of things. Of Gary Snyder Gunn said that he does not aim "towards a grand style to intrude between him and his perceptions. He patiently records the world, as an act of love, with all his senses opened to it."[37] Mark the first stanza of Gunn's poem:

The shadow of a pine-branch quivered
On a sunlit bank of pale unflowering weed.
    I watched, more solid by the pine,
The dark exactitude that light delivered,
    And, from obsession, or from greed,
Laboured to make it mine.

The faithfulness to the detail visually perceived is remarkable. But Gunn, as Clive Wilmer has remarked, is "quite consciously a writer of contrasts."[38] The shadow of the first line is contrasted with the sun light of the second, and as the poet develops intensity of attentiveness, he perceives a mutually contrasting "dark exactitude" which the "light" delivered. At this stage, the perception becomes an act of love and the desire to participate in the observed (field) develops into an obsession.

In an interesting comment upon Yvor Winters's poem "Quod Tegit Omnia" which is as follows:

Adventurer in
living fact, the poet
mounts into the spring,

upon his tongue the taste of
air becoming body: is embedded in this crystalline
precipitate of time.

Gunn wrote: ". . . he (Winters) came to view the writing of poetry as 'a technique of comprehension,' involving full use of the rational powers and moral judgment that he had deliberately avoided in his earliest work. The poet may still be 'embedded' in his subject-matter, but he now tries to view it in a context which can enable him to understand it."[39] Poetry for Gunn is also an exercise in self-exploration with words as medium to make him understand the nature of his environment. In the stanza quoted from "Words," the "it" of the last line obviously refers to the dark exactitude in the fourth line. In a world of light and shadow, the perception of permanence, and the desire for its possession, acquires the momentum of a quest:

In looking for the words, I found
Bright tendrils, round which that sharp outline faltered:
Limber detail, no bloom disclosed.
I was still separate on the shadow's ground
But, charged with growth, was being altered,
Composing uncomposed.

The poet's own existence is included in the overall fact of change in nature. That sharp outline that flickers (change) above and against the dark exactitude (permanence), and the failure to possess, much less retain, the dark exactitude, is conveyed by the cool, dejecting, somnolent phrase, "no bloom disclosed." This blatant and clear-cut refusal negatives speaker's attempts to unify himself with his locale. The share of "understanding" is palpitatingly a freak one: "I was still separate on the shadow's ground." "Still" deepens the sense of inchoate and dislocated experience. Poet's failure to synthesize the world divided into categories of light and shadow, is rationalised in the next line by the use of "But." The next part of the sentence explains the reality of change within which the concepts of growth and decay exist, and the basic fact of alteration nullifies poet's attempts of composing the uncomposed which becomes uncomposable. Gunn explained that "composing uncomposed is in a sense not having your cake and not eating it," [40] which means artistic detachment as a necessary condition for the task of poetic composition. Merle Brown points out that in "Words" Gunn fails to evoke a sharp contrast "between poetic composure and experiential discomposure,"[41] something, which, according to Brown, Gunn succeeds in doing in "Thomas Bewick" (*Jack Straw's Castle*).

About "From the Wave", Gunn has said that "Poems like 'From the Wave' were in some way answering an earlier poem like 'On the Move. . ."[42] "From the Wave," in its formal com-position, goes back to "Three." It is a poem of eight stanzas of four lines each with the rhyme scheme abab. The line length varies as does the stress-pattern from four to three, and then to two beat. The first stanza established the reality of the sea-tide and captures its movement by the use of rising and falling, long and short rhythms:

It mounts at sea, a concave wall
Down-ribbed with shine,
And pushed forward, building tall
Its steep incline

The poem develops a narrative and the supple images flow and make real sense only when grasped not in isolation but in the light of nature's cyclic movement. The second stanza brings "black shapes on board" upon the vacuous and turbulent sea-surface. These shapes, which are obviously human beings, do not try to impose their own mental frameworks upon the waves. Instead, they take a lot of pain, poise their weight, intimate, imitate, and re-enact the movement of the wave upon themselves. This is what sustains them and is the clue to their survival.

Clive Wilmer has argued, and rightly, that in "On the Move" "a gang of motorcyclists submerge their individuality in the uniformed group to assert their power of human will over nature. Man creates his own identity through choice (the philosophy is plainly existentialist) and here the symbol for that process is a manufactured object, the motorcycle. . . . the main impression is of man at war with nature. In 'From the Wave,' however, the protagonists are surfers who establish their identity by choosing the 'right waves' to ride. They too become what they are through 'movement,' but a movement now at one with nature."[43] The metamorphosis it furthers has completely attuned them to the shape, texture, and movement of the waves, so much that the protagonists seem grafted by the fact of foam "Half wave, half men." This is the best expression of the interpenetration of environment and human beings, in which each takes something of the other, in a harmonious and indivisible whole. Moreover, Gunn has been consistently thinking in terms of a world in which the balance is a formal triumph, the balance of reason and passion, instinct and intellect, soul and body, observer and the observed. When the surfers know that the waves are turbulent "they paddle in the shallows still" and wait for the right time and right waves to appear again so that they can maintain their balance.

In "Tom-Dobbin" sequence of poems, Gunn examines the nature of relationship between instinct and intellect. Tom-Dobbin is half-man, half-animal creature, and is another name for the protagonist whose multiple selves are present in every poem in some form or the other. "Tom-Dobbin" sequence is written in the third person. In the first of these poems are described the features of the protagonist. This is one poem in which Gunn has broken down the stanza pattern and rhyme. There is no punctuation from beginning to end, and each line is separated and distanced from the other in order to picture the man-beast creature clearly. This probably Gunn learnt from Gary Snyder on whose poem "The Spring," he remarked: "The lines of the first section are far more abruptly separated than the lines of the other poem. They do something Snyder is fond of—a naming of the tools and processes of a job, dryly, factually, using the terms of the workmen."[44] Describing Tom-Dobbin, Gunn's poem begins:

Light is in the pupil
    luminous seed
and light is in the mind
    crossing
in an instant
    passage between the two
seamless

From the minuteness of the physical detail of categories, there is a transition towards their dissolution as we proceed from the mind to the waist of the centaur. Centaur is the half-man, half-horse creature in Greek mythology. This dual aspect is described by the lines "there is the one/and at once it is also the other;" but this other in the poem is a blond whose name is Dobbin. The poem ends with a beginning of the sexual intercourse, while the second poem begins with the continuation of the same sequence of argument:

Hot in his mind, Tom watches Dobbin fuck,
Watches, and smiles with pleasure, oh what luck.

This poem is again organised in two stanzas of six and four lines each. The intensity of passion makes Tom's mind hot and he tries to maintain his composure by detaching himself from the intense sexual activity that is being carried on by Dobbin upon Tom's body. The interpenetration of the selves of Tom and Dobbin can only be enjoyed when the protagonist knows that he is not the doer but the medium of doing, and that the act of sexual intercourse is not a physical activity but the door-way towards the union of Tom and Dobbin. This can of course be done when Tom (mind) responds to Dobbin (the seeking self).

Tom withdraws his attention from the immediate act:

He sees beyond, and knows he sees, red cows.
Harsh green of grass, and pink-fired chestnut boughs.
The great brown body rears above the mare
Plunging beneath Tom's interested stare.

The next stanza comes as a climax and the reduction of union between Tom and Dobbin, for "only a moment," spreads the unified colours of spectrum into the variable fragments of time. The mind fails to strike a balance with instinct.

The third poem is a prose-poem dealing with the moment of ecstasy in the life of the protagonist. The desire to understand the instinct and the environment plunges Tom-Dobbin into sexual orgy. The exhilaration ensuing out of the orgy moves tbe protagonist in delightful eddies; then comes in the inter-penetration of the protagonist with the waves in the environment, nay, he becomes one with them:

> . . . It moves about
> him in easy eddies, and he enters their mingling
> and branching. He spreads with them, he is vined
> with sunshine.

The image of the sun dominates throughout *Moly,* either as light, or as fire or star. This fact has been noticed by Alan Bold.[45] In the second stanza, the protagonist, who has already identified himself with the minute particulars of his surrounding locale, continues the process of self-expansion. The place of eddies is taken by the cobalt gleam while the image of the sun lingers back. The minute accuracy of detail of the observed universe is remarkable. From the image, Gunn comes to direct statement: "The cobalt gleam of a peacock's neck, the course of a wind through grasses, distant smoke frozen in the sky, are extensions of self." Tom-Dobbin is undergoing a mystical experience made possible by the ritual of his plunging into the sexual orgy uninhibitedly. The expansion of the self is directly related to the expansion of energy in the human body, and its intercourse or interaction with the energy outside. This is what Hughes calls the elemental power-circuit of the universe. When a man experiences this level of consciousness, as certain mystics do, differentiation is lost in the unity of the self, which in turn, identifies itself with the essence behind every created object.

Fixed categories become fluid and dissolve themselves in the universal momentum: "And later something in him rises, neither sun nor moon, close and brilliant. It lights the debris, and brings it all together". The protagonist, as he experiences the change of expanded consciousness, feels the rise of another self in him, more wide, deep and unitive than the separate realities of Tom and Dobbin.

The fourth poem in "Tom-Dobbin" sequence might be taken as a celebration of the unity of Tom and Dobbin in terms of an old and a young mammal. The suggestion of the development of man from mammal is very much present in the poem. As earlier referred to, Hughes and Gunn are poets who write about the last phase of Christian civilization, a point noted by Merle Brown about Gunn.[46] The poem, therefore, might also be taken as celebrating the archetype of Christ's second coming.

The poem is in two stanzas of three and seven lines. In the first stanza, the first line tells that the old mammal is with her young and gives the statement, "She is unique". The second line goes millions of years back:

> Millions of years ago mixed habits gave
> That crisp perfected outline, webs, fur, beak.

The outlines of man's physical lineaments are the labour of millions of years, and the first line of the second stanza recapitulates the process of formation: "Risen from her close tunnel to her cave". The next two lines continue the theme of the birth of the mammal who lies ripe in her mother's stomach till one day the line of the old mother's belly breaks and brings the young mammal into the moisture of day. The next two lines describe the young mammal being hatched up by being given milk. The visual imagery is noteworthy. In the last two lines the poet comes forward and gives the statement:

> If you could see through darkness you could see
> One breaking outline that includes the two.

The outline in the stomach of the old mammal, although, has given birth to the young one, is still a symbol of the origin of the latter. The young mammal is not separate but part of the body of her mother. By analogy, Dobbin's existence as pure instinct or the female principle, has got no meaning in isolation; Tom as mind and male principle, helps its counterpart to realize herself with his association, as he realizes himself in the process too, and both become one. The last of "Tom-Dobbin" poems celebrates this oneness. The earlier "he" and "she" are dissolved into "we". The entire poem is:

> Ruthlessly gentle, gently ruthless we move
> As if through water with delaying limb.
> We circle clasping round an unmarked centre
> Gradually closing in, until we enter
> The haze together—which is me, which him?
> Selves Hoating in the one flesh we are of.

The first line exploits the inversion of word-order, like Shakespeare's line in *Macbeth,* scene I: "Fair is foul, foul is fair." Gunn's line pictures well the vigorous yet gentle, movement of the co-existence of two personalities, Tom and Dobbin, into "we," Their supposed movement through water, an image we met in "From the Wave," and which is a symbol of the ocean of life to be crossed, and which we also meet in Yeat's Byzentium poems, is natural enough. Water is also circumference and the need for centre is understood by those who seek for unitive vision. As Tom-Dobbin advance together, closing in with each other, toward the centre, the ego-distinction of "you" and "I" becomes indistinguishable, and the Tom-Dobbin selves float, in perfect harmony and balance with the world of nature, in one flesh. The unity is achieved at personal and environmental levels.

In his essay on Ben Jonson, Gunn remarks: ". . . all poetry is occasional: whether the occasion is an external event like a birthday or a declaration of war, whether it is an occasion of the imagination or whether it is in some sort of combination of the two. . . but it should be a starting point to which the poet must in some sense stay true. The truer he is to it, the closer he sticks to what for him is its authenticity, the more he will be able to draw from it in the adventures that it produces. . . ."[47]

"The Rooftop" starts as a response to an occasion:

White houses bank the hill,
Facing me where I sit.
It should be adequate
To watch the gardens fill

The poem deals with an experience that is aroused by Gunn's response to the landscape. Gunn is not a passive observer of objects, and the attentiveness of the "English detachment"[48] which he attempts to maintain, and the desire to plunge and participate in the experience provided by things, often leads him to a dilemma. Merle Brown holds that Gunn often fails to maintain his composure as a spectator and the "I," instead of being in the position of detached attentiveness, participates in the experience, thus blurring the distinction between attentiveness and poetic shaping of experience.[49]

The place where the poet sits has white houses and gardens surrounding it. The perception leads to joy as the poet gives details about the sunlight, washing tree, bush, and the year's last flowers. The third stanza introduces the problems of composing the uncomposed:

Perception gave me this:
A whole world, bit by bit.
Yet I cannot grasp it—
Bits, not an edifice.

As Yvor Winters said Truth is not relative; our apprehension of it is, so the perception of the infinite and the unknown[50] cannot be grasped by finite and limited man whose perceptions can only give him the world or its experience in bits and not in wholes. Our perception of reality is in categories and all acts of apprehension imply induction.

The activity of light as the giver of life is apparent from the fifth stanza onward. After the "I" has already turned down the gift of nature in the fourth stanza, the objectivity and detachment is remarkably seen in the stanzas that follow. The poet develops the symbolism of birth, death, and renewal, in terms of the life of the seed in nature. The heat which has been nourishing each visible object of nature till now, frets the earth, and the furious root, which implies the idea of flower, consequently implies exuberance, both in nature and in the mind of the observer. In the heat of the sun, the petals turn brown and loose, while the dry and white seed again bursts (seventh stanza) from the ground, going upward like a bone. This activity of life is paralleled by an activity of death, which epitomizes, in the life of the seed, the course of nature-cycle.

> Bouncing from rot toward earth,
> Compound of rot, to wait,
> An armoured concentrate
> Containing its own birth.

The edifice image occurs again in the ninth stanza. Whereas formerly, the poet was lamenting for the perceptions coming to him in bits and not in the form of an edifice, the development in the poet's understanding of his experience is marked by his conscious assertion that reality is "An unseen edifice." Gunn has said that "Writing poetry has in fact become a certain stage in my coping with the world, or in the way I try to understand what happens to me and inside me. Perhaps I could say that my poetry is an attempt to *grasp*, with grasp meaning both to *take hold of in* a first bid at possession, and also to *understand*."[31] The nature cycle in terms of seed is thus described:

> The seen, the tangles, lead
> From seed to death to seed
> Through green closed passages.

The poem also ends in the manner of cyclic movement: it ends with darkness into which gardens coldly rustle while it began with gardens filled with sunlight. "The Colour Machine" is another poem in which the nature of reality and the means to perceive it minutely are examined. It is a prose-poem written in three stanzas of varying length. The first stanza is in the third person, and the objectivity of description and faithfulness to perceived detail are remarkable. The colour machine is a symbol for the world-the world visualized in terms of variegated colours instead of as solid mass.

Visual details follow one after the other and make for the poem's narrative. During the night the people are sitting in the basement in front of the Colour Machine. As someone from among the people switches on the green and the red colours on the machine, a shape comes out riding through a dark-green sea, which is

> . . . like matter
> approaching and retreating from the brink of form.

The inability of the matter to malleate itself into form is the basic problem of existence. The poem depicts artist's attempts to articulate the unknowable, the mysterious. It also poses a metaphysical problem—whether we as formal imbroglios of matter, could apprehend the delicacies involved in the subtle fonn as seen on the Colour Machine—form, as distinct from the form or formal circumference of our own bodies. The inability to apprehend or understand this form results in a poetie play upon language:

> Where it has thickened it starts to turn transparent;
> Where it is almost transparent it starts to thicken.

and in a desperate bid to answer the vital question of the existence of this form, the poet ends miserably: "we cannot tell what it reminds us of," for it reminds of nothing worldly—something which is understood in terms of contraries as relations. Gunn has said that the idea precedes the act of its embodiment, and the truth or reality, which is what the "form" in the poem is, precedes even the idea, for we have or can have ideas only of things perceived, perceivable, or imaginable. Here poetry acquires magical overtones: "Looked at one way, idea preceded its embodiment; looked at another, particulars preceded induction. Neither process excludes the other here, because the process of writing a poem is something more comprehensive than either, and I think—in all seriousness and not as a mere playful metaphor—it is also connected with the processes of magic. It is a reaching out into the unexplained areas of the mind, in which the air is too thickly primitive or too fine for us to live continually."[52]

The logic of narration in the three stanzas shifts from "we" to "he" to "I." In the second stanza, the "he" who is one of the people encountered in the first stanza, gives himself completely to the Colour-Machine. This act of total self-surrender by "he," without caring for the inductive analysis for particulars about the machine, dissolves him into the textureless colours and rhythms of an altogether entirely different world. The limitation imposed upon the flowing and widening, terrific currents of the continuity of life, by the human mind and body, ends here. The "he" becomes invisible as the colours are; he becomes pure consciousness, beyond time-space limitations. Contraries are colours as each of the created object is, and our apprehension of them as relations, is based upon a perception of colours in contrast to, and distinct from, each other. Perception thus, becomes an act of categorisation of the reality principle into the particularised fragments of time. This precipitates the unity of things perceived and diversifies the synthesis of vision. In the third stanza the poet shifts on to himself, but the vices in him of being cowardly, selfish, and calculating, would not allow him to surrender to the Machine. The ego centres in the poet nullify his attempt to emulate his friend, and poet's hankering for courage and impulsiveness to achieve the state of his friend's mind, is no more than an impoverished, impotent attempt at self-mockery. The poet ends in sheer helplessness, for he is visible, has a body and analytical mind, and therefore, cannot understand things beyond mind.

"Street Song" might be taken as a companion piece to "The Colour Machine," as it also celebrates the effect of acid upon human personality. The poem has five stanzas of six lines each and the lines rhyme with each other. The poem is narrated in the first person. Only the last but second line of reach stanza has punctuation marks in between the lines. The first stanza gives us the picture of a habitual drug taker in dirty denim and dark glasses who asks everyone about *keys lids acid and speed.* The line is in italics and the loss of punctuation, as the use of words themselves, depicts magical madness and loss of conscious control. Commenting upon the acid trip and the use of metre, Gunn said: "The acid trip is instructured, it opens you up to countless possibilities, you hanker after the infinite. The only way I could give myself any control over the presentation of these experiences, and so could be true to them, was by trying to render the infinite through the finite, the unstructured through the structured."[53] In the second stanza the Speaker introduces himself in quite self-assertive lines: "My grass is not oregano./ Aomw of it grew in Mexico." And then his character as a typical salesman of drugs is revealed in supple rhythms:

> You cannot guess the weed I hold,
> Clara Green, Acapulco Gold,
> Panama Red, you name it man,
> Best on the street since I began.
> My methedrine, my double-sun,
> Will give you two lives in your one,

The speaker next asks us to taste the hash which burns sweet, smokes smooth, and makes one sharper. He is selling a world in the form of his drugs which open inexhaustible possibilities for man. The last stanza is an invitation for other men to join the druggist and enjoy a journey to whichever self one chooses. "Keys" stand for the opening of the gateway to the unknown regions of the unconscious; "lids" stand for eyelids which will see the world afresh; "acid" is of course the transforming drug and "speed" is the momentum of energy into which the taking of the drug will lead us.

"The Fair in the Woods" is another poem dealing directly with the transformation of man under the effect of drug. There are poems in which Gunn's treatment of man in the surroundings of nature seems like Wordsworth's treatment of the same subject. In the first stanza of the poem, for example, the, interpenetration of natural objects with woodsmen, sounds like the interpenetration of natural objects with the hermit in the first section of Wordsworth's *Tintern Abbey*. Here is the first stanza from Gunn's poem:

> The Woodmen blow their horns, and close the day,
> Grouped by some logs. The buckskins they are in
> Merge with ground's russet and with tree-trunk's grey,
> And through the colour of the body's skin
> Shift borrowings out of nearby birch and clay.

Gunn has entitled the first section of his essay on Gary Snyder as "Interpenetrating Things." In the concluding part of this section Gunn says: ". . . Snyder has worked to lay himself open to the feel, look, sound and smell of things. Attentiveness becomes in him as it does in Williams a form of moral discipline. The act of attentiveness is, too, one in which you can fully live, and its analogues are to found in the deer running, the mussels sucking, the man and woman making love, and the labourer at his job. These acts are a means of unifying categories and interpenetrating things".[54] That this applies to Gunn's own poems is indicated by the stanza from Gunn's poem above; it also brings Gunn closer to Wordsworth, particularly where Wordsworth's "I" is missing, and the description is visual and objective. The stanza quoted reminds us also of the clear, visual images engraved on the Grecian Urn as described by Keats.

Man in conjunction with nature is a "god's experiment," we are told in the second stanza, and the angel from God comes to supervise this experiment. The third stanza resumes the details of the first. The woodsmen are addressed as the "children of light," some of whom are clustered in the upper boughs of trees. From there they watch other people coming and going in the fair. The sun image comes to the fore in the fourth stanza, along with another archetypal image of nature who is addressed as a dancer:

Upon a platform dappled by the sun
The whole speed-family in a half round clapped
About the dancer where she arched and spun.
They raced toward stillness till they overlapped,
Ten energies working inward through the one.

The platform epitomizes the globe image where all life depends upon the energy of the sun. The woodsmen meet the dancer in the fair which is what our world is. The ten energies may refer to the nine channels of our own bodies[55] through which we receive sun's energy, the sun himself being the giver and the tenth. These ten energies are concentrated in the dancer "she", who is nature, through and in the background of whom, our life upon the "platform" depends.

The fifth stanza celebrates the unity after interpenetration of nature objects and men. All life is seen in terms of "lights fragmented" which join in one long dazzling burst of the unifying force of energy, just as horn closes over horn into one sound. The last stanza repeats the pattern of the fifth stanza.

The first half of this stanza deals with separated colours of bodily images:

Knuckle takes back hs colour, nail hs line.
Slowly the tawny jerkins separate
From bark and earth, but they will recombine
In the autumnal dusk, for it is late.
The horns call. There is little left to shine.

The second half tells us two things: first, that bodily images shall recombine with those of nature's at the return of the cycle, and second, that it is the night time, and before they again hine, it has to be the day. The poem begins with night, develops through the day, and ends in night again.

The next poem "Listening to Jefferson Airplane" is a two-line poem:

The music comes and goes on the wind,
Comes and goes on the brain.

The repetition of verbs, after the subject and before it, in the first and second lines, is done to mimic the sound movement of music. A reviewer quoted the entire poem and asked: "Is this the famous blowing of the mind?"[56] Gunn remarked to John Haffenden later: "What was reassuring to me was that of the reviewers I read on *Moly* most disliked it for different reasons."[57] "To Natty Bumppo" is a poem which combines the images of the familiar with the unknown, of abstract with the concrete, as it moves forward in time and enlarges in space, from a rude territory to a glistening continent. What Gunn said of Fulk Greville's sonnet "why how now Cupid, do you covet change?" (xx): ". . . ingenuity of thought combines with a conversational directness. . ."[58] can only be applied to his own poem under discussion. The first stanza is objective though the description of human lineaments presupposes a human being:

The grey eyes watchful and a lightened hand.
The ruder territory opening up
Fills with discovery: unoutlined land
With which familiar places overlap.

The grey eyes watchful and the lightened hand combine the serious with the comic. The next two lines contrast the rude and unoutlined with the "familiar places" of the fourth line. In the second stanza the speaker comes out and watches beyond the elm-topped rise a "there." This change in the speaker is obviously brought about by the drug, for this "there" is a new world opened within the brain of the speaker:

A plain, a forest, a field full of folk.
Footing the sun-shot turf beneath the trees,

They brandish their arms upward like the oak,
Their sky-blue banners rest along the breeze.
Open on all sides, it is held in common,
The first field of a glistening continent
Each found by trusting Eden in the human:
The guiding hand, the bright grey eyes intent.

Recalling his LSD trip later, Gunn said: "Raying out from the private there was a public excitement at the new territories that were being opened up in the mind. Golden Gate Park, the scene of so many mass trips and rock concerts, seemed like:

The first field of a glistening continent
Each found by trusting Eden in the human.[59]

"The Garden of the Gods," says P.R. King, "creates a mythic sense of divinity, a magical nature which is a rich profusion of delights and the source of fecundity in man. It is a beautiful description of an Eden-like garden in which 'It was sufficient, there, to be,' an existence in which meaning-as-expression was superseded by meaning-as-simply-experience. The conscious mind becomes perception within a fully living body."[60] Eden is the dominant image in the poem. The poem is written in seven stanzas of four lines each with lines rhyming abba. Eden is a perfect garden where even the minutest plant stays in its place in the total unity. But the reference is obviously to the tree of life because it also embodies the vision of human race. The tree's brightness is amazing and it transcends meaning by the sheer beauty of its intense dazzling light and white blossom.

The enamoured, enrapturing, or magical sense of self-contentment is so deep that the voice from within the speaker involuntarily forces the speaker to utter:

It was sufficient, there, to be,
And meaning, thus, was superseded.
—Night circles it, it has receded,
Distant and difficult to see.

Gunn has said, while reviewing Rod Taylor's book of poems, that a poet participates in the experience of the poem by the use of metaphor. The novelist participates in his characters by being unborn for a while.[61] The distinction between the thing and its meaning is an act of disintegrated perception. Perception implies a unity of the thing and its meaning; for the meaning does not exist apart from the thing. In the stanza quoted above, the perception of Eden has underscored the need for its explanation of its meaning; the experience as silence supersedes dividing categories of verbal detail. The garden is something like Yeats's Great Memory wherein lies the origin of created objects:

Where my foot rests, I hear the creak
From generations of my kin
Layer on layer, pressed leaf-thin.
They merely are. They cannot speak.

We are mere hypotheses of the reality principle which is Eden, not of the Bible,[62] but of the mind. The last stanza tells us that the garden is entwined in the breast and calf of the speaker and is rooted in the death-rich earth. This Edenic garden was discovered in the mind with the help of LSD.

About "Flooded Meadows" the following conversation took place between John Haffenden and Thom Gunn:

"Haffenden: Don't you have some sort of quarrel in the book *(Moly)* with too much cerebral life, the limitations of consciousness?

Gunn: Well, I don't think I explicitly come up against it. Haffenden: Perhaps in "Flooded Meadows"?

Gunn: No, I'd think the opposite. I think I'm being 'intellectual' there, as you'd say . . . The light is solipsistic in a sense, and conceals all the accretions of experience, simplifying it into maybe one marvellous LSD trance where the real world has been glamourised as pure abstract light. It's cancelled for a unity of ambiguous value, perhaps the unity of the moron—'the unity of unabsorbed excess' —and

I'm not using the word 'excess' in the sense Blake used it. So that's the intellect bringing back control at that point."[63]

The poem has fourteen lines rhyming abab with no octave or sestet. The water is not only a symbol of life; it is also a symbol of death. And just as death levels distinctions of name and form, so also "water has mapped irregular shapes that follow/Between no banks. . ." It is "water water everywhere" as the ancient mariner in Coleridge's poem says, but the drop of drinking water which he fails to get, is paralleled in Gunn's poem by the loss of all sense of value. Gunn's poem gives a vision of apocalypse though the poet is obviously on an LSD trip. The world of physical reality is changed into the abstraction of colour:

> . . . definition is superseded, for,
> In pools across the level listlessness,
> Light answers only light before the breeze,
> Cancelling the rutted, weedy, slow brown floor
> For the unity of unabsorbed excess.

The poet confronts nature's seeming listlessness by imposing upon it his mental framework of "unity" as he tells to John Haffenden.

"Grasses" is a response to an occasion in summer, and the participation in the experience of the poem by the speaker, results in his perception of the dualities that embody poet's vision of life. The visual details in nature and in man-created civilization mingle and coalesce:

> Laurel and eucalyptus, dry sharp smells,
> Pause in the dust of summer.
> But we sit High on a fort, above grey blocks and wells,
> And watch the restless grasses lapping it.

In poems specifically dealing with poet's response to a certain landscape, the poet sits in between the objects of nature and man-made things. Thus in "The Rooftop," "White houses bank the hill,/Facing me where I sit." This is one form of duality, contrast, intermingling, or reaction, of city and nature upon man. The second stanza continues visual details, and then the "we" in the poem separate from the poet's "I," in the third stanza, as happened in the Colour Machine. The sound of music in the fourth stanza gives added meaning and significance to the visual scenic beauty of the objects of nature. But the sound is like the one we hear in Keats's "Ode to a Nightingale," or in Arnold's "long withdrawing roar" in "Dover Beach." The clue to the meaning of the poem comes in the last stanza which emerges from the tune and is not imposed upon us:

A wail uneven all the afternoon,
Thin, slow, no noise of tramping nor of dance.
It is the sound, half tuneless and half tune,
With which the scattered details make advance.

Life is not only uneven; it is also monotonous. The sound which is half-tuneless, half-tune, captures the rhythmic ebb and flow of the contrasting colours of life. It is with the help of this sound, the universal motion, that the caravan of life advances from life to death back again to life.

"The Messenger" is a symbol of newly acquired powers of insight that one gets after taking the drug. The first stanza comprises one sentence and two subordinate clauses, and ends in a question mark for the identity of the messenger is not known. The rest of the stanzas elaborate messenger's nature who becomes an epitome of the dualities of life. The interpenetrating eye of the messenger is compared with a cat's, and the loss of speech in him implies sense of wonder at the newly opened channels of knowledge. And then we are told what the messenger stands for. The flower whose name the messenger does not know, embodies his and the universe's nature:

His body makes to imitate the flower,
Kneeling, with splayed toes pushing at the soil,
The source, crude, granular, and sour.

The secret of the beauty of the flower does not lie in the flower itself but in the crude, the granular, and the sour soil. In fact beauty will lose its very concept if it were not for the ugly soil to give it meaning. The simultaneously coalescent and co-existing opposed tendencies in the flower, are what the messenger is trying to imitate and see in his own body. The fourth stanza tries to see the flower's "unblown flame" in terms of messenger's stillness. The unblown flame is an abstract concept depicting the potentiality of flower in the flame, in a future yet to come and change itself into the present; this is how the beauty of the flower can be seen and enjoyed. But flower, in so far as it is all embodiment of the dualities of life, also transcends limits of human comprehension. Human beings can only bring ". . . their versions of the flower in small/Outward into intelligence." The last stanza shows the messenger gazing into the flower in order to become it. The flower is the ideal and the messenger is a symbol of humanity which is trying to attain to that ideal.

"Being Born" is written in eight stanzas of four lines each, in the rhyme scheme abba. The first two stanzas describe the pre-birth haze, mist and smoke; the speaker's search for self origin is negatived by the absence of embodied figures, the "unfleshed giant presences. . ." This pictures well the haze in the stomach. The child, from within the stomach, sees two shapes and takes momentary consolation in the hope that he will adventure in the new world soon. These are the shapes of the midwife and the doctor, who bring on to the land the new-born. But no sooner does the child come on to the land, he has already lost contact with the hazy world he was an inhabitant of, and which has now become an abstraction for him:

Must I rewrite my childhood? What jagg'd growth
What mergings of authority and pain,
Invading breath, must I live through again
Are they the past or yet to come or both?

To see the past and future of life embodied in an instant of the present has always been man's quest through history; the nature of reality, however, has won over man, and man's inability to answer the last question in the stanza quoted, is based upon man's habit of apprehending everything in terms of diversified categories and pair of opposites. Blake wrote in the opening song of his Songs of Experience: "Hear the voice of the Bard/ Who past, present and future sees." This perception integrates; the perception in Gunn's poem fails to unify categories of time. Catharine R. Stimpson says: "How can the flesh, of man, woman, or nature, become word? . . . Though language is inseparable from the physicalities of sight and sound, it is involved with the physical world rather as a ghost is. The poet who metamorphizes place into text must, as he writes, feel the solid melt away, and the reader, as he acts as a random perturbation of the system of the text, not material, but mental spaces."[64] "At the Centre," like "The Signs," is divided into three sections, and deals with the unity and expansion of consciousness of the protagonist of *Moly.* 'Richard Howard writes: 'The—effort, and in such poems as 'The Colour Machine,' 'The Pair in the Woods,' 'The Garden of the Gods,' 'The Messenger,' and chiefly, 'At the Center,' the effort *is* not only made but mastered—is to get beyond definition, questions like 'What place is this,' 'What am I', and into identification, into surrender of the separating will which may then merely—merely! acknowledge, acquiesce."[65]

The first stanza of the poem's first section states that the speaker is not bound by the "weathered boards" or the "barbed wire" at the stair. He has steered clear of the confines of the place ('what place is this'). In the second stanza, an attempt is made to grasp the "component lights" in terms of which we understand the sky. But the gulf between sensuous apprehension and the fact of abstraction ('lights') tells:

You cannot keep them. Blinking line by line
They brim beyond the scaffold they replace.

In the second section we come across "pouring" which is the reduction of the universe of categories into a fluid, of which every created thing is a part. While this gives unity, it destroys the individual character of events and objects in time and place. "Oh, wonder" sounds inappropriate and rhetorical. The gradual devebpment of images from widening and braiding to blending, unites them to their source, the "one all-river." This river is the river of life whose roar is" . . . unheard from being always heard." The speaker next discovers that the mind is also fluid and part of this ever-flowing river, ". . . open to the pull/And on the underside twined deep with it." The first line of the third section epitomizes the tension of the self-contrasting nature of existence, "Terror and beauty in an single board," while the next line rationalizes the loss of individuality in the life river, by giving the analogy of "—a tracery Pronded and ferned, of woods inside the wood." The self-surrender of will, which Gunn failed to achieve in "The Colour Machine," is finally achieved here. The knower and the known, the observer and the observed, are blended in a harmonious unity. This unification, from personal to impersonal level, is extended to the last section of the poem:

Later, downstairs and at the kitchen table,
I look round at my friends.
Through light we move Like foam.
We started choosing long ago
—Clearly and capably as we were able—
Hostages from the pouring we are of.
The faces are as bright now as fresh snow.

The last but second line reminds of Wordsworth's line "Trailing clouds of glory do we come" in the "Immortality Ode." But Wordsworth achieves unity of existence without distorting the physical lineaments of the universe; Gunn achieves it by reducing the world into the abstraction of light and colour; human beings arc etherealised as all other objects are—moving masses of foam upon the ever-flowing river of life.

"The Discovery of the Pacific" and "Sunlight" are considered by Alan Bold as "the two most lyrical and beautiful poems."[66] The title of the first poem recalls the title of Yvor Winters's last book *Forms of Discovery*. "The Discovery of the Pacific" is written in six stanzas of four lines each in the rhyme scheme abab. It deals with a couple, who, by analogy, are the male and the female portions of the personality of *Moly's* protagonist. The couple are on a journey and the direction of journey is determined by the course of the sun. The environmental emptiness of things soon becomes an existential emptiness, and then the lady wakes:

> . . . she had woken
> To resin-smell and to the first slight sound,
> And through their sleeping-bag had fiet the broken
> Tight-knotted surfaces of the naked ground.

The rifted and cracked lineaments of natural objects do not encounter any separate will of the couple. The intermingling of the couple with nature is gradual but sure. This resolves the dilemma of Gunn's earlier poems in which the poet would maintain his ego and remain separate.

> And now their skin is caked with road, the grime
> Merely reflecting sunlight as it fails.
> They leave their clothes among the rocks they climb,
> Blunt leaves of iceplant nuzzle at their soles.

In the final stanza the couple achieve perfect unity. The image O water as motion and source of life is again used; the intermingling of couple with natural objects now reduces itself to the intermingling of male and female parts of the body into an embrace.

In "Sunlight," the sun is shown as the source and lord of all life. The poem is written in seven stanzas of four lines each in the rhyme scheme abab. The first two stanzas elaborate water and metallic images in relation to the sunlight:

What captures light belongs to what it captures:
The whole side of a world facing the sun,
Re-turned itself to what created it,
And wearing green in sign of its subjection.
It is as if the sun were infinite.

The recurrence of the sun in its daily course makes it a symbol of human desire which is as persistent as the sun. Merle Brown says: "It is the pain of holding the known and the desired up against each other that gives 'Sunlight' its power."[67]

Desires and knowledge touch without relating.
The system of which sun and we are part
Is both imperfect and deteriorating.
And yet the sun outlasts us at the heart.

The sun is like the sunflower but different from it, for it is without any root or stem. It gives colour and shape of identity to objects, and, while defining them thus, recreates them too. Gunn has remarked in his essay on Gary Snyder that "Discovery of a meaning is always also the creation of it, and creation is an act of discovery."[68] The last stanza is in the form of an invocation to the sun. Completely in submission the speaker seeks to embody sun's qualities of passionless, impartial but intense love, and, in life's journey from circumference to centre, attain to an innocence which the petals of light have attained by completely submerging themselves in the innocence of sun itself.

Commenting upon Robert Duncan's *Moly* poems Gunn said that the protagonist, the boy, "lives in 'the incompletion of desires,' both longing for the fulfilment of simple lust and longing for that fulfilment to have meaning."[69] This is the basic problem of Gunn's own *Moly* poems, where the protagonist feels himself incomplete, changes himself or is changed by Circe, into half-animal, half-man, or half-man and half-woman. The transformation is taking place in every poem. In some poems the hero dissolves himself into the nothingness of colour and light, while in others, he returns to live the experience and make it his own. The problem of making the non-verbal, the inarticulate, and the disembodied, is the basic problem of *Moly,* the hovering between "being and non-being,"[70] as Gunn said of Duncan's *Moly* poems. The sun image, which is at the background of most of the poems, is itself a symbol of the unity of all life, and the protagonist's desire to absorb sun's qualities of pure and intense love and innocence, is an argument towards the unity of his own being.

Notes and References

1. Thom Gunn, *Moly* (London: Faber, 1971), p. 11.
2. *Poetry Book Society Bulletin,* No. 68 (Spring 1971), henceforth abbreviated *PBSB.*
3. Ibid.
4. 'Merle Brown, *Double Lyric: Divisiveness and Communal Creativily* in *Recent English Poetry* (London: Routledge & Kegan Paul, 1980), p vii.
5. *Ibid.,* p. 130.
6. Thom Gunn, *The Occasions of Poetry: Essays in Criticism and Autobiography,* ed., Clive Wilmer (London: Faber, 1982), p. 173.
7. *Ibid.,* p. 182.
8. For a detailed consideration of this problem see R.C. Zaehner, Mysticism: Sacred and Profane.
9. Thom Gunn, *The Occasions of Poetry,* p. 182.
10. *Ibid.,* p. 186.
11. *Ibid.,* p. 183.
12. *Ibid.,* p. 119. Neil Rennie titled his unfavourable review of Gunn's *Moly* as "Mystic Wisdom,' See *London Magazine,* Vol. 11 (June-July 1971), No. 2.
13. *Ibid.,* p. 188
14. *PBSB,* No. 68 (Spring 1971).
15. Thom Gunn, *The Occasions of Poetry,* pp. 130-31. Blake's *The Four Zoas* is also a dream of Val a (Nature) into nine nights, where Urizen, Los, Luvah, Tharmas, their spectres and emanations, rise from the being of Albion and merge into him as the poem moves from disintegration into integration.

16. *Ibid.*, p. 162.
17. Gunn says of Tony White: " . . . he was a model as well as a friend. He helped me to shape my thoughts. It was he who first got me to read Sartre's plays and Camus's novels," *The Occasions of Poetry*, p. 163. Tony White also played the role of romantic-existentialist characters like Mark Anthony *(Julius Ceaser)*, Petruchio, Romeo and Cyrano, etc. *Ibid.*, p. 162.
18. *Ibid.*, p. 143.
19. It also reminds of Ted Hughes's *Gaudete* where Mr. Lumb sings hymns in praise of a female goddess at the end of the poem. Alan Bold compares the poem with Ted Hughes's "View of a Pig" (Lupercal). See his *Thorn Gunn and Ted Hughes* (Edinburgh: Oliver and Boyd, 1976), p. 91.
20. Thom Gunn, *The Occasions of Poetry*, p. 181.
21. "The father-figure, the symbol of authority, is to be dispensed with so the poet can return to mother earth. . ." See his *Thom Gunn and Ted Hughes*, p. 91.
22. Thom Gunn, *The Occasions of Poety*, p. 38.
23. Thom Gunn, "William Carlos Williams," *Ibid.*, p. 22.
24. Merle E. Brown, *Double Lyric*, p. 141.
25. Michael Schmidt, *Fifty Modern British Poets* (London: Heinemann, 1979), pp. 381-82.
26. *The Occasions of Poetry*, P. 24.
27. In Yoga terminology too, the body is called the field *(Ksetra)*, while he who knows it is called the knower of the field *(Ksetrajna)*. See S. Radhakrishnan, *The Bhagavadgita* (London: George Allen & Unwin, 1970), p. 300.
28. *Thom Gunn and Ted Hughes*, p. 89.
29. Thom Gunn, *The Occasions of Poetry*, p. 33.
30. *PBSB*, No. 68 (Spring 1971).
31. *The Occasions of Poetry*, pp. 181-82.
32. *PBSB*, No. 90 (Autumn 1976).
33. *The Occasions of Poetry*, p. 25.
34. First published in 1973.
35. *The Occasions of Poetry*, pp. 151-52.
36. *Ibid.*, pp. 25-26.
37. *Ibid.*, p. 46.
38. *Ibid.*, p. 11.
39. *Ibid.*, p. 15.
40. "Thom Gunn" in *Viewpoints: Poets in Conversation with John Haffenden* (London: Faber, 1981), p. 48.
41. Merle Brown, *Double Lyric*, p. 189.

42. John Haffenden, *Viewpoints,* p. 47.
43. Clive Wilmer, "Definition and Flow: A Personal Reading of Thom Gunn," *Poetry Nation Review,* Vol 5 (1978), No. 3, PP. 54-55.
44. Thom Gunn, *The Occasions of Poetry,* p. 39.
45. See his *Thom Gunn and Hughes,* p. 89.
46. *Double Lyric,* p. 130.
47. *The Occasions of Poetry,* pp. 106-07.
48. William Carlos Williams considered Eliot as "The American poet who has acquired an 'English' detachment, turning to the dead ash of European subject-matter." Gunn's approval of Eliot's impersonality theory is already referred to in the first section.
49. *Double Lyric,* pp. 188-89.
50. Gunn had a lot of praise for Robert Duncan who emphasized poet's reach into the unknown through the act of writing. See his *The Occasions of Poetry,* p. 183. Gunn, for a while, also developed the theory of poetry as 'loot,' a word which occurs in the fifth stanza, which meant "a prize grabbed from the outside world and taken permanently into the poet's possession." *Ibid.,* p. 156.
51. *The Occasions of Poetry,* pp. 185-86.
52. *Ibid.,* p. 152.
53. *Ibid.* , p. 182.
54. *Ibid.,* p. 42.
55. A theme with which Gunn is concerned in his latest book *The Passages of Joy* (Faber, 1932).
56. Neil Rennie, "Mystic Wisdom," *op. cit.,* p. 130.
57. John Haffenden, *Viewpoints,* p. 49.
58. *The Occasions of Poetry,* p. 56.
59. *Ibid.,* p. 181.
60. P.R, King, *Nine Call temporary Poets: A Critical Introduction* (London: Methuen,]979), p. 101.
61. *The Occasiolls of Poetry,* p. 136.
62. Gunn said, "I am for ever grateful that my brother and I were brought up in no religion at all." *The Occasions of Poetry,* p. 170.
63. John Haffenden, *Viewpoints,* p. 48.
64. "Thom Gunn: The Redifinition of Place," *Contemporary Literature* (Summer 1977), p. 404. Quoted in Merle Brown, *Double Lyric,* p. 198.
65. "Ecstasies and Decorum (Gunn, Stafford)," *Parnassus* (Spring/

Summer 1974), p. 216. Quoted in Merle Brown, *Double Lyric,* p. 178.
66. *Thom Gunn and Ted Hughes,* p. 94.
67. *Double Lyric,* p. 77.
68. *The Occasions of Poetry,* P. 43.
69. *The Occasions of Poetry,* p. 129.
70. *Ibid.,* p. 134.

5

The Window and the Wheel

THE first section of the chapter will introduce Charles Tomlinson's volume of poems *Seeing is Believing,* focussing on aspects necessary for an understanding of the text; the second section will discuss *Seeing is Believing* poems. The third section will introduce *Renga* and will comment upon its structure; the fourth will discuss *Renga* poems. Parallels from mythology will be drawn, where demanded, by imagery or by thought, of a particular poem.

I

Seeing is Believing is Charles Tomlinson's third collection of poems[1] which is "both substantial and representative."[2] Donald Davie holds that Tomlinson had achieved his style in *The Necklace* which, in *Seeing is Believing,* he has ". . . adapted, refined and elaborated so as to serve a much wider range of experience. . ."[3] Tomlinson himself has remarked that the consideration of the role of syntax in arranging shapes of sentences according to the way we perceive things, helped him develop his style, and write his "first full-scale book, *Seeing is Believing* (1960)."[4] Tomlinson's poetry manifests an awareness to the type of visual image which extends in space, occupies it, until it develops into a design or a painting. The associative expansion of images seldom acquires symbolical or allegorical overtones; it extends its associative diameters into space, the given reality, there, on the empty page. Particularly Tomlinson's first three collections of poems should be studied alongside his experiments in painting. Tomlinson's visual images present something of the character of Chinese written language. Tomlinson, after coming down from Cambridge in 1948, wrote filmscripts which were rejected. But, as Octavio Paz thinks, this left him with two interests: "in the image in motion, and in the idea of a literary text as support for the image. Both elements reappear in the poems and the collages."[5] Tomlinson's association with American poets is well known: "Critics have sometimes related my own work to the American poets, and this is just."[6] Tomlinson might have drawn inspiration for his painting from FenolMlosa's essay on the Chinese written character, published by Ezra Pound and subtitled by him, "An Ars Poetica." As Davie thinks, "the uniquely poetical value of Chinese rests in its combining this temporal (sequacious) feature with the density and angularity of 'things,' the peculiar contribution of painting and sculpture."[7]

This is what precisely Tomlinson was trying to bring about in his poems. And his return to painting in *Written on Water* (1972) more than speaks for such an endeavours Writing on the Chinese sentence "Man Sees Horse," Fenollosa says: "Chinese notation is something much more than arbitrary symbols. It is based upon a vivid shorthand picture of the operations of nature. . . the Chinese method follows natural suggestion. First stands the man on his two legs. Second, his eye moves through space: a bold figure represented by running legs under an eye, a modified picture of an eye, a modified picture of running legs, but unforgettable once you have seen it. Third stands the horse on his four legs".[9] "Man sees Horse" presents a situation, a whole, a structure, and this structure has been broken down in Fenollosa's account into interrelated parts, the texture, as technically called in painting: "the texture of the visual design at any location within it consists of the relations among the small parts at that location."[10] Speaking about poems "Wakening with the Window over Fields" *(Relations and Contraries)* and "Fiascherino" *(The Necklace)*, which we'shall presently consider, Tomlinson said that ". . . the fragments of sensation seemed to knit up into a more organic whole."[11] The unity of vision in Tomlinson's poems and paintings is simultaneous and should be seen as such. In fact, our point is, that paintings have helped Tomlinson widen his vision and technique in pvetry. Octavio Paz writes: "In this first phase of his painting, the results were indecisive: *frottages* in the shadow of Max Ernst, studies of water and rocks more or less inspired by Cezanne, trees and foliage seen in Samuel Palmer rather than in the real world. Like other artists of his generation, he made the circuit round the various stations or modern art and paused, long enough to genuflect, before the geometric chapel of the Braques, the Legers and the Oris's. During those same years—getting on towards 1954—Tomlinson was writing the splendid *Seeing* is *Believing* poems".[12]

Immediately relevant to Tomlinson's arriving at the unity of "fragments of sensation" in *Seeing is Believing* are poems related to the window image. Window is an image as well as a mask. Seeing without a window into the open reality of space, one is always open to the danger of getting lost in the universal vacuity; the nothing; this would imply a loss of objects, and therefore a loss of interrelations among them, as also the loss of contraries which make interrelations possible. "The poet, also, faced by a water world—a world, that is, where, in the old formulation, everything flows—must also discover his way through that given reality, using craft, knowledge, experience,"[13] Window narrows our vision, gives us an angle to look at the object world, and it is by *narrowing* the vision that it reveals. Roughly about the time when Tomlinson was writing *Seeing is Believing* poems, he was "obsessed by Gaudi and by the memory of the dining-room windows in Casa Batllo. He drew them many times: what would happen if we could look out from these windows on the lunar landscape?"[14] Tomlinson, in order to perceive seeming diversity as unity, like microcosm in the macrocosm and vice versa, was trying to surrender himself to an impersonal reality to the extent of himself becoming an automatism —a condition, where man becomes an involuntary medium for the universal perceptions of unity among parts, and where parts just pour out from organism's microcosmic lineaments to imprint themselves, inordinately, on the page. This happens in an artist's life by accident, though accident presupposes a great deal of labour and self-endeavour.

Tomlinson was finding an answer to the equivalent in painting, of rhyme (given) in poetry. Rhyme is an instance of accident, but once it comes unsummoned, it becomes a rule. In "The Chances of Rhyme" *(The Way of a World,* 1969), Tomlinson wrote: "The chances of rhyme are Hke the chances of meeting -/ In the finding fortuitous, but once found, binding:/." Oscar Dominguez answered Tomlinson's question by a method in painting that is called *decalcomania,*[15] Tomlinson later said: "Then, I conceived of the idea of cutting and contrasting sections of a sheet of *decalcomania* and fitting them into the irregular windowpanes. . . Scissors! Here was the instrument for choice. I found I could draw with scissors, reacting *with* and *against* the *decalcomania.* . . Finally I took a piece of paper, cut out the shape of Gaudi's window and moved this mask across my *decalcomania* until I found my monoscape. . . The 18th of June 1970 was a day of discovery for me: I made my best arabesque of a mask, fitted it round a painted blot with geometric lines. . ."[16] What this process helped Tomlinson achieve was a double function of image: the image as a verbal metaphor in time, and the image as visual design in space: "Gaudi's windows, converted by Tomlinson into masks, that is, into objects which *conceal,* serve him to *reveal.*"[17]

In the poem beginning "Wakening with the window over Fields" *(Relations and Contraries),* which, Tomlinson said, "was the first poem of mine where I seemed to hear a world beyond myself that defined its existence in terms of a syncopated melody (thus pulling away from traditional metric) and also in terms of space, light and air."[18] The poet tries to come in contact with the objects of the world through the mask of a window, which is what he imagines his mind to be. This mind sees objects in terms of their sound that appears like "coin-clear harness-jingle" floating. The print of hooves that fall upon the ground, occupy a space:

> The hooves describe an arabesque on space;
> A dotted line in sound that falls and rises
> As the cart goes by, recedes, turns to retrace
> Its way back through the unawakened village.

The dotted line, apart from implicitly denoting the passage of the cart, carries something of the existential rhythm in it of the world which is both the object in space and the sound in time. The rhyme invariably comes in, without any sense of intrusion or labour. Such rhymes guide us through the text and lead to the process of discovery. The movement of the cart that goes by is elastic-like. It will return to the place it originated from. The appearance, before it is destructed, is saved by life-rhythms that never die. These are muscular rhythms of Tomlinson's poetry as also the saving graces. The sound spreads in space as opposed to the physical reality which is localised therein. This expansion of sound counter-stresses and balances the lilting hoof that falls and breaks upon the ground.

While Tomlinson himself felt about this poem: "I knew now what I wanted to do, though I did not know how to do it;"[19] "Fiascherino" *(The Necklace)*, however, is an extension of the window image, which culminates the experience of the former poem by achieving unity among parts. The images that dominate this poem are contrasting in nature; they depict the ebb and flow of life within the contrasting framework of existence wherein also lies clue to the survival:

> . . . The map-like interplay
> Of sea-light against shadow
> And the mottled close-up of wet rocks
> Drying themselves in the hot air
> Are lost to us. Content with our portion,

Where, we ask ourselves, is the end of all this
Variety that follows us? Glare
Pierces muslin; its broken rays
Hovering in trembling filaments
Glance on the ceiling with no more substance
Than a bee's wing.

The image of sea-light contrasts with shadow; rocks that are wet, dry themselves in hot air to continue existential process, while the pertinent nihilism of the question concerning the end of life is balanced and affirmed by the rhetorical question which is also an answer, "Variety that follows us?" Then again the substance of life is reduced to the barest minimum ('bee's wing') only to 'thicken' as the poem approaches end. Of the two poems discussed, the syntactical changes in the shape or structure of sentences are clear. Moreover, Tomlinson's desire to imitate syncopated melody of rhythm in life has done away completely with meter or rhyme. In the earlier poem from *Relations and Contraries,* which contains three stanzas, second and third lines rhyme in the first stanza, first and third lines rhyme in the second, while in the third stanza, first line rhymes with the third, second with the fourth. The depersonalization is common to both the poems.

Simultaneous with the widening of Tomlinson's vision is another event in his career as a painter. By considering it we shall better be able to see the use of colour imagery in his poems and the corresponding meaning and movement therein. Tomlinson often used black colour which would make his compositions stiff. In a letter to Octavio Paz, he wrote: "I wanted to reveal the presence of objects, but all I managed to do was thicken the outlines,"[20] which exaggerated the contours, Then took place an event which not only resolved Tomlinson's artistic problem; it also solved his existential dilemma by which he absorbed the dualities of life (signified by black and white) by widening the contours of his own self. Paz has narrated this as follows: "Tomlinson was wise to have chosen Hercules Seghers. . . Seghers's lesson is: do not abandon black, do not resist it, but embrace it, walk round it as you walk round a mountain. Black was not an enemy but an accomplice. If it was not a bridge, then it was a tunnel: if he followed it to the end it would bring him through to the other side, to the light."[21]

A blackness or negation in life or in art cannot be countered by an effort of the same nature in the same direction (Ted Hughes's *Crow* does it but fails). One of the remarkable features of paintings on Buddha is his settled, self-assured, calm composure, which wins over contradictions by its sheer simplicity of outline. Buddha had attained this after his passive resistance to the attempts on his life by the demon Mara. Passivity is not inaction or inertness, and what Paz admires in Indian paintings, according to Tomlinson, is the mixture of gravity and ecstasy.[22] The dualities of life can be transcended not by a reasoning negative but by a positive affirmation of negatives. After Tomlinson had learnt this, his next problem was to give this experience its verbal equivalent-the visual echoes, correspondences, resonances and reflections of the world of nature. To paint natural objects or give their verbal equivalents, Tomlinson needed unconsciousness of the immediate, the sef-transcendence. Window-masks, earlier referred to, helped him here. They gave him: "Not the real world: an emaginary landscape. What began on the 18th of June 1970 was a fantastic morphology. A morphology and not a mythology: the places and beings which Tomlinson's collages evoke for us reveal no paradise or hell. Those skies and those caverns are not inhabited by gods or devils; they are places of the mind . . They are the product of the confabulation—in the etymological sense of that word—of accident and imagination."[23]

This brings us to an important stage in countering *Seeing is Believing*. The above quotation will reveal that seeing the world in a grain of flower, or an imaginary landscape as Paz calls it, was no ordinary seeing. It has passed through the rigours of imagining oneself more and other than what one otherwise is; the mask of window implies engrossing and expanding awareness of the minutiae of existence within the complex of a single organism. When such a man casts his eyes upon the object world, the question of right and wrong, true and false, is already dissolved by the sheer absorption gained by affirmative "everlasting yea." Blake said, "If sun and moon should doubt. They would immediately go out," and Tomlinson, influenced as he is by his readings of Blake,[24] thinks perception as an act of self-identification. This self-identification means two different things to a poet and a mystic; in the latter case it results in silence which is its own language and its own expression; in the former case, in so far as the poet maintains communication between Creator and Created on the verbal plane, it (perception) takes delight in contemplation of the objects identified and in description of their inter-relatedness. The self never subsumes objects; it keeps them out there. Merle Brown rightly remarks: "Poetic perception, at least as it works in much of Tomlinson's earlier poetry, *is* a form of awareness presupposing and depending upon a series of fundamental distinctions, those between the real and the unreal, world and self, space and time, exterior and interior, and the necessary and the contingent. The title of Tomlinson's second book, *Seeing is Believing* (Oxford, 1960), means in effect that, if one looks with care and alertness, he will see what is really there, he will see objectively and not subjectively, the world and not the self."[25]

II

In 1977, Michael Schimdt asked Tomlinson about his following statement which appeared in *Poems in Folio* series: "The hardness of crystals, the facets of cut glass; but also the shifting of light, the energizing weather which is a result of the combination of sun and frost—these are the images for a certain mental climate, components for the moral landscape of my poetry in general."[26]

Tomlinson replied:" I take your point about that formulation being couched in exccssively acsthetic terms—it doesn't really even explain the book on which it appeared as a blurb, namely *Seeing is Believing* (195S). As an early formulation, however—and it actually grew out of *The Necklace,* completed between 1950 and 1953—for me it contained the right promises, the right "base for a continuity. I wanted precision. This was at the time when Dylan Thomas represented one of the norms in poetry, and the weaker side of Thomas—his playing with words :as if they were plasticine—seemed to me a threat to what I should call a *civil* language."[27]

Precision, control, civil language, are qualities called for by Movement poets, and Tomlinson has maintained them in each of his poems' collection produced so far. *Seeing is Believing* ends with a poem called "Epitaph," whose first section runs as follows:

> Enamoured by
> 'The unlettered muse'
> Now outdoes
> Her favourite
> Device of rhetoric—
> Namely, the pretence
> Of having none.

Seeing is Believing begins with a poem called "The Atlantic," which, says M.L. Rosenthal, is "a poem of the most accurate observation of the movement of a wave breaking on a shore, which is marked not only by its kinetic precision but by its dose adherence to its theme through all the stages of the wave's movement and its retreat."[28] Most of Tomlinson's poems begin by their almost unparalleled fidelity to observed detail, and the final message comes not through image as symbol or poem as allegory, but by a widening and deepening or awareness of things already seen and perceived during the compass or the poem. "The Atlantic" begins:

> LAUNCHED into an opposing wind, hangs
> Grappled beneath the onrush,
> And there, lifts, curling in spume,
> Unlocks, drops from that hold
> Over the shoreward.

The wave is maintained as a metaphor in the poem, an entity not named but manifesting itself, in the activity of the event that is taking place. Each alternate line is indented, and the rhythmic movement of lines, with the use of verbs often twice ('lifts, curling . . ./ Unlocks, drops . . .') imposes the reality and movement of the wave upon the stationary solid shores and sands of sea's reality. Over and against this solidity of the sea, which is just a sea and not a sea of life, the wave dapples below and above:

> Then, curded, shallow, heavy
> With clustering bubbles, it nears
> In a slow sheet that must climb
> Relinquishing its power, upward
> Across tilted sand . . .

Tomlinson the moralist, often comes out as here in the third line, shown by the use "must," which, however, refers to an existential reality. The ebb and flow of the wave is repeated in the poem four times and the use of four full-stops indicates it. The poem does not so much stress the theme of interrelatedness as of movement versus stasis:

> . . . Neither survives the instant
> But is caught back, and leaves, like the after-image
> Released from the floor of a now different mind,
> A quick gold, dyeing the uncovering beach
> With sunglaze. That which we were,
> Confronted by all that we are not,
> Grasps in subservience its replenishment.

We are part of a higher reality irrespective of our knowing or not knowing it, accepting or contradicting it. The physical fact of movement and flexibility of the wave, which gets its reality because of the static solidity of the beach and the shore, which stay there, does not refer to the wave and the shore in themselves; they are referents of Being and Becoming. Calvin Bedient comes near the point when he describes

Tomlinson's nature poetry as "unique in its classical temperateness as in its classical consecration to the Being of Space, to the face and actions of our natural environment."[29] Henry Bergson, 'who influenced a great deal modern art theories, and recognised as such by Davie in his *Articulate Energy,* says: "It is true that if we had to do with photographs alone, however much we might look at them, we should never see them animated: with immobility set aside immobility, even endlessly, we could never make movement. In order that the pictures may be animated, there must be movement somewhere. The movement does indeed exist here; it is in the apparatus".[31] This presence of "the other" is central to Tomlinson's poems.

"Winter Encounters" is a poem about place and people. It unites the human with the non-human. Tomlinson said: "Two themes—sometimes related and sometimes. not—which recur in my poems, are the theme of place and that of return."[32] The reality of life is brought to light by the juxaposition of static, spatial images (House, Village) with kinaesthetic images of environment-winter and rain—which are part of a simulacrum. The poem begins with adescription of "ceaseless pairings" (continuum of life) within which are situated a house and a village, each accompanied by a hollow and a valley-side. Peter Levi has remarked: "Charles Tomlinson's house, which I have visited only once, seemed to me intimately related to his admirable poetry. . , It stands in the quietest valley I have ever penetrated in Western England, steep-sided with hanging woods and a stream."[33] This localises the basic event of the poem. In Tomlinson, verbs are seldom used in singular form; the addition of "s" helps evoke reasonances of nature world and multiply relationships. Moreover, the conscious play upon sound-effect mingles with sounds of nature:

. . . The hedges' barbs
Are bared. Lengthened shadows
    Intersecting, the fields seem parcelled smaller
As if by hedgerow Within hedgerow . . .

The plurality of verb is contrasted with the singularity of the subject (noun). Most of the lines have pauses and the sense of easy inertness which they foster, implies harmony between people and place: ". . . Inanimate or human,/The distinction fails in these brisk exchanges—." Tomlinson said: "The fact is, each poem seems to demand its own formal shape."[34] People's encounter with winter does not spring sense of surprize. Winter's

> Encounter enacts itself in the conversation
> On customary subjects, where the mind
> May lean at ease, weighing the prospect
> Of another's presence.

The process of change in nature is assimilated in the psychic nerves and temperaments of people and places inhabiting landscape, and the identical movement of rhythm in people and places is mingled in a larger continuity which soon brings in the probability of rain (spring). Changes in nature and their filial relationship with man are instances which hold a sense of wonder in themselves as they happen in a cataclysmic play before the nudity of the eye. But they are not responsible for their happening:

> These, though of moment in themselves,
> Serve rather to articulate the sense
> That having met, one meets with more
> Than the words can witness. One feels behind
> Into the intensity that bodies through them
> Calmness within the wind, the warmth in cold.

Objects in nature will serve their purpose if they compelled man to think for their creator. The intensity that keeps people, places, and objects of nature, breathing morsels of life, owes its existence to "the other." Seeing and believing are part of a larger argument. What we see is what our eyes perceive; this is also what we believe. But this belief is preceded by our belief in ourselves, which, in turn, is dependent on our belief in a transpersonal reality, which is beyond people, places, time and space reality. Hence the network of belief does not spring from one object encountering another object; it springs from one object already in belief with itself, its creator, and environment, encountering another object which is again part of the same belief-pattern.

The image of the merry-go-lucky round would better explain what it means, for it also includes the changing cyclic process of life and nature. The central pole of the round would then imply the idea of a Being, personal and impersonal both and simultaneously. Dependent upon the strength, integrity, solidity of this pole are the artificial horses tied to the iron-round; and the children who sit upon these animals to enjoy the merry round, are in turn dependent, without knowing it, upon the entire belief-pattern that preceded them. In Tomlinson there is an interpersonal reflection of the reality of one object upon the other. Nature is full of objects but blind and unlike in Wordsworth, where nature becomes the source of everything including moral perception, in Tomlinson, the role of human will is emphasized:

> . . . Nature is blind
> Like habit. Distrust them. We, since no mirrors,
> Are free both to question this deployment
> And to arrange it—what we reflect
> Being what we choose . . .

The idea of every created thing being part of a larger continuum runs through every poem of Tomlinson. "Reflections" also emphasizes the idea that the mind is not a passive receptor of a given reality; it reacts, chooses, moderates, and transforms:

> Like liquid shadows. The idea is thin
>   Whose mirror smears them as it intercepts
> Withdrawing colours; and where the crust,
>   As if a skin livid with tautening scars,
> Whitens, cracks, it steals from these deformations
> A style too tenuous for the image.

P.R. King comments: "The use of this image—suggesting that the shadows are being broken across by the cracks in the ice and that the cracks are like scars—reveals how the initial perception of the scene has been transfigured into a sharpening vision by the observer's imagination."[35]

"Ponte Veneziano," subtitled "Two Figures," contemplates the relation between two figures and their looking at the object world. The piercing nature of their staring transcends prow, and blazes the canopy which shades a boat. The transition of colours is well pictured by these lines:

. . . The canopy
Which shades a boat
Flares from the line through which they gaze
    Orange against coolness.

The object of the glance of figures is to apprehend the nameless, colourless reality of noumenon. The glance is thwarted, sometimes by figures themselves, and sometimes by a reality, that is too hard for their glance to pierce through:

Undistracted, their glance channels itself
Ignoring the whiteness of a bridge
To cross beneath, where,
Closed by the vault,
It broods on the further light.

This seeming sense of defeat leaves the protagonist in a world where realities of time and place stand irresolute. The stillness, both of the scene and of figures, seem to torture and tantalize:

They do not exclaim,
But bound to that distance,
Transmit without gesture
Their stillness into its ringed centre.

This is protagonists' reconciliation with the given reality, and the seeming sense of defeat is transformed into victory by the passive contemplation which helps figures transmit their stillness to the centre. The relationship between figures and place becomes positive and they believe what they see.

Tomlinson's perception is sensuous or sensuously passionate, and its tendency is towards sensuously abstract. Tomlinson told Michael Schmidt: "I knew French poetry earlier than I knew English—though I have never translated much of it—and I envy its power of sensuous abstraction."[36] Tomlinson is ever shifting the contours of the self to adjust it to an everchanging complex of colours, smells, sounds, which, nevertheless, are given. This desire to attain "primordial freshness,"[37] inspires in Tomlinson a "distrust of the fixities of the self. . . If one can elude such demands, as one can in any genuine relationship. . .; if one can respond to the given and avoid merely secreting one's precious essence over everything one encounters, there occurs the chance of deepenings and renewals."[38] It is for this reason that we find "self" not imposing itself, or reacting against, its environment but surrendering to it. Calvin Bedient's remark about "Reflections:" ". . .this would seem, rather, an instance of being chosen, and the declaration of self-determination does not convince,"[39] is applicable to some other poemsas well, as for example, "Ponte Veneziano."

"Oxen: Ploughing at Fiesole" expounds the need for self to surrender, and the moralistic overtones in the poem become much too evident. The lines of the poem move in an easy manner as there is no resistance from the bulls in the poem. They realize the need for work. Their motto is "Giving and not conceding/Your premises. Work/ Is necessary, therefore:"

> 'We will be useful
> But we will not be swift: now
> Follow us for your improvement
> And at our pace.'

By submission one must improve and not by resistance. Submission, though, is surrender, but not the loss of identity.

Calvin Bedient rightly says: "What Tomlinson values in human beings is a similar facing away from the self, a rock-like, disciplined submergence in *being*."[40]

"The Mediterranean" is one of those poems where Tomlinson departs from Romantic poets' common abhorrence of the city. The poem demonstrates that the act of imaginative perception does not distinguish the object world into categories. The poem is divided into three sections. The first section poses the problem by using internal rhymes and lines varying in their stress and rhythmic movement:

In this country of grapes
Where the architecture
Plays musical interludes, flays
The emotions with the barest statement
Or, confusing the issue and the beholder,

The second section reminds of the influence of Hopkins's sprung rhythm though all lines in the poem are not four-stress. The choice of words and their arrangement, however, give the impression of sprung rhythm. Tomlinson called his usual four-stress line, "a version of sprung rhythm."[41]

The sea
Whether it is 'wrinkled' and 'crawls'
Or pounds, plunders, rounding
On itself in thunderous showers, a
Broken, bellowing foam canopy
Rock-riven and driven wild
By its own formless griefs—

This devouring sea, which is part of nature, is set over against the work of human civilization in the final section:

The imagination cannot lie. It bites brick;
Says: 'This is steel—I will taste steel.
Bred on a lie, I am merely
Guidebooks, advertisements, politics.'

The sea laps by the rail road tracks.
To have admitted this also defines the sea.

Calvin Bedient says: "Several of the poems give a sharp rap to the skull of Romanticism, consistently conceived as an egotistic imagination bringing to birth frenzied and false worlds of its own."[42] "The Mediterranean," likewise, attacks Romantics' hatred of the city, particularly of industrial civilization ('This is steel—I will taste steel').

"Distinctions" is another poem in which Tomlinson "chides Pater for indicating that the blue of the sea gives way to 'pinks, golds, or mauves.' "[43] Tomlinson's acute observation of nature phenomenon is revealed in another poem "Icos." Keats is also generally known as the poet of sensations, but Keats's sensations form human images in terms of natural landscape which they interpret and are affected by. Tomlinson's sensuously passionate evocation of natural objects seldom concerns crickets, bats, gnats, owls, or nightingales, mush less human beings; it concerns the evocation of colours in terms of which he visualizes the primordial freshness of his mental landscape. This settlement of things "out there" should not be distorted by human endeavour to resettle them according to his own scheme and desire. Desire breeds discontent and frustrates human vision of the unity of things. Hence Tomlinson is often content[44] to observe nature objects and things created by humans (houses), having no plans to improve over them or bring them down.

White, a shingled path
Climbs among dusted olives
To where at the hill-crest
Stare houses whiter
Than either dust or shingle.

This is pure passionate fidelity to the objects as they stand in themselves, something Tomlinson learnt not only from Williams but also admired in Marianne Moore: "Miss

Moore is ready to accord to objects and to animals a life of their own."[45] After having juxtaposed houses and nature objects without infiltration, nature creatures are glanced at with the same detached passionate observation though "willing eye"—

Above, piercing the empty blue,
A gull would convey whiteness
Through the sole space which looks it
But, there, scanning the shore,
Hangs only the eagle, depth
Measured within its level gaze.

John Press rightly says: "He (Tomlinson) stares intently at a landscape or at an object and gradually reveals the shape, the texture, the physical objects of what he is contemplating; he also conveys the relationships of these things to ourselves and to the world in which we live."[46]

Among the poets of the Romantic period, Charles Tomlinson, in his attitude to nature creatures, comes nearest to Walt Whitman who said of animals in his poem "Animals" *(Song of Myself)*: "How calm and peaceful they are/I wish I could be like them." But in Tomlinson, the emphasis is towards meditative perception of things as they stand in the universal scheme. "How Still the Hawk" derives its beauty by a certain empathy in rhythm and detachment in observation:

How still the hawk
Hangs innocent above
Its native wood:
Distance, that purifies the act
Of all intent, has graced
Intent with beauty.

The plain style treats the poetic subjects plainly; the identification does not take place between the perceiver and the perceived; the poet strives in contemplation towards self.

submission to the peaceful environment, the setting, which gives the hawk its beauty and artist the grace of intent.

Merle Brown compares this lyric with Tennyson's poem "The Eagle" and Hughes's "Hawk Roosting." Whereas in Tennyson's poem, the bird is predatory, falls because of taint of disease and obscenity; in Hughes's poem ". . . Hughes pretends that he is hawk and so enjoys being wicked innocently."[47] Tomlinson has given importance to civic concerns in his poetry, and what do they imply, as Michael Kirkham has said, is "civility. . . to live willingly within the boundaries of the possible and from a human social centre, ..."[48] Tomlinson's poetry exhibits this civic sensibility in the unique combination of has Augustan frame of mind, restrained rhythms, healthy perception, and a desire to remain within classical limits, never losing himself in romantic megalomania or Freudian insomnia. This does not mean he does not achieve artistic self-transcendence. His poetry revolves round a centre of existence of things which balances as it perceives, renovates as it meditates, liberates as it empathizes.

Writing on *Written on Water,* Tomlinson said: " 'The mind is a hunter of forms' . . . and this is certainly human experience, not only that of poef or political thinker. This search for forms, for patterns of order, for meaningful relationship with people and place, is the basic human act of faith."[49] The patterns of order, lying always in nature though invisible, are perceived by the poet who is the "anchorite of appearances," "an ascetic of the eye."[50] The religio-historical phenomenon of the enactment of ritual is a variation upon the theme of eternal return, to which Tomlinson has referred. Rituals are also forms of memory which they emphasize by their recurrence, and they preserve history. This phenomenon, especially manifest in tribal societies, does not die but changes its form in societies detribalised and civilized.

Tomlinson, more or less from the start of his poetic career, has been deeply concerned to place his identity in historical context. His poems on political or historical themes are part of the same endeavour. Tomlinson once said: "Involved in history, men are sometimes equal to it, though seldom in terms of the kind of success they seek."[51] The theme of the recurrence of desire and its relative fulfilment and non-fulfilment, re-enacts itself in the form of recurrence of ritual in religion or culture. The poem, in so far as it embodies rhythms and nerves of history in terms of verbal monuments, is a form of ritual in literature: "In the poet's weighing and measuring—even to the point of counting ten syllables or five beats to his life—there is a dwelling on the inner rhythms of events that is as fundamental and as primitive, if you like, as ritual. And like ritual, the poem dwells on the event, to force us to a consciousness of the meaningfulness of that event. Like ritual, the poem is pointed outward s from its own contemplative pausing, towards life at large."[52]

The task of the poet in terms of his understanding of historical events as rhythmic layers of ritual, becomes to evoke those rhythms by means of language. Language becomes not so much an aggregate of words which convey meaning; it becomes an empathic embodiment to the identity process, which, as it evokes primordial rhythms of freshness, also renews and sublimates the protagonist who enacts events.

The drama of such evocation of ritualistic rhythms Tomlinson carries in "The Mausoleum:" ". . . whether a shot-red could invade/Decorously so impoverished a kingdom." The tomb is seen as an eternalization of the ritual not only of death but also of rebirth.

> The dead
> Have buried their dead and the living
> Can approach it without fear and push open
> (as one may find it) the frayed door
> To stand where a child might and where children do
> Play under the bare shelves of stone tiers.

The repetitive character of ritualistic rhythm, which corresponds to the repetitive rhythms of language, has an element of tragic intensity. The influence of Octavio Paz cannot be ruled out here, whose poems of "tragic intensity"[53]

Tomlinson has great admiration for. The following lines imply great tragic potential:

Swarming the base of the narrow walls
    As far as the raised arm can incise
Graffiti and beyond that as high as stone
    Can be aimed against stone in such a confine
The legend is complete however it is simple,
    Is plain, though under this dimmed
Clerestory the darkness liquifies it,
    And the work, however many the hands, one.

The initial four run-on lines in succession place the destiny of man against the Eden of his desire, and the history behind the monumental erection of man's mortal monument concerns the recurrence of a single ritual in many forms, as the last line quoted above tells us. All history and its endless process is an attempt to concentrate itself to the reality of an impersonal being, "the other," the immovable mover of the world, the still centre of the ever-moving wheel of history. We are the protagonists of history, and our actions, big or small, re-enact, in some way or the other, the archetypal ritual of life and death, and by so doing, let us transcend—

Into that world to which this silence
    Scarred by so many hands in prologue,
You will concede that they have gained it whole
    Whatever they have lost in its possession.

Tomlinson wrote on his poem "The Compact at Volterra" *(Written on Water)*: ". . . I describe the eroded landscape of this town, where, despite the constant collapse of earth into a vast ravine, the farmers go on training their vines along the very edges of that ravine. In a way their action repudiates that of poet and thinker. . ."[54] The continuity of the act of training their vines upon the ever-falling edges by farmers gives their activity a ritualistic character, whose rhythms were already immanent in the psyche of the poet. The same is true of "The Mausoleum" where history is visualized as a process, and man its helpless protagonist who tries to immortalize himself in time by enacting again and again the ritual of building mausoleums of unfulfilled desire.

Another history poem, "Antecedents: A Homage and Valediction," is a sequence of six interrelated poems in which an artist encounters literary tradition and the need for a sense of self-identity makes him pay homage to some writers while. bidding farewell to others. Tomlinson's attitude recalls T.S. Eliot: "I think one is inevitably influenced by T.S. Eliot,"[55] and also echoes Croce's ideas on tradition: "An actor on the stage of history must in everyone of his acts illustrate both conservation and revolution, constancy and change, conservation being the necessary basis for revolution and constancy for change."[56]

Tomlinson, writing on the poem, said: "I began rather crudely and naively with history in 'Monuments, Variations on a Theme of Yeats' in *Relations and Contraries* (1951) . . . Then, in *Seeing is Believing* there is a long, actually comic poem, 'Antecedents', which is a capsulated history of late romanticism and asks, out of a very concrete and historic situation, where do we go from here"?[57]

The first poem "Nothing: a Divagation" strikes Tomlinson's basic attitude:

> Not the calm—the clarity
> After the storm. There are
> In lucidity itself
> Its crystal abysses
> Perspective within perspective:

Tomlinson recalls that Dylan Thomas played with words, while he himself wanted "resistance in language and subject-matter-hence the rather self-conscious talk about facets and crystals. . ."[58]

In the second poem "Praeludium," poetry has become history as learned allusions[59] tighten rhythms to the point of indigestion.[60] The sun-set, a key image henceforth, is used to deploy the inevitability of time as succession. This poem narrates the birth of French Symbolist Movement after the end of Romanticism. The third poem hints at the need for modification of tradition:

> Our innate
> Perspicacity for the moderate
> Is a national armoury.
> I have not Read him;
> I have read about him:'
> In usum delphini—for the use
> Of the common man.

Tomlinson's poetic universe has the hard crystals of rational intellect where imagination is equally welcome. He is trying to involve himself in history to give himself and the common man a civic language. For this purpose, the need is not to act out parts of historical characters that have already been played, but to enforce choice upon oneself by keeping eyes open to the current time and place:

> And thus
> Rimbaud the incendiary,
> Gamin contemporary
> With Gosse, the gentleman
> Arrived late. He was dressed
> In the skin of a Welsh lion, or the lion
> Wore his—for the light
> was dubious,—

Tomlinson tells us, "There are the vignettes in 'Antecedents' of Rimbaud and Dylan Thomas,"[61] and in lines quoted,. says Davie, ". . . the Mallarmean syntax . . . acts out . . . the anachronism of Thomas playing in 1940 the Rimbaud game for which the right time was 1870."[62] Tomlinson, however, is "not going to make the mistake he diagnoses in Thomas, of playing Laforgue as Thomas played Rimbaud, a half-century too late."[63]

The symbolist dilemma of the poem as closed universe sprang from symbolist poets' imposition of their subjective mental states upon the outer reality:

> weaving the smoke, subjective
> Faun with a cigarette Stephane assembled one:
> The page (the horns gone glacial)
> Discovered its landscapes
> As arctic gardens,
> A luminous aura, hinting the penetration
> Of green skeins, a snow-light
> Bruising the mind.

'The fifth poem "The Bells: A Period Piece," takes us to the post-symbolist period, where medium is out of control of the messenger of history:

> . . . now silence breaks:
> Secure no larger in their theme
> Or violence of its repetitions,
> The generations abdicate
> To us the means to vacillate

History repeats itself but not without changing its tones, colours, textures. The direction is provided in the final poem, "Something: A Direction," a poem remarkable for syntactical clarity" as for musical, and more than usual flow and flexibility in rhythms. This is simultaneous with artist gaining his direction:

> Out of the shut cell of that solitude there is
>   One egress, past point of interrogation
> Sun is, because it is not you; you are
>   Since you are self, and self delimited
> Regarding sun . . .

When the poet's self has identified with the symbol it has created (and the symbol is a displacement of the reality 'out there' into the 'shut cell' of the poem), the basic law of relativity of created things disappears in a false sense of self-sufficiency which the symbol imposes, however temporarily, upon the landscape of human mind. In Tomlinson's universe, the protagonist of history should keep himself separate from the thing observed. Tomlinson proceeds from a perception of things out there to his interior landscape, always conscious though, to maintain restrained, hard, crystal-like separation between the observer and the thing observed, for this is an artistic need. Calvin Bedient remarks upon the poem's stanza quoted: "Observer and observed stand apart, then, as the necessary poles or substantiated being. The eye is the first of philosophers; seeming, turns up the soil of ontology. Beholding thus applies to the spirit a metaphysical balm. The 'central calm' of appearances, their very theirness, gives a floor to the world. So Tomlinson walks and looks, and he finds it enough."[64]

The poem further emphasizes the need for, protagonist to become submissive to an impersonal reality, which impels the historic process, and thereby human beings, to enact and re-enact their forms of desire. The return to ritual in the poem is, unmistakable:

> Your returns may enter, welcome strangers
> Into a civil country (you were not the first
> To see it), but a country, natural and profuse
> Unbroken by past incursions, as the theme
> Strung over stave, is rediscovered
> After dismemberment in the canon, and over stave
> Can still proceed, ...

The lines have archetypal significance, and the area of their visionary framework extends from creation to apocalypse back to creation.

"The poem, in itself, is a ceremony of initiation. It leads us' into and through and out on the other side of an imagined experience. It is a rite of passage through a terrain which, when we look back over it, has been flashed up into consciousness in a way we should scarcely have foreseen. . . The poem tries to celebrate the fact that the help we gain from alien phenomenon . . . the help is towards relation, towards grasp, towards awareness, of all that we are not, yet of relationship with it . . . In doing so we are at once chastened and initiated into a new world of meaning and possibility. The poem is the ceremony which attempts to keep clear its differentiations . . ."[65] We are part of a larger continuum, bubbles upon the flow of time river. Each of us is, trying to swim across to the other side of the shore; this shore furthers away from us as we approach it. What we can do is to invoke its presence with the help of rituals by living within the bounds of a civil country. The poem is the world and the world is the poem; both of them become subject and object to each other as we effect variations upon distancing or the act of looking. This reality is meaningful to us in so far as we are able to perceive given relationships with the help of the medium.

In "Northern Spring," Tomlinson contrasts changes in nature, the clash among natural objects, and, in such an environmental setting, shows, how man can give meaning and definition to his existence, and to the existence of his environment, by building a structure of possibility (house, civil country) against the impossibility of nature.

Trees
Fight with the wind, the wind eludes them
Streaking its cross-lanes over the uneasy water
Whose bronze whitens. To emultate such confusion
One must impoverish the resources of folly,
But to taste it is medicinal.

The rapid changes in weather are not for their own sake; they are giving reality and meaning to the solitariness and chaos of existence. The meaning of their existence, in turn, depends upon man's efforts to articulate himself (using nature as tool and medium) by bringing in conscious elements of will and choice.

Where should one look
In the profession of possibilities?
One conceives
Placing before them a square house
Washed in the coolness of lime, a hub
For the scattered deployment, to define
In pure white from its verdant ground
The variegated excess which threatens it.[66]

Tomlinson's submission and submergence is not to visual reality lying or standing there; it is to a reality standing behind them objective and impersonal. Whereas romantic poets humanised nature (Wordsworth called her 'mother') and imposed their subjective mental states upon natural objects, which later led to the development of symbolist movement in literature,[67] Tomlinson, ascetic as he is of the eye and the appearance, never confuses, corroborates, or imposes, his subjectivity upon the objects outside. This is one reason his poems are not in the folk-tale or ballad tradition. Tomlinson is the type of sage who has lived in the city first and in the village only afterwards. Therefore, he sees no reason why city and nature should be seen as two contrasting images of the rhythm of life.[68] His contribution to romanticism is precisely here, that he qualifies the city by placing it in the context of nature, as nature is qualified by being placed in the context of the city. Both of them fulfil each other, and by so doing give meaning and significance to the reality of their being. Tomlinson's restrained rhythms, hard, solid images, solid even when they maintain their kinetic character, the logic of contraries in terms of colours, sounds, smell, etc.. expounds the same basic economy of attitude, both classical and romantic, and enlivens us by its sheer all-inclusiveness, all apprehending nature.

One the chief occupations of Tomlinson as artist lies in his protrayal of world as relative and his submission to a reality neither relative nor casual but beyond them both. The reality of time and place, learned so laboriously from Williams and Moore, could not blind Tomlinson to the vision of a reality that stood beyond objects and places. It is to be recalled that Tomlinson criticised Williams for sticking irresolutely to th e physical, which devoided him of width, metaphysical depth, and range in poetry. The ascetic detachment, itself a metaphysical quality, helped Tomlinson move from outward to inward, and not from inward to outward, as symbolists did. "On a Land; scape by Li Ch'eng" is a poem of remarkable fidelity to artist's detached temperament and his sincerity to the visual detail of a painting. The objectivity and the literalness of detail enmeshes us again into the logic of contraries forming relations of meaning:

> Look down. There is snow.
> Where the snow ends
> Sea, and where the sea enters
> Grey among capes
> Like an unvaried sky, lapping
> From finger to finger
> Of a raised hand, travellers
> Skirt between snow and sea.

What interests Tomlinson, says Octavio Paz, "is the process which leads it to be the object that it is. He is fascinated—with his eyes open: a lucid fascination—at the universal busyness, the continuous generation and degeneration of things. His is a poetry of minimal catastrophes and resurrections of which the great catastrophe and resurrection of the worlds is composed."[69]

"More Foreign Cities" is prefaced by Kingsley Amis's statement made during the fifties in D.J. Enright's anthology *Poets of the 1950's:* "Nobody wants any more poems about foreign cities. . ." which Tomlinson rejects:

> Not forgetting Ko-jen, that
> Musical city (it has
> Few buildings and annexes

Space by combating silence),
Against walls of transparent stone
Unsettling all preconception—a city
For architects (they are taught
By casting their nets
Into those moving shoals);

While the internationalism of Tomlinson's cities is obvious,[70] the charge of subjectivity imposed upon the object world, which Tomlinson laid upon romantic poets and French Symbolist poets, may, in turn, be laid upon him. Davie says upon this poem: "Symbolist poetry characteristically seems to have run the traffic . . . to the point indeed at which the reality of the supposedly objective world, as anything as a phantasmal reflection of the subjective, becomes highly questionable. Tomlinson too may run the traffic this way, as when he answers Amis's notorious 'Nobody wants any more. . .' by conjuring up cities imagined so as to correspond to states of mind."[71]

The fact is there are no absolute theories for poetry much less for poetic practice. The ascetic distance, for the sake of objectivity, which Tomlinson so assiduously maintains, does relapse, here and there, into the symbolist dilemma of identification of mental states with physical objects. Such reading of mental states into objects also occurs in poems like "Sconset" and Fire in a Dark Landscape." The former poem begins:

I have never been
To Sconset, but the gleam
Of painted houses
Adding a snow-tone
To the sea-tone in the mind's
Folder of the principal views
Full of contrasting play of colours,

In the latter poem the mind first mistakes the blackness of shadow for white:

And where it falls, a quality
Not of the night, but of the mind
As when, on the moonlit roofs,
A counterfeit snow
Whitely deceives us.

But in the end is made clear the real origin from which the sensibility, generated by the play of shadows, ensues:

the winds'
Chimera of silk, twisting
Thickened with amber shadows,
A quality, not of the mind
But of fire of darkness.

"Farewell to Van Gogh" chides Van Gogh, the painter, for his excessive involvement with the theme of violence. What is in conflict with Van Gogh is Tomlinson's detached, meditative, observant eye and mind, which, as it sees the beauty and wonder of creation, wants to go on seeing, and thereby believing in an endless process of contemplative stasis, for what else there is for an artist to do? Can he improve upon God's creation? But this is what Van Gogh does:

The quiet deepens. You will not persuade
One leaf of the accomplished, steady, darkening
Chestnut-tower to displace itself
With more of violence than the air supplies
When, gathering dusk, the pond brims evenly
And we must be content with stillness.

The quiet deepens. The objects stand naked, mute, in the absorbing exuberance which is their very beauty, enamouring and meditative. But the "more of violence" comes as an infiltration upon the mystic silence of the scene. While it is true that Tomlinson has brought city near and in juxtaposition with nature; nature, Tomlinson does not think, is against human endeavours of a civil country, as was thought by romantic poets.[72] In Tomlinson's art, each word that stands naked on the page without rhetoric or ornament, imposes its mute presence like engraving on a tomb, sad but enrapturing, in their re-enlivening the memory of the dead. This is what Tomlinson calls the tragic potentiality of history which fascinates him.

Man cannot improve creation. Such attempts, if history is any proof, have only imbalanced the monumental balance of nature:

> Farewell, and for your instructive frenzy
> Gratitude. The world does not end tonight
> And the fruit that we shall pick tomorrow
> Await us, weighing the unstripped bough.

M.L. Rosenthal says that "For all these qualities (of Van Gogh) the speaker is grateful, yet at the end he argues, in his concretely evocative post-imagistic manner, that the frenzy is not really warranted . . ."[73] Opposed to such human infiltration, as distinct from human context of poems, are "Frondes Agrestes" and "Geneva Restored"—poems which acknowledge their debt to John Ruskin. Consider the objectivity of these lines from "Frondes Agrestes." The rose is shown

> Gathered up into its own translucence
> Where there is no shade save colour,
> the unsymbolic rose.

Calvin Bedient quotes these lines to show Tomlinson's "equal felicities of the imaginative power of augmenting and interpreting appearances without denying them . . ."[74] Tomlinson acknowledged his debt to John Ruskin: . . . "I have been definitely influenced first of all by a prose writer, and that is John Ruskin, in actually looking at nature and considering what it has to offer one. . ."[75] Tomlinson further said, talking of M. Moore and Wallace Stevens. ". . . She has this Ruskinian open-ness to the creative universe in looking at the surfaces that it offers one, just as Stevens at his best has."[76] Mark the celebration of nature-images Ruskinian open-ness in the following stanza from "Frondes Agrestes":

Nature's difficulties, her thought
Over dints and bosses, her attempts
To beautify with a leopard-skin of moss
The rocks she has already sculpted,
All disclose her purposes—the thrush's bill,
The shark's teeth, are not his story.

Nature has a purpose, is not callous and blind; somehow the story of man's ('his') civilization has not run parallel to that of nature. Man's attempts to improve, upon nature prove, if anything, the augury of his own attempts. The same indebtedness is acknowledged to Ruskin in "Geneva Restored":

Close roofs on a gravel height,
Building knit into rock; the bird's nest of a place
Rich in protestant pieties, in heroic half-truths
That was Ruskin's. Guard and rebuild it.

Such poems reveal Tomlinson the conservatist and moralist.

Sometimes, the otherness, to which most of Tomlinson's poems demand obeisance and submission, seems unresponsive, unwilling to partake or share the devotion of the worshipper of appearances. These are the lines from "Cezanne at Aix":

And the mountain: each day
Immobile like fruit. Unlike, also
—Because irreducible, because
Neither a component of the delicious
And therefore questionable,
Nor distracted (as the sitter)
By his own pose and, therefore,

Doubly to be questioned: it is not
Posed. It is. Untaught
Unalterable, a stone bridgehead
To that which is tangible
Because unfelt before. There
In its weathered weight
Its silence silences, a presence
Which does not present itself

While it is a pure instance of seeing which is believing, Davie, also quoting the entire poem, says: ". . . far more characteristically (and spccifically so as to escape the Symbolist vertigo about whether the objective exists), Tomlinson runs the traffic the other way, insisting upon the irreducible Otherness of the non-human world, its Presence in the sense of being present, its being bodied against the senses, as the irreplaceable first principle of all sanity and all morality. Of many statements of this (for it is after all what gives the book its title), I take 'Cezanne at Aix . . .'"[77] Davie contradicts the anticipated objection of poems being non-human though allowing for five unsuccessful poems in the volume *(Seeing is Believing).*[78] It should be recalled that *Seeing is Believing* belongs to the earlier phase of Tomlinson's career, which is analogous to his career as a painter. Octavio Paz tells us: "In this first phase of his painting, the results were indecisive: frottages in the shadow of Max Ernst, studies of water and rocks more or less inspired by Cezanne, . . ."[79] Paz's statement will explain the absence of human context in Tomlinson's poem.

Tomlinson himself answers this objection in another of his poem on painting:

Art
Is complete when it is human. It is human
Once the looped pigments, the pin-heads of light
Securing space under their left restrictions
Convince, as the index of a possible passion.
As the adequate guage, both of the passion
And its object.

Light is an element which dominates Tomlinson's poems. It is in terms of light in fact, which later changes into and mainfests as colours, that we apprehend fluid objects of the world. The creator, the imperceptible being behind the changing kaleidoscopic colours of creation, is also an artist, and He qualifies this function of His by deftly placing pin-heads of light in well-marked patches of space. A human artist, if he is able to perceive this phenomenon of objects as colours, both in space and in time, with a passion that does not take us to the possibility of nature as chaos, but enlivens us by his deft ascetic restrictions of perceived objects within a civil country he is an artist who renews the reality of object "out there" with the help of passion "inside" his own personality. Tomlinson said: "English have rather sloppy ideas about the relation between mind and feelings and one can only sigh and go on believing there is such a thing as passionate intellect. I was surprized that even Leavis in his recent put-down of Valer's 'Le Cimitere Marin' should have proved so impervious to the sensuous cerebration of that poem."[80]

There is a great deal of misunderstanding about the concept of passion, feeling, on the one hand, and reason, intellect, mind, on the other. This may well endanger the understanding of the concept of seeing as believing itself. The most simple fact about the act of perception is that it does not admit a schism between mind and passion. The "sensist" and "intuitionist" schools of approaching reality emerge out of different sets of historical needs, and this is the only difference they have between them. "Every concrete and real sensation is always a complete intuitive organism,"[81] declares Croce. He further says: "Sensism, like intuitionism, was therefore not only efficacious in its negative task of rousing a stronger awareness of what thought and the criticism of thought are, but was also efficacious in the positive work of bnnginp out the then neglected and rejected virtue of scnse, that is intuition, und (herewith of fancy, poetry, art, and the whole aesthetic world. 'Aesthetic' is a word derived from 'aisthesis,' sense, and the definition was *Scimtia cognitionis sensilivae,* while Vico ascribed to the poets the sensitivity of the human race."[82]

Almost all of Tomlinson's poems abound in images which combine the open-ness of sense with the restraint of mind at an intense degree of perceptive process, where sensing the object involuntarily becomes intuitive, while seeing transforms its lf into believing. Questions concerning the reality and non-reality of objects constitute the history of perception in decadence. ". . . the distinction between reality and non-reality is extraneous, secondary, to the true nature of intuition."[83] An integrated act of perception combines the "outside" and the "inside," as Tomlinson might have learnt from Blake whose quarrel with Locke was precisely this. The latter imagined thought to be physical process, while the mind is a *tubula rasa,* imprinting upon itself, what it perceived and received from outside. For Blake, the mind not only reacted to what it perceived, it also transformed it by the power of Imagination, the Divine Body in each one of us. Tomlinson's passivity and contentedness is not to be confused with inertness and mental resignation. By resigning himself from the immediateness of things, Tomlinson is able to enact the drama of artistic distancing (something Blake failed to do according to T.S. Eliot), which changes physical landscape into mental and imaginative reality. This is what Tomlinson was trying to achieve by putting the mask of the window upon the prismatic outflow or his mental rays. This levelling of the states of perceived experience has given Tomlinson images in motion, and the world they present is not the real one (is it any value to have one?), but "an imaginary landscape," to borrow a phrase from Octavio Paz.

The act of writing a poem is an encounter not only with things outside as objects and the poet as subject, but the poet as object before the mute creator who stands behind the minutest particles of dust, lets objects speak by contrasting with them his metaphors of silence. The poem becomes a penitential hymn in the verbal ocean of mind; the creator of the poem stands mute before a still creator of his own being, in sheer feelings of egolessness; the rite of the poem, disregarding symbolist's interior passage, takes the poet where things really are, silent, disembodied, naked, in their rhythmic structures: "We can never know all that reality, but the rite of the poem has, so one hopes, brought us into closer relation with it. We put down the book. We put aside the mask. We go on living. But it is the book and it is the mask that bring to bear the mystery and the qualities of the process of living."[84]

The vision of Tomlinson's poems is the vision exclusively of a religious ascetic, a poet-mystic, whom God sends into the world giving him tools—of words, pen, ink, mind, to perceive and experience things—and who fulfils this function as assiduously and faithfully as possible, by imagining the world as a poem of colours, sounds, textures, where each object is an image not of itself but of a reality that always stands behind, unseen, felt but inexpressible.

This is where Tomlinson also unites East with West in the former's view of art as a medium to approach the creator. The imperceptible creator of Tomlinson's poems seems very much like the unseen presence manifest in Tagore's *Gitanjali*, of which Octavio Paz said: "The expressionism of some of Tagore's ink drawings, with their violence, compensates us for the sticky sweetness of many of his melodies."[85] Tomlinson presents his poems to his creator by bowing down before Him in feelings of humility and reverence, holding them like a bouquet, the incense of whose flowers touches the unfathomed filaments of each created phenomenon. The poems pay a great homage and a touching tribute to each object of the created world, which renew themselves as they expand their lineaments into the wider coteries of a new awareness inhabited by the presence of their creator. ". . . as Tomlinson puts it best: 'to reconcile the I that is with the I that I am.' In the nameless, impersonal I that is, are fused the I that measures and the I that dreams, the I that thinks and the I that breathes, the I which creates and the I which destroys."[86]

III

Tomlinson's search for articulating the anonymous

absolute moment of noumenic experience into the frameworks of words having poetic contexts, takes him to another poetic venture. We have noted Tomlinson's appreciation for William Carlos Williams's poetry where, as Robert Creeley said, writing is an emotional system, which feels as it sees.[87] Tomlinson also appreciated Williams's habit of marrying words with things, things with ideas[88] respecting the native scene, unlike Eliot, who cast an "egoistic veil over the world."[89] What Tomlinson himself was looking for, was a transcendence of words, things, and ideas, simultaneously.[90] This transcendence, Tomlinson was "bit, to achicve in as early a volume as *Seeing is Believing* (1958, 1960), in personal terms. This personal transcendence of objects became a collective transcendence of experience when, in April 1969. Tomlinson, along with three other poets, Octavio Paz (Mexico), Jacques Roubaud (France), Edoardo Sanguineti (Italy), gathered at a hotel in Paris, to write a poem called *Renga,* published originally, under the same title, in French in 1971, and simultaneously published in Canada and New York, in an English translation, done by Tomlinson himself.[91]

Renga, as Octavio Paz himself defines in his Introduction to the book, is "a chain of poems, chain of poems-poets, chain of chains."[92] To put it more simply, *Renga* is a link of two or more poems inter-connected, in which every linked part maintains its individual identity in the total unity of the poem, compared well with a pyramid by Charles Tomlinson. Poetic forms often owe their origin to the dovelopment of civilizations, architecture is whose most important symbol. Poetic forms are an imitation of, and based upon, the pattern and movement of astronomical bodies—sun, moon, seasons, planets, etc., or the zodiac. This is particularly truc about countries where myth, religion and art were indistinguishable in the early stages of their civilization. Renga is an oriental poetic form of Japan which demands labours of several poetic talents simultaneously for its composition. It has its origin in Buddhism. Professor D.T. Suzuki, an authority on Japanese Buddhism, says: "When Mahayana Buddhism[93] was introduced to Japan, the Prince Shotoku (A.D. 593-621) embraced it at once saying that Japan was truely the land fit for the Mahayana teaching. By this, he meant that the Mahayana was the teaching truely appealing to the Japanese mind. . ."[94] As Claude Roy says in his "Foreword" to *Renga:* "The renga is a collective poetic form which was extremely popular in Japan where it developed between the Heian period (794-1192) and the Moromachi, in the fourteenth and fifteenth centuries."[95] Claude Roy further says: "The oldest example of a 'collective poem' offered to us by Japanese literature is to be found in the classic mythology of Manyoshi, most of the poems of which were composed between 600 and 750 AD."[96]

Shintoism was the term by which Buddhism came to be known in Japan. The term means "the way of the Gods." Japanese also express themselves, while responding to their environment, by the phrase *kannagara,* which means "to be like the gods" or "to reflect in oneself the image of the gods."[97] Dr. Suzuki says: "To be or to act in accordance with the gods was to take Nature as she is and not to exercise any human intelligence over nature. This is gleaned from *The Collection of Ten Thousand Leaves (Mannyo-shu)* which is the collection of the ancient Japanese poems compiled probably by Otomo-no-Yakamochi in the latter part of the eighth century."[98] Claude Roy quotes one poem by Yakamochi to show the brevity of the lines, and "the symbolic implicitness of the themes of water and fecundity, the erotic significance of which has been fairly constant from Sanskrit literature to the poetry of Eluard."[99]

In the Heian period (AD. 897-1185), to which Claude Roy also refers in the quotation above, Japanese outlook on environment outside, underwent a change. Instead of regarding nature as not to be interfered with human intelligence, they now read their emotions into the changes of seasons, objects animate or inanimate. The *kannagara,* as a result, was replaced by the expression *mono no aware. Mono* meant "things," *no* corresponded to "of," and *aware* meant "emotional response." "When the autumnal moon peeps into a humble hut, or when the spring foliage shines in the sun, or when the winter field is cowred all white with snow, the Heian poets feel various emotions moving in Nature as the seasons alternate . . . *Mono* means things in general; not only are natural objects *mono,* we sentient humans are also *mono.* When four hearts are released from egocentric impulses and rationalistic subtleties, they become resonant with the spirit of the gods, which is *kannagara,* and are enabled to see deep into the value of human emotionality. This is when they read *mono no aware* in all phases of our social activities calling forth our emotional responses in all their varieties."[100]

Octavio Paz, in his Introduction to *Renga,* writes: "The Renga is divided into various sequences or modes. The model for this arrangement is the movement of the seasons or that of the twenty-four hours of the day, the passage from dawn to night. A linear and circular composition, a design of extreme simplicity and extreme elegance which, in the sphere of music, corresponds to melody."[101] The movement of the moon, a recurring image in *Renga,* is the basis of the daily, weekly, monthly, and yearly cycles in Buddhism as in most other religions. Particularly the four days in each lunar month, the full and the new moons, are sacred. The symbolism of four in *Renga,* related as it is to the four seasons, is related, in a more vital way, to Buddhist spells *(dharani).* Spell is a musical term having a certain duration in time; but its ritual and magical character consists in that when its performance is taking place, it succeeds in actualising and articulating human motivations that went into performing it.

The composition of *Renga* by four poets, and each poet contributing seven sonnets, may be said to have at its basis the following story about Buddha: "In the *Atanatiya sutta (Digha,* iii, 194), the four Great Kings with their troops visit Buddha. Vessavana (Kuvera), Great King of the north, gives Buddha a form of 'protection' (rakkha) against evil-disposed non-human beings, . . . if monks, nuns, laymen, and lay women will repeat the spell, such beings will protect them. The spell itself is in verse and consists of homage to the seven Buddhas and to the four Great Kings. Buddha afterwards repeats it to his monks, so that it becomes part of the Buddha-word."[102] Moreover, to determine the genuineness of a passage as to whether it belongs to Buddha-word or not, Buddha is said to have composed four rules. Each time a monk utters a sermon before the public and attributes it to Buddha, it is to be compared with *Vinaya,* or the teaching of the Master.

These passages are quoted to show the tendencies that might have gone into the birth of the Renga form of poetic composition. The idea of poetry as collective might sound' Marxist, but it is Buddhist. In India, the historical conditions which necessitated the birth of Buddhism, among others, were extremely individualistic character of *Upanishads* and the *Bhagavadgita.* The "I" is extolled to the position of becoming a god. Buddha supplements this concept of liberation as individualistic with liberation as collective by organising *sangha,* association. Whosoever will become a member of it, follow rules, will attain liberation. What is important here is that the individual character of the attainment of liberation is not distorted; it is given added dignity by being woven into a chain of succeeding liberations to be attained within the boundaries of a group. A seeker does not become a cloister by going to some solitary place; he stays in the world, subordinates his personal "I" to the "we" of the group, and thus achieves liberation.

In the last quotation above, what is further to be noted is that Buddha does not keep the secret of liberation he discovered on to himself; he passes it on to the group. On the other hand, the group does not attain its identity in isolation; it attains meaning and liberation by constantly developing contexts whose centre is always Buddha. This gives us the logic of variation (group) versus constant (Buddha), as Claude Roy says: "We rediscovered together constants in our preoccupations and preoccupations in our constants which were not our own, nor did they seem like our own special prerogative. . ."[103] The form of delivering the sermon, moreover, contributes to this process where the monk would sit on a platform and people admitted to the order (*sangha*) would sit surrounding him. What the Monk says, people repeat, and the repetition of this process develops a spiral-like, gyrating movement round a centre. The "I" constantly subordinates to the "we," and the "we" constantly gets its metaphor of meaning with reference to the "I." Octavio Paz writes: "The practice of the renga implies the negation of certain cardinal Western notions, such as the belief in the soul and the reality of the I. The historic context in which it was born and developed did not know of the existence of a creator god and denounced the soul and the I as pernicious illusions. In the Japan of tradition the social cell, the basic unity, was not the individual, but the group. Further, each in its own way, Buddhism, Confucianism, and Shintoism, fought against the idolatory of the I. For the first it was a chimercial entity: from the point of view of true reality (emptiness) the ego is not so much an infirmity as an optical illusion. Confucianism and Shintoism, for their part, restrict the individual within the double yoke of 'filial piety' and loyalty to the feudal lord. For all these reasons, it seems to me that the renga must have offered to the Japanese the possibility of going out from themselves, of passing from the anonymity of the isolated individual into the circle of exchange and recognition. Also it was a way of liberating themselves from the weight of hierarchy."[104]

Buddhism emphasizes individual's quest for truth *through* the Order and not out of it. It is by remaining in Order (Paz's 'weight of hierarchy') that the individual transcends the Order, the Group, and himself. The formal structure of renga consists of odd/even verses, which recapitulates the logic of word/echo, of the sermon by the monk and its repetition by the people in Order. Of the struclure of *Mahayana* Buddhist *Sutra,* E.J. Thomas tells us: "It consists largely of verse, but these passages are embedded in prose, which often repeats the matter of the verses."[105] The transplantation of Buddhist texts from India to Japan and China, and of Buddhism in general, is now a historical fact.[106]

The account above may well take care of the historical context to which renga poetic form may owe its development. There is also a mythological aspect to this poetic form. While referring to Buddhist cycles, we said that they are based upon the lunar movement. Buddhist festivals, as most of the other great mythological events, are associated with the movement of the moon, change in seasons, etc. Of Buddhist festivals, Melford E. Spiro says: "They all fall at various transitional points of either the agricultural or the climatic year: the beginning or end of the monsoon, the beginning or end of the paddy cultivation cycle, and so on."[107] Claude Roy writes on the mythic motif in *Renga:* "In myth, subterranean retreats augur always the unfolding of a harvest: the harvest of wheat which Persephone descends into Hades to gain as her reward, the harvest of life which Alcestis descends to Tartarus to obtain, for her egoistic husband, the harvest of wisdom which all the heroes of initiations go to bring ripeness and gather in the dark of the underworld."[108]

The mythological figures referred to are Persephone, Alcestis, and initiation heroes. Persephone is the daughter of Zeus and Demeter, the Cretan goddess of agriculture and fruitful soil. The myth of Persephone runs: ". . . the maiden was playing, . . . in a meadow, culling flowers with the daughters of Okeanos, god of the all-embracing sea, when she spied a glorious plant with a hundred blossoms spreading its fragrance all about, which had been sent up expressly to seduce her by the goddess Warth (Gaia), at the behest of Hades, the lord of the underworld. So that when she hurried to pluck its flowers the earth gaped and a great god (Hades) appeared in a chariot of gold, who carried her down into his abyss despite her cries."[109] With Persephone's departure for the underworld, the earth loses its fecundity and decay in nature occupies the theme of growth. With the intervention of Zeus, however, Persephone "returned to Olympus in glory, and, as though by magic, the fields were covered again with flowers and the life-giving grain."[110]

Alcestis, as G.S. Kirk tells us, is the subject of Euripides' play of that title, "who had reluctantly offered to die in place of her husband Admetus, . . ."[111] and whom Hercules descended to save. In the context of *Renga,* she equals the function of Persephone, and her return to the world is a victory of egolessness over the ego of her husband, of fertility over aridity. The initiation myths give another context to the same myth. The initiation heroes go on a journey from this world to the underworld and emerge after killing some demon for the benefit of the human race. Initiation myths also concern the rites of marriage. Children are taken in a group, put to various trials before they become marriageable. From singular they become plural, from plural again singular. This again celebrates the marriage of aridity with fertility.[112]

IV

Renga begins with the sonnets of Octavio Paz; the metaphorical beginning of the poem coincides with the physical circumstances of the particular month of the year during which the poem was begun. In the second sonnet, Paz tells us: "March thirtieth I was a skull already, in the shadow of her immense felt hat." The theme is obviously a description of the underworld with which the poem begins, the onset of autumn in nature. In the Introduction Paz has written: "From the first day, in the basement room of the hotel St. Simon and during the following days, from March the thirtieth to April the third, irritation and humiliation of the I."[113] The Buddhist new year begins not in January but in April as March thirty-first marks the end of the previous year. *Renga,* likewise, begins in the underworld of March thirtieth and thirty-first.[114] The movement is from diversity, the darkness of the underworld, to the unity of four poets into one. The metaphor of a lover seeking his beloved, lurks behind each sonnet of *Renga,* which culminates in the lover discovering his bride at the end of the poem, as protagonists come from the underworld to the world we inhabit. Mark the description of the underworld:

> The sun advances over bones benumbed:
> in the underground room: gestations:
> ants ooze already at the mouths of the metro.
> An end of dreams, and the fight of tongues begins:

In his Introduction Paz described five conditions that went into the making of *Renga.* Briefly, they are:

"A feeling of abandonment, rapidly changing into disquiet then into aggressiveness . . .
A senstation of oppression: for a Japanese the circle of the renga is a space which oepns up, for me it is a snare drawn tight. A trap.
A feeling of shame: I write in front of the others, the others in front of me. Something like undressing in a cafe, or defecating, crying before strangers.
A Feeling of voyeurism: I see myself manipulating sentences. I see them come together, fall apart, come back into shape . . . . Beautiful and terrifying promiscuity of language. A feeling of returning: I go down into the magic cave . . . underground room (Prosperpine, Calypso) . . . Passage from anguish to laughter ... I laugh at myself in laughing at you and thus I honor myself and honor you."[115]

These five stages roughly correspond to the five spokes of the Buddhist wheel of becoming. The five spokes signify five destinies, beginning from the bottom—hells, animals, ghosts, gods, and human beings.[116] Claude Roy says: "But what seems to interest Octavio Paz in the Buddhist attitude, and in the philosophies which prefigure and join with or derive from it Taoism, Shintoism, or Zen, lies perhaps in the deliberate refusal to accord belief or absolute values to the permanence of an unchanging spirit: self, ego, soul, jivatman."[117] E.J. Thomas reminds us of Buddhist wheel of becoming that "The whole is to be represented as swallowed by Impermanence (anityata) . . ."[118]

The first stanza of the sonnet quoted shows, by the use of the word "benumbed," a sense of abandonment, involuntariness, overtaking the alert human nerves and arteries, contributing to the progress of a looming sense of inertia, even nausea. The last two stanzas of the sonnet introduce four new images—the stone, the cave, the ghost, and the sand:

For the stone is perhaps a vine
the stone where ants jet out their acid,

a spoken word that readies itself within this cave:
Princes! tomb and showcase, I heaved up ghostly saliva.
my jaw gnawed its syllables of sand:

I was relic and clepsydra through the panes of the West: Joseph Campbell tells that there are many stories about the journey of the dead to the other land: "According to one, the soul entering the cave is immediately blocked by the guardian spirit, Le-hevhev, to whom the boar-offering is presented . . . the voyager, then allowed to pass, goes through the cave and emerges on the coast, along which he walks to a certain rocky place, well known, where he lights a fire to summon the ferryman. The latter comes in a ghost canoe, . . ."[119]

The movement is from the human world to the Hades, and if we look at the qualities associated with each spoke of Buddha's wheel, which also corresponds to Paz's hierarchy enumerated above, we shall find that in Buddha's wheel of becoming, the hierarchy is from human beings to gods, from gods to ghosts—an hierarchy immediately relevant to the lines quoted from the sonnet. In the quotation from Campbell, the source of the images of cave (Paz's 'magic cave'), stone (rock), and ghost, is easily discernible. The poet is entering the cave after imagining himself as dead on the land; "Princes" of the stanza from the sonnet corresponds to "gods" of the Buddhist wheel of becoming, who have already changed into "tomb and showcase"—ghosts—in both, the poem and Campbell's account. The source of the images of sand and stone is to be understood from this passage from Campbell. Hactcin is the name of a black shaman tribe. Once, one Hactcin tried to bring back the sun which had disappeared. He "made a sand-painting with four little coloured mounds in a row, into which they (people) put the seeds. The birds and animals sang, and presently the little mounds began to grow, the seeds began to sprout, and the four mounds of coloured earth merged and became one mountain, which continued to rise."[120] The sand-relic, which the poet becomes, is explainable in terms of the sand-painting, and the stone, which in the sonnet is also referred to as "perhaps a vine," is clearly explainable in terms of the mountain in Campbell's account, which has merged in itself the fecundity of the earth. Therefore, in Paz, it has become a stone, maintaining yet the fertile nature of vine.

The second sonnet advances the argument of descent into Hades: the soul is seeming to leave the body; the feeling of the fullness of environment, filled with the presence of objects, is being supplemented by a feeling of void and emptiness. The feeling of the poct as human being is being supplemented by the poet as a living carcass, a ghost. By the time of March thirtieth, the poet has become a skull, and the images of the underworld come on the surface one after the other:

> While I write, scraps of moons shower over me,
> nails torn from stuffed leopards, skulls, little laughs,
> Dispersion from a verbal boneyard, rain of anecdotes,
> across my page run graceful mice in their ring-of-roses.

Paz himself referred to the creatures of the underworld in his Introduction: "Moles, rats, worms. Venerable serpents, august dragons. . ."[121]

The third sonnet introduces further, the images of the underworld—perspex debris, spools of forgotten films. We have advanced from March thirtieth to March thirty-first. The sonnet also introduces the eros theme, by having recourse to three levels in philosophy which are, obviously, the human, the animal, and the non-human. The desire to live on the instinctual level results

> in figures tightly embracing:
> they are practicing the second level:

This is what Paz has called the beautiful and terrifying promiscuity of language. The figures are, as Tomlinson tells us, "Donne's unmoving lovers of *The Extasie,*" who "become the Extruscan couple of the Ville Giulia: they embodied the erotic side of our poem, celebrated the personal and at the same time translated it into the sculptural."[122] The references to Henry Rousseau, the painter, and Arnaut, etc., have involuntarily gained access into the poem as Tomlinson tells us.[123] This is what happens when poetry is written at a pitch of consciousness when things lose their thinginess to become presences in an ever-flowing continuum. Blake said of Abraham and Moses, that they are not two personalities but mental states. Paz, likewise, says of Homer: "Homer is not so much a real historical being, as a formal, aesthetic condition of the artistic work."[124]

The feeling of voyeurism results in the poet's unsuccessful manipulation of sentences (fourth sonnet). As the pleasure derived by the poet (since he is already a skull) is not real but imaginary, the abstractness of language never quite articulates itself into meaningful associations of speech. The theme of darkness complicates the suffocation in the underworld, which is highlighted in the fifth sonnet.

> Among ruins which are filth: tin cans, portraits
> of actors, sonnets, excrement:
> a sunday evening in the quiet
> country, at the hour of sunset, when you get back into
> the car:

The sixth sonnet introduces the theme of water:

> Over tattered utopias, over the erotic
> second-hand clothes shop, debris of the industrial era,
> fall sparks from the genital conflagration:
> rain!—incandescence, sonnet, garden of flames:
> Rain into the carnage of trees, among the words
> of the subterranean sentences. . .

Claude Roy has already noted the erotic significance of water in his Foreword to *Renga*. The water is related with famous story of Actaeon having seen Diana bathing naked as Ovid tells us, and in the art of tantric Buddhism, as Campbell has noted, the creation of world is represented "in the image of a divine male and female in sexual embrace."[125]

The "genital conflagration," while it refers to the metaphor of rain, repeats the basic archetype of creation, or rather re-creation, after the descent into the underworld. The journey is in process as the recurrence of the image of "mouth of the cave" tells us. The growing sense of emptiness annuls everything into the void of existence.

The second sonnet-sequence is written by the French poet, Jacques Roubaud, and he starts from where Octavio Paz has left. The love theme dominates this section, and the archetypal motif behind this theme is the marriage of Persephone to the land (imaged as lover) she was taken away from, in her journey underground. Thc lovers are part of Buddhist wheel of becoming, and the existential process, which is ever in motion, extends to the underworld and to the world above. The lover says to the beloved:

> This is the way, my sphere, you dream suspended
>   within me:
> tender, you breathed into being a sky, and I seek
>   inside myself;
>   seek your poles to see whether
> your tongue is my wheel, . . .

The aridity of the land above corresponds to the loss of the reality of Persephone's being into abstraction of a sphere, and the identification of her tongue with wheel by the lover, not only captures Persephone in the cyclic activity of change which she cannot withstand; it also speaks of the dominance of male over female ('you dream suspended within me'). We know that Persephone is in subjection of Hades, who is the lover in the poem. In the myth also "The god was Hades, lord of the underworld, and in the land of the dead she becomes his queen."[126] Females, however, are symbols of fertility and generation, and their subjection can only lead to earth powdering away everything in the emptiness of *stupa*. *Stupa* is a Pali name for tomb, a solid, high structure, which contains the bones of the dead Buddha, to be opened again only by the future Buddha.

Persephone's relapse from the consciousness of her imaginative fertility into inertia of the spherical activity, where she is with her lover, reduces everything to "ashes and end" (second sonnet), and brings only a clouded moonrise. Moon, as noted earlier, is a recurring image, and it is associated not only with Buddhist calendar, it is also associated with Hekate, the moon-goddess, the colours and textures of whose personality Persephone herself appropriates:

> Out of the gloom a gloomy path we entered
> like the teeth of ink into a blotting paper
> (and so we must: the squid moon was at the edge of dark)

The gloom, a sound variation upon "moon", dominates the environment of the sonnet. The third sonnet again pictures the journey in motion:

> And love, a command no more, to each one
> the way lies clear through the comity of vine, of stone:

The vine and stone images have met us before.[127] The fact that lovers have lost unity and command explains for the aridity and fallowness of the land. The fourth sonnet introduces celebratory images (of harvest time) as the process of the recognition of Persephone for what she is begins: ('I recognise you in the wine, in the stone:/ I read with you elementary oracles. . .'). But from a recognition of the lineaments of Persephone from what she was in the past, we immediately come to

> The subdued color of a bombardment of flowers
> books of ivy crossed by a rapid white
> which flares over the quiet of the palisades

The earth, at the behest of Hades, had caused a fragrant flower to bloom. When Persephone came to pluck its flower, the earth gaped and Hades took away the maiden.[128] The reference to (the subdued colour of bombardment flowers is a reference to this, and the quiet palisades are the adamantine bars of the underworld, which will never break, change or pass, till the coming of next spring. The fifth sonnet shows the lover trying to transplant the lineaments of Persephone into the texture of his own being in order to declare the unity and command in love:

> I grasp you without force with ozone with straw
> I repeat your music at start of each *laisse*
> day by day (the nights are this *canso capfinida)*
>
> you open and close (brackets) your eyes, and this text
> gives, denies, gives (lips, teeth, tongue) its meanings
>
> in this branchwork labyrinth of glance and feature
> these lines that are life-lines,
> these veins vines:

The beauty of these lines not only parallels but transcends the beauty of lady's physical features and contours. The opening and closing of lady's eyes captures existence between moments of articulation and the fear of its loss (gives, denies, gives), while the text becomes the playground of the interplay of contrasting lines of glance and feature, trying to measure their own reality (and validity) by the "life-lines" (of Persephone). The attempt to make lady's veins, vines of fertility logic, is well conveyed by the last line, appended softly, involuntarily, to the line that precedes it. Jacques Roubaud's each poem contains only eleven lines as compared to fourteen by Octavio Paz. The stanzas are of three and two lines, which makes them dialectical of passions, of affirmation, denial, and negation. In the sixth poem the lady is identified with water. She asks the lover:

> 'Look at the moon,' and looked—at her, not at the moon:
> And my face was a reflection in water (in the hollow
> of a hand) and she herself, perhaps, the water
> the hollow of water where I had lived badly:

The following quotation from Joseph Campbell will show where the logic of the poem is moving: ". . . there is a trinity of goddesses identified with the local food plants, the pig, the underworld and the moon, whose rites ensure both a growth of the plants, and a passage of the soul to the land of the dead."[129]

The lady's asking the lover to look on the moon, therefore, implies the onward march of the soul to the land of the dead in the underworld. The water is part of water-libation ritual. In Buddhism, it is associated with Buddha's life himself: "When Mara, the Evil One, arrives with his hosts to oust the Buddha from under the *bodhi* tree, he points to his army as validation for his claim. The Buddha, in turn, points to the Earth, as witness to his many meritorious deeds, to validate His claim. Thereupon, the Earth appears in the guise of a woman (Withoudaya), and to display the Buddha's accumulated merit she squeezes from her hair the water that had been poured on the earth to commemorate. His meritorious deeds. They are so numerous that the water creates a flood, causing Mara and his hosts to flee."[130] In the poem the lover recognises the lady for what she is ('. . . she herself, perhaps, the water'), but his own predicament is indicated by his failure to live where he aught to in order to strike a balance between male and female principles, so essential for the renewal of life. Water is also a symbol of purity, and its sprinkling during religious ceremonies in Buddhism, implies purification. The seventh poem ends with lover's understanding" . . . if/water invites you follow it."

The poem of the Italian poet Edoardo Sangumeti are again written in fourteen lines divided into stanzas of varying lines and line lengths. Sanguineti again takes up the theme of the underworld and his first sonnet elaborates it in terms of confusion, insects, scabies, etc. The sonnet ends with the phrase "nuptial sea"—the sea which is what our world as underworld is, and out of which the primordial marriage of earth and environment, in terms of beloved and lover, is to take place. The attempts of the lover towards transplantation of lady's lineaments on to himself for attaining mythic unity in terms of fertility, fail to dislocate the sense of imm diateness of the presence of lady's reality as and, fallow, and drought (second sonnet):

> and in the to-and-fro of syllables in search
> of marriage, meaning, what I find
> is the given woman, the mythless presence
> and quotidian certainty of your heart and mind:

The stanza, prior to this, describes how the lover, living with the lady, in the underworld, gets lost in the portals of her being, and loses sense of balance and self-control—things needed for renewal:

> I am breathless against the wool you flaunt in
> gong I oscillate beneath the sharps of your laughter

The laughter refers to the fertility and growth in nature that is yet to take place, while the "gong" is an instrument struck at the time of the birth of spring, return of Persephone to the upper world: "A bronze gong was struck at this moment, a young priestess representing Kore herself appeared, and the pageant terminated with a paean of joy."[131] As the poem passes from its middle towards the end, the lover who has been constantly transplanting lady's limbs on to himself, and who personifies the environment, now tries to transplant lady's sexual organs in his attempt to renew the land while changing Persephone from an object to a subject:

> I have inscribed on my brow the wrinkles of your uterus,
> the soft rings of your menstrual moss:
> I have poured livid liquors into the pages of your calen-
> dars:
> I have cultivated mushroom and fern on the beaches of
> your lakes:

The inscription of lady's womb (uterus), wrinkles upon the brow of the lover, "prophecies" (a word which occurs in the last line of second stanza), rebirth, and the image of the "menstrual moss," extends the logic of "nuptial sea," met in the first sonnet of this sequence.

In the fourth sonnet the lover attempts rebirth by swimming in the river, as aspect of the lady—her veins, arteries, glances, features, etc., but fails to transform aridity into fertility. The mention of the figures of Narcissus and Euclid, the geometrician, who are supposed to be tracing their figures in the sandy desert,[132] are not answered in the affirmative as the prophecy of renewal is yet to materialise.

The protagonist of the poem is one and the personalities of four poets always transform their consciousness into the single verbal image in time. Persephone, in the fifth sonnet as in the fourth, is referred to as "outside":

> Where—and what? What is 'outside'? That
> in whose creation I had no part, which enters me now
> both image and other; marriage or loss
> of memory: . . .

All females are part of Mother-Nature, and are usually created by a God figure. But in some mythologies, female is the *primum mobile,* the first beginning and the material matrix.[133] In the poem's stanza above, the protagonist has to make this female his bride, who is also the land. She enters into the male figure, who has to respond to the seeking self by marrying the reality of his being to the mythic image of the female goddess. Only then the outside of his being will become inside, and the memory will change into imagination.

The sixth sonnet introduces journey images, while the protagonist is busy inventing the outside within himself. The seventh sonnet takes us to a very important stage of the journey—introducing two new images of the city and the tree. Cities and gardens in anthropomorphic tradition are often identified with the body of a female Eleusis, a city near Greece, has for long been a centre for the performance of rituals by farmers concerning Persephone. It was in this city that Demeter, Persephone's mother, along with Hekate, sat by a well known as the Well of the Virgin, and served as a nurse in a kingly household, while praying for the return of Persephone from the underworld. The sonnet is Petrarchan which is the most proper form of expressing love, especially courtly love. The objective "outside," the body of the lady, which the lover has desperately been trying to imagine as "inside," and whose centre and point of reference he has been exasperatingly trying to discover, now expresses itself in the language of silence which is more powerful than the verbal form of language. Identification has taken the speech of lovers, and the lady has become "O my America, my new-found-land explored,/ unspeaking plenitude of the flesh made word,": much in the manner of Metaphysical tradition. The lady has become not only a city, but a centre as wen, where voices, faces, songs, meet and get their terms of reference.

> the faces inhabiting a single face,
> Persephone, my city: from whose prodigal
> ground, branches a tree of tongues, twining of voices,
> a madrigal.

The tree image rightly occurs at this time, as the recognition of the lady's true identity, is a discovery not only for the lover, but a context for the lady herself, which validates her existence and gives her meaning. In Buddhism, the full moon of May is observed as a day of Enlightenment for the Buddha, and the ceremony is marked by watering the bo tree, under which Buddha attained Enlightenment.

Tomlinson's sonnets again are of fourteen lines and fixity of pattern is replaced by stanzas of varying line and line-lengths. The second stanza of the first sonnet indicates where have we come:

> alphabets, numbers. . .
> cereals of Ceres, pomegranates of Persephone,
> seed, peoples, races beneath earth: epochs?

When Demeter, Persephone's mother, fasted for nine days

for Persephone's release from the underworld, Zeus at last caused her to be released. "She had eaten, however, a seed of the pomegranate in the world below and, as a consequence, would now have to spend one-third of each year with Hades."[134]

The recurrence of the wheel image in the final stanza, at whose centre is Persephone, sweet, blind and limp, shows that the movement has been from one epoch to another. For formerly, whereas Persephone was subject to the movement of wheel, now she occupies its centre, spilling life in place of aridity. The second sonnet is celebratory in nature and it is the time of revelry: "once more my Nile conceals its hard head of a monster:/ (I see hooves); (I hear tails); I play chess; (zblanc's'):" The third sonnet continues the theme of interjection, transplantation and the consequent loss of the lover in the beloved, beloved in the lover. There is a pun on Babel (babble) soundwise. Babel obviously refers to the Tower of Shinar (Genesis XI) where God confused the speech of man. But the loss of speech in the poem is because of two segregated personalities merging into the unity of the pyramid of fourteen tiers. The fourth sonnet introduces the garden image which the lady has become, the light and the sun images. When Persephone was taken underground nobody knew of her existence except the sun, and the recurrence of sun image at this stage is but appropriate. "Demeter met the moon-goddess Hekate, and together they proceeded to the sun-god, Phoebus, who had seen the maid abducted and could tell them where she was..."[135] The poem says: "we met in a clearness of light. The sun/eats my shadow in the lion-colored arena of your belly."

The shadow of the lover eaten, is the shadow which caused him Persephone appear as "outside." The "clearness of light" refers to the Buddhist festivals of light which fall on the full moon of October. On this day Buddha descends from heaven "The myth has it that a few years after attaining Enlightenment, the Buddha ascended to heaven on the full moon or *Wa-zou,* where he spent the entire Lent expounding the intricacies of Buddhist metaphysics and ontology *(abhiddhamma)* to the gods, and especially to his mother. Completing his discourses at the end of Lent, he descended to the earth on *Thadin-jut,* preceded by myriads of heavenly torches which lit his way."[136] In the Persephone myth itself, we come across the account that Demeter, Persephone's mother, "wandered over the earth, holding a long, staff-like torch in either hand."[187] The last stanza of the sonnet subordinates the "I" of lovers to the *sangha or* group: "But Baucis and Philemon (superannuated lovers) disappeared in the collectivisation of gardens and vines, and the inspector of gramophones." The concluding lines of sonnet four remind of what Octavio Paz has called in Introduction: "In the Japanese renga linear succession triumphs: the poem flows; in the Western renga succession proceeds in a zigzag, by opposition then reconciliation of terms . . ."[138] The lovers in the poem have clearly triumphed over linearity of time into the unity of life's melody. The fifth sonnet further elaborates the same theme:

> He)
> She) said (green swaying roof above
> "this dialogue of one"): "We saw by this it was not so:
> City, we saw not what did move":
> We stayed like this, year on year, silent, expressionless,
> stretched above our sarcophagus:

The sixth and final sonnet celebrates personal unity in terms of group and environment:

> I have become four voices that encircle
> a common object, defining a self
> lost in a spiral of selves, a naming:

Buddha, very much conscious of a priori structure of the world, did not identify individual with any form of determinism, natural, theistic, or karmic. The individual is given freedom to work out his own salvation and alter his own condition from imprisonment to liberation. Buddhist sermons are written in stanzas as said earlier, and they are recited mainly for the purposes of liberation—liberation from desire, disease, prison and body. Tomlinson writes: "We rose from our underworld, not on the third, but on the fifth day. . .":[39] which obviously refers to the five spokes of the Buddhist wheel.

It is this movement of the wheel which had attracted Paz, for the seeker does not go either to heaven or to hell, after completing his journey. He remains in the movement, the stream of consciousness (*Vinnana sata*), the dynamic continuum. In his criticism of sixty-two theories regarding man and the universe, Buddha compares himself with a razor's edge (*Digha Nikaya, Sutta* 1), "which will steer clear of certain theoretical pitfalls like eternalism and annihilationism, materialism and idealism, determinism and indeterminism, and value relativism and value absolutism."[140] Octavio Paz also says: "Renga: a poem which effaces itself as it is written, a path which is wiped out and has no desire to lead anywhere. Nothing awaits us at its end: there is no end, anymore than there is a beginning: all is movement."[141]

Notes and References

1. Originally published in America in 1958 by Mc-Dowell, Obolensky. British edition (London; Oxford University Press, 1960). The first two collections are *Relations and Contraries* (Hand & Fowler Press, 1951) and *The Necklace* (Oxford: Fantasy Press, 1955).
2. Donald Davie, "See, and Believe," review of *Seeing is Believing,* Essays in Criticism, Vol IX (January 1959), No. 1, p. 188.
3. *Ibid.*
4. *Poetry Book Society Bulletin,* No. 97 (Summer 1978).
5. Octavio Paz, "Black and White: The Graphics of Charles Tomlinson," trans. Michael Schmidt, *Poetry Nation* (1975), 5, p. 94.
6. *PBSB,* No. 96 (Spring 1978).
7. Donald Davie, *Articulate Energy: An Enquiry into the Syntax of English Poetry* (London: Routledge & Kegan Paul, 1955), p. 34.
8. Oxford University Press exhibited Tomlinson's paintings and

collages to mark the appearance of *Written on Water.*

9. Quoted in D. Davie, *Articulate Energy,* pp. 34-35.
10. Monroe C. Beardsley, *Aesthetics: Problems in the Philosophy of Criticism* (Indianapolis: Hackett Publishing Company, 1981, p. 169.
11. *PBSB,* No. 97 (Summer 1978).
12. Octavio Paz, "Black and White: The Graphics of Charles *Tomlinson,*" p. 91.
13. Tomlinson in *PBSB,* No. 75 (Christmas 1972).
14. Octavio Paz, "Black and White: The Graphics of Charles Tomlinson," p. 92.
15. In this method, black goauche is spread out on a sheet of white glossy paper with the help of black thick brush. This sheet is pressed by another sheet which is lifted after some time. There is, obviously, an involuntary design on the page, accidental, which parallels the instance of rhyme in poetry.
16. Tomlinson's letter quoted in Octavio Paz, "Black and White: . . ." *op. cit.,* p. 92.
17. Octavio Paz, *Ibid.*
18. *PBSB,* No. 97 (Summer 1978).
19. *Ibid.*
20. Octavio Paz, "Black and White, . . ." p. 91.
21. *Ibid.*
22. ". . . in the art of India (above all the sculpture of Kali) he (Paz) admires that combination of ecstasy and gravity which, in another form, characterises much of his own mature poetry." C. Tomlinson, "Introduction: A Note on Octavio Paz," in C. Tomlinson, 'ed., *Octavio Paz: Selected Poems* (Penguin, 1979), p. 13.
23. Octavio Paz, "Black and White: . . .," p. 92.
24. "A poet whose first influences were Blake and Yeats. . ." Peter Jones and Michael Schmidt, eds., *British Poetry Since 1970: A Critical Survey* (Manchester: Carcanet Press, 1980), p. 57.
25. Merie E. Brown, *Double Lyric,* p. 147.
26. Quoted in M.L. Rosenthal, *The New Poets: American and British*

Poetry Since World War II (N. York: Oxford University Press, 1967), p. 245.

27. "Char]es Tomlinson in Conversation," *PN Review*, Vol. 5 (1977), No. 1, p. 35.
28. M. L. Rosenthal, *The New Poets*, p. 245.
29. Calvin Bedient, *Eight Contemporary Poets* (London: Oxford University Press, 1974), p. 4.
30. D. Davie, *Articulate Energy*, pp. 6-9.
31. Henry Bergson, "Form and Meaning," in Richard M. Gale, ed., *The Philosophy of Time: A Collection of Essays* (London: Macmillan, 1968), p. 398.
32. *PBSB*, No. 82 (Autumn 1974).
33. "Fifteen Ways of Looking at Charles Tomlinson," *PN Review*, Vol 5 (1977), No. 1, p. 40.
34. "Charles Tomlinson in Conversation," *PN Review*, Vol. 5 (1977), No. 1, p. 36.
35. P.R. King, *Nine Contemporary Poets*, p. 54.
36. "Charles Tomlinson in Conversation," *op. cit.*, pp. 36-37.
37. *Ibid*, p. 37.
38. *Ibid.*
39. Calvin Bedient, *Eight Contemporary Poets*, p. 19.
40. *Ibid.*, p. 6.
41. "Charles Tomlinson in Conversation," p. 36.
42. *Eight Contemporary Poets*, p. 13.
43. *Ibid.*
44. 'The man will follow, each/As the other's servant/Content to remain content,' "Oxen. Ploughing at Fiesole."
45. Charles Tomlinson, ed., *Marriane Moore: A Collection of Critical Essays* (New Jersey: Prentice-Hall, Inc., 1969), p. 1.
46. "Fifteen Ways of Looking at Charles Tomlinson," p. 40.
47. Merle E. Brown, *Double Lyric*, p. 151.
48. "Fifteen Ways of Looking at Charles Tomlinson," p. 43.
49. *PBSB*, No. 75 (Christmas 1972).
50. Calvin Bedient, *Eight Contemporary Poets*, p. 3.

51. *PBSB,* No. 75 (Christmas 1972).
52. Charles Tomlinson, *The Poem as Initiation* (New York: Colgate University Press). Lecture delivered at Kappa Convocation, Colgate University, October 30, 1967.
53. Tomlinson, ed., *Octavio Paz* (Penguin, 1979), p. 14.
54. *PBSB,* No. 75 (Christmas 1972).
55. "Charles Tomlinson," in *The Poet Speaks: Interviews with Contemporary Poets,* ed., Peter Orr (London: Routledge, 1967), p. 251.
56. Benedetto Croce, *Philosophy Poetry History: An Anthology of Essays,* trans. Cecil Sprigge (London: OUP, 1966), p. 596.
57. "Charles Tomlinson in Conversation," *PN Review* (1977), Vol 5, No. 1, p. 35.
58. *Ibid.*
59. "Will Tomlinson be told to bear his learning more lightly?" Davie in "See, and Believe," *Essays* in *Criticism,* Vol. IX (Jan. 1959), No. 1, p. 190.
60. Davie acknowledges poem's merit but thinks it limited as it offends "Sidney's injunction that the poet should not confound himself with the historian." *Ibid.*
61. "Charles Tomlinson in Conversation," p. 36.
62. D. Davie, "See, and Believe," p. 192.
63. *Ibid.*
64. *Eight Contemporary Poets,* p. 5.
65. Tomlinson, *Tire Poem as Initiation.*
66. The Romantic poets, instead of building a human house amid natural impossibilities, surrendered themselves to it; the variegated excess of nature led them to think in terms of an excessive vision concerning nature's beneficient aspect. In "Tramontana at Lerici," Tomlinson says: 'And the chill grows. In this air/Unfit for politicians and romantics/ Dark hardens from blue, effacing the windows:' The windows are human centres of vision, and their loss implies loss of the possibility of a civil country. See also Irving Babbit, *Rousseau and Romanticism,* in which he held that Romantic poets jacked centrality of vision.
67. Tomlinson introduces the idea in the second section that

symbolist movement was a natural consequence of romanticism ("Antecedents").

68. Blake alone, among Romantic poets, chided Wordsworth for seeing in nature what was in his own mind.

69. "Black and White: The Graphics of Charles Tomlinson," pp. 87-88.

70. "From the start Charles Tomlinson has been internationalist in outlook" -- Donald Wesling, "An Avant-Garde Careful and Bold," in "Fifteen Ways of Looking at Charles Tomlinson," p. 43.

71. D. Davie, "See, and Believe," pp. 192-93.

72. "Charles Tomlinson in Conversation," p. 36.

73. *The New Poets,* p. 246.

74. *Eight Contemporary Poets,* p. 15.

75. "Charles Tomlinson," in Peter Orr, ed., *The Poet Speaks,* p. 250.

76. *Ibid.,* p. 251.

77. Davie, "See, and Believe," p. 193.

78. *Ibid.,* p. 194.

79. "Black and White: The Graphics of Charles Tomlinson," p. 91.

80. "Charles Tomlinson in Conversation," p. 37.

81. B. Croce, *Philosophy Poetry History,* p. 75.

82. *Ibid,* pp. 75-76.

83. B. Croce, *Aestheticism,* trans. Douglas Ainslie (London: Vision Press, 1967), p. 3.

84. Charles Tomlinson, *The Poem as Initiation.*

85. "Black and White: . . .," p. 89.

86. Octavio Paz, *Ibid,* p. 94.

87. C. Tomlinson, ed., *William Carlos Williams* (Penguin, 1972), p. 209.

88. *Ibid,* p. 27.

89. *Ibid.,* p. 29.

90. Tomlinson, however, criticised Williams's poetry for being

too limited to the physical realities of time and place.

91. The American publisher is George Braziller, Inc., One Park Avenue, New York, NY. 10016. In Canada it is published by Doubleday Canada Ltd.

92. Octavio Paz, "Introduction," in C. Tomlinson, ed., *Renga* (New York: George Braziller, 1971), p. 22.

93. *Mahayana* Buddhism is one of the four schools in which Buddhism got divided in India after Buddha's death.

94. D.T. Suzuki, "Japanese Thought," in S. Radhakrishnan and others, ed., *History of Philosophy: Eastern and Western* (London: George Allen & Unwin, 1952), p. 600.

95. Claude Roy, *Renga,* p. 8.

96. *Ibid.*

97. D.T. Suzuki, "Japanese Thought," *op. cit.,* p. 596.

98. *Ibid.*

99. Claude Roy, "Foreword," *Renga,* p. 9.

100. D.T. Suzuki, "Japanese Thought," p. 603.

101. Octavio Paz, "Introduction," *Renga,* p. 26.

102. Edward J. Thomas, *The History of Buddhist Thought* (London: Kegan Paul, Trench, Trubner & Co., Ltd., 1933), p. 186.

103. Claude Roy, "Foreword, "*Renga,* p. 10.

104. "Introduction," *Renga,* p. 21.

105. E.J. Thomas, *The History of Buddhist Thought,* p. 180.

106. See, for example, Prof. Aneski, *Some Problems of the Textual History of the Buddhist Scriptures;* and *The Four Buddhist Agamas in Chinese,* trans. Asiatic Society of Japan, XXXV, Parts 2 & 3, 1908; *Le sagatha-vagga du Samyutta-nikaya el ses versions chinoises,* Museon, 1905, pp. 23 if. Also, Prof. Akanuma, *The Comparative Catalogue of Chinese Agamas and Pali Nikayas* (in Japanese), Nagoya, Japan, 1929.

107. *Buddhism and Society* (London: George Allen & Unwin, 1971).

108. "Foreword," *Renga,* p. 7.

109. J. Campbell, *The Masks of God: Primitive Mythology* (London: Souvenir Press, 1973), p. 183.

110. *Ibid.,* p. 185.

111. *The Nature of Greek Myths* (Penguin, 1977), p. 191.
112. See pp. 112-16 in J. Campbell, *Primitive Mythology.*
113. "Introduction," *Renga,* pp. 21-22.
114. In Burmese variation of Buddhist myth, the king of the gods, "the chief Thagya . . . annually descends to the earth, where he remains for the last two days of the old year. . . Completing his work, he returns to his abode in the Ta-wa-deing-tha (Pali, Tavatim sa) heaven on the third day, his return marking the beginning of the New Year." Melford E. Spiro, *Buddhism and Society,* p. 220.
115. Octavio Paz, "Introduction," *Renga,* pp. 22-24.
116. See p. 68 in E.J. Thomas, *The History of Buddhist Thought.*
117. "Foreword", *Renga,* p. 12.
118. *The History of Buddhist Thought,* pp. 68-69.
119. *Primitive Mythology,* pp. 450-51.
120. *Ibid.,* pp. 237-38.
121. "Introduction," p. 23.
122. "The Unison: A Retrospect," *Renga,* p. 36.
123. *Ibid.*
124. "Introduction," *Rmga,* p. 19.
125. *Primitive Mythology,* p. 64.
126. *Ibid.,* p. 183.
127. See quotation no. 120.
128. J. Campbell, *Primitive Mythology,* p. 183.
129. *Ibid.,* p. 186.
130. Melford E. Spiro, *Buddhism and Society,* p. 214.
131. *Primitive Mythology,* p. 186. The wool image refers to the 'web of wool' which Persephone wove, and on which she made a picture of the universe, while hiding in a cave, where her mother Demeter had put her on her journey from Crete to Sicily, *Ibid.,* p. 101.
132. For the sand image refer to quotation no. 120.
133. See J. Campbell, *Primitive Mythology,* p. 63.
134. *Ibid.,* p. 185.

135. *Ibid.*, p. 184.
136. Melford E. Spiro, *Buddhism and Society*, p. 225.
137. Campbell, *Primitive Mythology*, p. 184.
138. Octavio Paz, "Introducttion," *Renga*, p. 26.
139. Charles Tomlinson, "The Unison: A Retrospect," *Renga*, p. 36.
140. Padmasiri de Silva, "Two Paradigmatic Strands in the Buddhist Theory of Consciousness," in Ronald S. Valle and Rolf Von Eckartsberg, ed., *The Metaphors of Consciousness* (N. York: Plenum Press, 1981), p. 275.
141. "Introduction," *Renga*, p. 27.

Conclusion

The foregoing examination of British poetry after the Movement has demonstrated that myth forms an important part in the poetry of Hughes, Gunn and Tomlinson. The study discovers the idea of serpent's usurpation of God's throne, found in so many of *Crow* poems, in Greek myths as described by Joseph Campbell. The source of Crow myth I discover among the Gros Ventre tribe of North Montana, upon which is based Hughes's entire poem. The source of other images and concepts in *Crow* – "laughter," "stone," "rock" and "worm" among others, is also discovered for the first time. Moreover, to explain Hughes's religious postion, I have taken recourse to Hughes's reviews of books on myth and history, which helps me collocate Hughes's message in *Crow*. By analysing Thom Gunn's *Moly* I incline to the view that Gunn's poems can best be understood as an argument in the metaphors of self. Adjustment of self with its environment, which is also Hughes's chief concern, is exhibited by many of Gunn's poems, especially the ones written after taking the drug. Most often, Gunn has recourse to two personas: the "I and the "you" which continue to shift and merge their identities into each other.

Tomlinson's *Seeing is Believing,* I approach through the image of window which is also a metaphor, and *Renga,* till now not analysed, I analyse here. The source of most of the images and concepts in *Renga* I locate in Buddhism. Since 1950, I conclude, there has been no significant movement in

British poetry. The character of British poetry has grown individualistic: Hughes, Tomlinson, and Gunn, have come out of Movement aims and ideology; they do not feel any need to subscribe to any school, nor do they have their own predetermined poetic frameworks, as the poems discussed demonstrate. The empirical attitude of Movement poets, which had confined both poetic experience and its linguistic expression, is now broken in favour of what Blake Morrison and Andrew Motion, in their anthology *Contemporary British Poetry* (Penguin, 1982) say, a "preoccupation with relativism," which they consider as a "radical departure" from the previous poetry.

Ted Hughes's poems discussed, demonstrate his interest in mythology, narrative, and linguistic innovation. There are no set formal structures; the language is to depict the elemental power-circuit of the universe, and to this end it is used without punctuation marks, traditional meters, or rhetorical devices. Tomlinson, in his rejection of fanaticism of any sort, either with regard to language or experience, is an example of a poet whose "civil country" has demonstrated how it could be different from the civil language and experience of Movement poets. Tomlinson has also demonstrated that a poet is the kind of consciollsness where impressions from different traditions get imprinted, and take their shape and texture involuntarily on the page, some time or the other. Tomlinson is also an example of a poet, who tells by what he writes, that novelty in poetry within traditional meters can be achieved only when the poetic consciollsness encountering experience, sees with its own eyes, naked, what is in front of it. It is at this level that strangeness is added to the ordinariness of experience, and poetic language merely frames it later into words.

Both Ted Hughes and Charles Tomlinson have provided angles of vision which places human activity in more than human contexts, the presence of "the other," which is sometimes terrifying, sometimes ennobling. As compared to both these poets, Gunn has remained somewhat autobiographical in his poetic range, experimenting both in traditional metrics and going out of it. Blake Morrison and Andrew Motion, who claim to be deliberately conscious of Alvarez's *The New Poetry*, draw from latter's anthology the inference: "The implication of *The New Poetry* that a correlation necessarily exists between gravity of subject and quality of achievement is one that many young writers—James Fenton, for instance—regard with scorn: . . ." This is an inference *The New Poetry* would not allow. Blake Morrison and Andrew Motion further say: ". . . he (Alvarez) presented language as a mere instrument in a therapeutic transaction between writer and reader."

If writing an Introduction to an anthology means deliberately to be different from the preceding anthology, such disagreements from Introduction might better be avoided. Alvarez had said in 1962: "What poetry needs, in brief, is a new seriousness. I would define this seriousness simply as the poet's ability and willingness to face the full range of his experience with his full intelligence; not to take the easy exists of either the conventional response or choking incohetence." On language and treatment of them, Alvarez evokes the qualities of skilfulness, originality, and intelligence, without rigid adherence to the cult of impersonality. Would Blake Morrison and Andrew Motion deny the need for such qualities for a poet? Alvarez's praise for Lowell is based on latter's avoidance of a language of mannerism, and not couching his experience in Catholic or theological terms. This is what Alvarez calls coping with experience naked, without evasion. Alvarez's "new seriousness" has been wrongly interpreted as "gravity of subject' by Blake Morrison and Andrew Motion. A poet can be serious even in his gay treatment of a comic situation. Shakespeare created Falstaff, not by remaining separate, non serious. from his character, but by losing his own sense of personality in him for the time being. Seriousness is an artistic necessity, implying fidelity to the formal treatment of subject, which may, in itself, be serious or comic.

The present study purports to the view that British poetry since 1963 has seen the fulfilment of Alvarez's criteria of "new seriousness," both in its attitude towards language and experience, which, the study equally holds, the anthology of Andrew Motion and Blake Morrison also advocates, though in a different garb—the extension of "imaginative franchise."

There is, however, another way to approach Motion's and Morrison's anthology—their intention to bring poetry back on the street, and his desire to include tooth-brushes and light-switches, as Motion told *The Guardian* (May 12, 1983). Will it mean the type of poetry the Movement has been a witness to? Poems which can endure rigours of time, attitudes, and tastes, cannot but be "difficult" in some sense or the other, from the standpoint of poetry-reading public. Whether Motion wilt bring about a poetic revolution by conforming poetry to the public taste, or he will care for poetry in itself as an aesthetic activity, is yet to be seen. I do not see two activities contrary but they never quite work out into a degree acceptable both to the esthete and to the man in the pub or on the street. To generalise is to be an idiot, said William Blake, and truth is never so simple as to be understood by a fool. Whether big things have become small for Andrew Motion, as in the form of death, one will have to wait and see. If poets like Thomas Hardy, R.S. Thomas, Philip Larkin, constitute British tradition, to which tradition do William Blake, W.B. Yeats, T.S. Eliot and Ted Hughes belong? I feel the degree of public involvement in poetry in England is to be decided once and for all, and no absolute criteria are set for poetry writing. Why after all a poet of great talent should confine himself to public taste and not listen to the demands of his genius which is for creating larger frameworks of meaning?

I feel the meaning of Motion's dictum: "I want people to feel reading poetry is a normal, unembarrassed way of life"(The Guardian, May 12, 1983), is too clear to be misunderstood, and while the need for poetry to be simple has its own value, simplicity, combined with a sense of imaginative reality (transcendence of periodicity?), again tends to become "difficult." In fact simplicity is its own difficulty and the language of great poetry cannot escape it. Blake's Songs of Innocence and Experiencc arc examples.

Select Bibliography

CRITICISM (BOOKS, ARTICLES, REVIEWS, OTHER THAN THOSE BY POETS STUDIED)

Abse, Dannie and Howard Sergeant, *Mavericks,* London, 1957.

Allsop, Kenneth, *The Angry Decade,* London: Peter Owen, 1958. Alvarez, A. *The Shaping Spirit,* London: Chatto & Windus, 1958.

——, *Beyond All This Fiddle,* London: Allen Lane, 1968. Anon, "Four Young Poets," *Times Educational Supplement,* July 3-August 3, 1956.

——, "Speaking of Writing XiII: Philip Larkin," *Times,* February 20, 1964.

Bateson, F.W. "Auden's (and Empson's) Heirs," *Essays in Criticism,* 6, 1957.

Beardsley, Monroe C., *Aesthetics: Problems in the Philosophy of Criticism,* Indianapolis: Hackett Publishing Company, Inc., 1981.

Bedient, Calvin, *Eight Contemporary Poets,* London: Oxford University Press, 1974.

Bergonzi, Bernard, "After the Movement: English Poetry Today," *Listener,* August 24, 1961.

——, "Critical Situations: From the Fifties to the Seventies," *Critical Quarterly,* 15, 1973.

Bergson, Henry. "Form and Meaning," in Richard M. Gale, ed., *The Philosophy of Time: A Collection of Essays,* London: Macmillan, 1968.

Blavatsky, H.P., *The Secret Doctrine,* Madras: Adyar, 1971.

Bold, Alan, *Thom Gunn and Ted Hughes,* Edinburgh: Oliver and Boyd, 1976.

Bradbury, Malcolm, *Eating People is Wrong,* London: Seeker & Warburg, 1959.

Bragg, Melvyn, "Kingsley Amis Looks Back," *Listener,* February 20, 1975.

Brown, Merle E., *Double Lyric: Divisiveness and Communal Creativity in Recent English Poetry,* London: Routledge, 1980.

Campbell, Joseph, *Hero With a Thousand Faces,* New York: Meridian Books, 1956.

——, *The Masks of God: Primitive Mythology,* London: Souvenir Press, 1973.

Cox, G.B., "New Beats for Old," review of *Wodwo, Spectator,* July 28; 1967.

——, and A.R. Jones, "After the Tranquillized Fifties," *Critical Quarterly,* Vol 6, 1964.

Croce, Benedetto, *Philosophy Poetry History: An Anthology of Essays.* trans. Cecil Sprigge, London: Oxford University Press, 1966.

——, *Aestheticism,* trans. Douglas Ainslie, London: Vision Press, 1967.

Dekker, George. "Donald Davie: New and Divergent Lines in English Poetry," *Agenda,* 14, Summer 1976.

Delta, No. 8, Spring 1956 and No. 10 Autumn 1956, carry special issue on Movement.

Dodsworth, Martin, *The Survival of Poetry,* London: Faber, 1970.

Eliade, Mercia, *Shamanism: Archaic Techniques of Ecstasy*, London: Routledge, 1964.

——, *Myth and Reality*, London: George Allen & Unwin, 1963.

Falck, Colin, "Opinion: Poetry and Ordinariness," *New Review*, April 1974.

——, "Dreams and Responsibilities," review of Alvarez's *The New Poetry*, *The Review*, No. 2, June-July, 1962.

Fass, Ekbert, *Ted Hughes: The Unaccommodated Universe*, Santa Barbara: Black Sparrow Press, 1980.

Fraser, G.S. "The Poetry of Thorn Gunn," *Critical Quarterly*, Vol 3, Winter 1961, No. 4.

——, *The Modern Writer and His World*, Harmondsworth: Penguin, 1964.

——, *Vision and Rhetoric: Studies in Modern Poetry*, London: Faber, 1959.

Frazer, J.G., *The Golden Bough*, New York: Macmillan, 1963.

Frye, Northrop, *The Anatomy of Criticism*, N. Jersey: Princeton University Press, 1973.

Gardner, Philip, *Kingsley Amis*, Boston: Twayne Publishers, 1981.

Gifford, Terry and Neil Roberts, *Ted Hughes: A Critical Study*, London: Faber, 1981.

Haffenden, John, *Viewpoints: Poets in Conversation with John Haffenden*, London: Faber, 1981.

Hamilton, Ian, "Four Conversations," *London Magazine*, November 1964.

——, *A Poetry Chronicle: Essays and Reviews*, London: Faber, 1973.

——, ed., *The Modern Poet: Essays from the Review*, London: Macdonald, 1968.

Hartley, Anthony, "Critic Between the Lines," *Spectator*, January 8, 1954.

Hecht, Anthony, "Writers' Rights and Readers' Rights," review of *Wodwo, The Hudson Review,* Vol. XXI, Spring 1968, No. 1.

Hirschberg, Stuart, *Myth in the Poetry of Ted Hughes,* Dublin: Wolfhound Press 1981.

Hugh, Graham, *Image and Experience.*

James, Clive, "Kingsley Amis," *The* New *Review,* Vol. 1, July 1974, No. 4.

Jones, Peter and Schmidt, Michael ed., *British Poetry Since 1970: A Critical* Surrey, Manchester: Carcanet Press, 1980.

Kermode, Frank, Review of Thorn Gunn's *A Sense of Movement, Listen,* Vol. 2, Spring 1958, No. 4.

King, R.P., *Nine Contemporary Poets: A Critical Introduction,* London: Methuen, 1979.

Kirk, G.S., *The Nature of Greek Myths,* Harmondsworth: Penguin, 1977.

Martin, Graham, "Poets of a Savage Age," review of *Wodwo, Listener,* July 6, 1967.

——, and P. Furbank. *Twentieth-Century Poetry: Critical Essays and Documents,* Open University Press, 1963.

Morrison, Blake, *The Movement: English Poetry and Fiction of the 1950s,* London: Oxford University Press, 1980.

O'Conner, W. Van., *The* New *University Wits,* Carbondale, 1963.

Orr, Peter, ed., The *Poet Speaks: Interviews, with Contemporary Poets,* London: Routledge, 1967.

Paz, Octavio, "Black and White: The Graphics of Charles Tomlinson," trans. Michael Schmidt, *Poetry Nation,* 5, 1975.

Powell, Neil, Review of Thorn Gunn's *The Passages of Joy, PN Review,* Vol. 9, 1982, No. 4.

Press, John, *Rule and Energy,* London: Oxford University Press, 1963.

Raban, Jonathan, *The Society of the Poem,* London: Harrap, 1971.

Radhnkrishnan, S., ed., *The Bhagavadgita,* London: George Allen & Unwin, 1970.

——, ed., *History of Philosophy: Eastern and Western,* London: George Allen & Unwin, 1952.

Radin, Paul, *The Trickster: A Study of American Indian Mythology,* New York: Schocken Books, 1956.

Rennie, Neil, "Mystic Wisdom," review of Thorn Gunn's *Moly, London Magazine,* Vol. 11, June-July, 1971, No. 2.

Roscnthal, M.L., *The New Poets: American and British Poets Since World War II,* New York: Oxford University Press, 1967.

Sagar, Keith. *The Art of Ted Hughes,* Cambridge University Press, 1978.

Saurat, Denis, *Literature and Occult Tradition: Studies in Philosophical Poetry,* trans. Dorothy Bolton, London: G. Dell, 1910.

Schmid Michael, *Fifty Modern, British Poets,* London: Heinmann, 1979.

——, and Grevel Lindop, ed., *British Poetry Since 1960: A Critical Survey,* Oxford: Carcanet Press, 1972.

Schober Plath, Aurelia, ed., *Sylvia Plath Letters Home Correspondence 1950-1963,* New York: Bantam, 1977.

Singh, Charu Sheel, *The Chariot of Fire: A Study of William Blake in the Light of Hindu Thought,* Salzburg: Salzburg University Press, 1981.

Sisson, C.H., *English Poetry 1900-1950: An Assessment,* London: Rupert Hart Davis, 1971.

Spiro, Melford E., *Buddhism and Society,* London: George Allen & Unwin, 1971.

Summerfield, G., ed., *Worlds: Seven Modern Poets,* Harmondsworth: Penguin, 1974.

Suzuki, D.T., "Japanese Thought," *History of Philosophy: Eastern and Western,* ed., S. Radhakrishnan, London. George Allen & Unwin, 1952.

Symons, Julian, "Moveable Feet," review of *Wodwo, New Statesman,* June 16, 1967.

Thomas, Edward J., *The History of Buddhist Thought,* London: Kegan Paul, Trench, Trubner, 1933.

Thwaite, Anthony, "The Two Poetries," in D. Abse, ed., *Poetry Dimension,* 2, 1964.

——, *Twentieth-Century English Poetry,* London: Heinmann, 1978.

Valle, Ronald S. and Rolf Von Eckartsberg, ed., *The Metaphors of Consciousness,* New York: Plenum Press, 1981.

Wilkins, Charles, *Bhagvat-Geeta or Dialogues of Kreeshna and Arjoon,* London, 1785.

Wilmer, Clive, "Definition and Flow: A Personal Reading of Thom Gunn," *PN Review,* Vol. 5, 1978, No. 3.

Zaehner, R.C., *The Bhagavadgita,* London: Oxford University Press, 1957.

——, *Mysticism Sacred and Profane: An Enquiry into Some Varieties of Preternatural Experience,* London: Oxford University Press, 1957.

BOOKS, ARTICLES, REVIEWS AND INTERVIEWS OF POETS STUDIED

Gunn, Thom

Collection: Creative

Fighting Terms, Oxford: Fantasy Press, 1954; revised edition, London: Faber, 1962, 1970.

The Sense of MOl'ement, London: Faber, 1957, 1968.

My Sad Coptains, London: Faber, 1961, 1974.

Positives: Verses by Thom Gunn, Photographs by Ander Gunn, London: Faber, 1966, 1973.

Touch, London: Faber, 1967, 1974.

Moly, London: Faber, 1971.

Jack Straw's Castle, London: Faber, 1976.

The Passages of Joy, London: Faber, 1982.

Collection: Critical

The Occasions of Poetry: Essays in Criticism and Autobiography, London: Faber, 1982.

Poetry Book Society Bulletin, No. 68, Spring 1971.

Poetry Book Society Bulletin, No. 90, Autumn 1976. "Introduction to American Poetry," *London Magazine*, Vol. 3, 1956, No.8.

"My Suburban Muse," *Worlds: Seven Modern Poets*, ed., G. Summerfield, Harmondsworth: Penguin, 1974. *Editorship Poetry from Cambridge*. 1951-2: *A Selection of Verse by Members of the University*, London: Fortune Press, 1952.

With Ted Hughes, *Five American Poets*, London: Faber, 1963.

Selected Poems of Fulke Greville, London: Faber, 1968

Ben Jonson, London: Penguin, 1974.

Hughes, Ted

Collection: Creative

The Hawk in the Rain, London: Faber, 1957.

Lupercal, London: Faber, 1960.

Meet My Folks, London: Faber, 1961.

The Earth-Owl and Other Moon-People, London: Faber, 1963.

How the Whale Became, London: Faber, 1963.

Nessie the Mannerless Monster, London: Faber, 1964.

Wodwo, London: Faber, 1967.

The Irom Man: A Story in Five Parts.

Crow: From the Life and Songs the Crow, London: Faber, 1970.

Season Songs, London: Faber, 1976.

Gaudete, London: Faber, 1977.

Cave Birds, London: Faber, 1978.

emains of Elmet, London: Faber, 1979.

Collection: Critical

Poetry in the Making: An Anthology of Poems and Programmes from Listening and Writing, London: Faber, 1967; published as *Poetry Is,* New York: Doubleday, 1970.

"Janos Piliniszky: An Introduction," *Poetry Nation Review,* No. 6, 1976.

Editorship

With Patrica Beer and Vernon Scannell, *New Poems* 1962, London: Hutchinson, 1962.

With Thom Gunn, *Five American Poets,* London: Faber, 1963.

A Choice of Emily Dickinson's Verse, London: Faber, 1968.

A Choice of Shakespeare's Verse, London: Faber, 1971.

Crossing the Water by S. Plath, London: Faber, 1971.

"Ted Hughes and *Crow*", 1970.

"Ted Hughes and *Gaudete*", 1977, Both the interviews appear in E. Fass, *Ted Hughes: The Unaccommodated Universe,* pp. 197-215.

"Betjeman en Bloc," *Ibid.,* 3, Spring 1959.

"Not the Place's Fault," *Umbrella,* 1, Summer 1959.

"Wanted: Good Hardy Critic," *Critical Quarterly,* 8, 1966, No.2.

"A Conversation with Philip Larkin," *Tracks,* 1, Summer 1967.

"Four Conversations," *London Magazine,* 4, November 1964.

Tomlinson, Charles

Collection: Creative

Relations and Contraries, London: Hand & Flower Press, 1951.

The Necklace, London and New York: Oxford University Press, 1966; first published by Fontasy Press, 1960.

Seeing is Believing, New York: Mc-Dowell,Obolensky, 1958; London: Oxford University Press, 1960.

A Peopled Landscape, London: Oxford University Press, 1963.

American Scenes and Other Poems, London: Oxford University Press, 1966.

The Way of a World, London: Oxford University Press, 1969.

Renga, with other poets, New York: Park Avenue, 1971; Doubleday, Canada, 1971.

Written on Water, London: Oxford University Press, 1972.

The Way In, London: Oxford University Press, 1974.

The Shaft, London: Oxford University Press, 1978.

Collection: Critical

The Poem as Initiation, New York: Colgate University Press, 1967. "The Middle Erow Muse," *Essays in Criticism,* Vo1. VII, April 1957, No.2.

"Poetry Today," in Borris Ford, ed., *The Jorfodern Age,* Harmondsworth: Penguin, 1973.

"Black Mountain Revisited," *New Review,* Vo1. 1, June 1974, No.3.

Poetry Book Society Bulletin, No. 82, Autumn 1974. "Fate and the Image of Music: Rosenberg's Plays," *Poetry Nation,* No.3, 1974.

Poetry Book Society Bulletin, No. 75, Christmas 1975.

Poetry Book Society Bulletin, No. 96, Spring 1978.

Selected Poems, Ibid., No. 97, Summer 1978.

"New Mexican Places," *Poetry Nation Review,* Vo1. 7, 1980, No.5.

Tomlinson interviews Report Creeley in *The Review,* No. 10, January 1964.

"Charles Tomlinson in Conversation," *Poetry Nation Review,* Vol. 5, 1977, No. 1.

"Charles Tomlinson at 50: A Celebration," *Poetry Nation Review,* Vol. 5, 1977, No. 1.

"Fifteen Ways of Looking at Tomlinson," *Ibid.*

"Eight New Graphic Works by Charles Tomlinson," *Ibid.*

Editorship

Marianne Moore: A Collection of Critiral Essays, N. Jersey: Prentice-Hall, Englewood Cliffs, 1970.

William Carlos Williams: A Critical Anthology, Penguin, 1972.

Anthologies

Allott, Kenneth, ed., *Penguin Book of Contemporary Verse*, Harmondsworth: Penguin, 1962.

Alvarez, A., ed., *The New Poetry*, Harmondsworth: Penguin, 1962.

Bold, Alan ed., *Cambridge Book of English Verse* 1939-75, Cambridge: Cambridge University Press, 1976.

Conquest, R., ed., *New Lines I*, London: Macmillan, 1956.

——, *New Lines* 2, London: Macmillan, 1963.

Hobsbaum, Philip and Edward Lucie-SmIth, ed., *A Group Anthology*, London: Oxford University Press, 1963.

Horovitz, Michael, ed., *Children of Albion*, Harmondsworth: Penguin, 1969.

Larkin, Philip, ed., *The Oxford Book of Twentieth Century English Verse*, London: Oxford University Press, 1973.

Lucie-Smith, E., ed., *The Liverpool Scene*, Donald Carroll, 1967.

——, *British Poetry Since 1945*, Harmondsworth: Penguin, 1970.

Macbeth, George, ed., *Poetry 1900 to 1965*, Longmans, 1967.

Morrison, Blake and Andrew Motion, ed., *Contemporary British Poetry*, Harmondsworth: Penguin, 1982.

Roberts, Michael, ed., *The Faber Book of Modern Verse*, revised Donald Hall, London: Faber, 1965.

Robson, J., ed., *The Young British Poets*, London: Chatto & Windus, 1971.

Summerfield, G., ed., *Worlds: Seven Modern Poets*, Harmondsworth: Penguin, 1974.

Index

G

H

Q

R